FROMMER'S

COMPREHENSIVE TRAVEL GUIDE

NEW ORLEANS
'91-'92

by Susan Poole

PRENTICE
HALL
PRESS

NEW YORK • LONDON • TORONTO • SYDNEY • TOKYO • SINGAPORE

FROMMER BOOKS

Published by Prentice Hall Press
A division of Simon & Schuster Inc.
15 Columbus Circle
New York, NY 10023

ISBN 0-13-334434-7
ISSN 0899-2908

Manufactured in the United States of America

CONTENTS

MAPS

> *To Bill, the lagniappe of my life*

ACKNOWLEDGMENTS

Seldom, if ever, have I met with such cooperation—to say nothing of friendliness and downright eagerness to help—as during the preparation of this guide. The first acknowledgment should simply be to New Orleans itself, for once again taking me in and seeing to it that I found what I was looking for. So, although the following were *specifically* my guiding angels in this project, I'd also like to make an upfront blanket statement of gratitude to the clerks, artists, bartenders, and fellow tourists who are imbued with a love of this city and to the scores of others who pointed me in the direction of yet another "find" to pass along to readers.

My very first thanks must go to Mrs. Junius Underwood, a gracious host and landlady who understands New Orleans with an enthusiasm and a passion that she readily shares with her guests. Similarly thanks to Beverly Gianna, of the Greater New Orleans Tourist and Convention Commission, who serves up warm affection for the city along with any and every sort of information requested. Gayle Burchfield, Audrey Krust, and Mary Sue Griffith, of the Louisiana State Office of Tourism, made sure that I found my way around New Orleans's environs via little-known restaurants, interesting people, and background facts that added vibrancy and color to my journey. And Jim Monaghan, a good friend and dedicated New Orleans Booster, has again proved an unfailing source of places to go and things to do that I might otherwise miss on every trip.

INTRODUCING NEW ORLEANS

There's no other place quite like it in our country. Call it the "Crescent City," because it sits in a deep bend of the Mississippi River; call it the "City that Care Forgot"; call it "America's Most Interesting City"—by any name, New Orleans holds a unique place among American cities.

It also holds, I'm quick to confess, first place in my affections. I've never been able to put my finger on exactly why this should be so. Maybe it's the intriguing architecture of the French Quarter, or the Old South appeal of the Garden District, or the food that is so special it can make me homesick just remembering when I'm far away, or the uninhibited gaiety of Bourbon Street, or the joyous jazz of Preservation Hall. Maybe it's a little of all those things. But I think perhaps it is really the *people* of New Orleans who first won my heart many years ago and have held it captive ever since. Although I grew up in the tradition of hospitality that is the hallmark of the South, I've found over the years that the word *hospitality* takes on richer meaning in this city. It isn't only that you're warmly welcomed—New Orleanians seem *overjoyed* that you've chosen to come, and they can't wait to make sure you enjoy your stay! Tales abound of those who have come on a "passing-through" basis and remained to join the ranks of residents. It's unlikely you'll escape a similar inclination after only a day or two.

Who can resist that sense of history as you walk narrow streets lined with centuries-old buildings dripping with fancy ironwork and still as functional today as when they were built. The imagination would have to be nonexistent not to people sidewalks, courtyards, and restaurants with frock-coated gentlemen and hoop-skirted ladies. Visions of black women in calico balancing baskets of sugary pralines on their heads; swashbuckling privateers swaggering through the streets while their leader, Jean Lafitte, huddles with Gen. Andrew Jackson in the Old Absinthe House, deep in plans for a cooperative defense against the British; or glittering, candlelit ballrooms in the very buildings you pass by, dine in, or call "home" during your visit—all come as automatically as a reflex.

But don't for one instant imagine that you'll be stuck in New Orleans's past. That brassy jazz sound filling the streets is very much of the 20th century. And if it occasionally turns into the low moan of blues that echo past sorrows, you're likely to hear a very modern echo in your heart. A look across Canal Street from the French Quarter will propel you even further into the present and the future —with skyscrapers, once thought impossible to build on this swampy site, sharing the skyline with skeletonlike frameworks of others yet to come. The Louisiana Superdome pays homage to a modern-day preoccupation with sporting events, while the towering International Trade Mart and the sprawling Rivergate Exhibition Center serve the interests of commerce. And the rejuvenated riverfront has come alive with shops, eateries, and entertainment.

And then there are the people. Artists "on the fence" around Jackson Square; musicians sitting in at jazz clubs or Preservation Hall; shopkeepers displaying exquisite imports alongside inexpensive souvenirs; taxi drivers hopping out to open doors (unheard of nowadays); natives happily sharing tables with tourists at the Café du Monde for an any-hour café au lait and beignets (more about those later)—they come in all occupations, shapes, sizes, nationalities, colors, and accents. The population "stew" that comes from this marrying of flavors is a natural result of New Orleans's long history, a past that has seen widely differing groups gather here to oppose one another in the beginning, only to join hands in mutual self-interest in the end.

A LOOK BACKWARD

In 1718 a Canadian-born Frenchman, Sieur de Bienville, set out to find a suitable location for a settlement to protect France's holdings in the New World from British expansion. His brother, Sieur d'Iberville, had planted a cross at the great bend of the Mississippi River in 1699, and Bienville found this place a strategic point for his "city." Although it was almost 110 miles inland from the gulf by river, the city had an easy portage route to a little stream (Bayou St. John) that provided easy water transportation directly into Lake Pontchartrain. From a military standpoint, this was a convenient "backdoor" for defense or escape, depending on the fortunes of war should the British get serious. And, of course, it was a perfect trade route for the fabled Indian gold that Bienville hoped to ship back home. Following the plan of a late French medieval town, a central square (the Place d'Armes) was laid out, with streets forming a grid around it—a church, government office, priest's house, and official residences fronting the square and earthen ramparts dotted with forts on its perimeter. In honor of the then Regent of France, the Duc d'Orléans, the little town was named New Orleans.

Today we know that section of the modern city as the Vieux Carré (it means "Old Square" and is pronounced "Vyew Ka-*ray*") and the Place d'Armes as Jackson Square. Rude huts of cypress filled in with moss and clay were erected, and a tiny wooden levee was raised against the mighty river, which persisted in flooding periodically to turn streets into rivers of mud.

The fabled gold turned out to be just that, a fable. But there were furs aplenty, and Bienville needed settlers to trap them, run farms to feed the colony, and fight off hostile Indians. The French government saw this as a perfect opportunity to rid itself of all its misfits at home and sent out the dregs of its prisons, some bonded servants, and slaves from French Caribbean settlements. They were the first ingredients of New Orleans's population "stew." Among them were "fallen women" who somehow managed to leave no direct descendants—if you can believe today's New Orleanians, who proudly trace their ancestry to French or Spanish nobility and the respectable "casket girls" brought over by Ursuline nuns in 1727 (carrying all their worldly goods in casketlike trunks), with never a mention of those earlier women of the streets.

Lured by the first real estate scam in this country's history (a flamboyant speculator named John Law painted the appealing picture of a virtual paradise on earth in the new settlement), wealthy Europeans, aristocrats, merchants, exiles, soldiers, and a large contingent of German farmers arrived to find only mosquitoes, a raw frontier existence, and swampy land that resisted all but the most heroic efforts to put it to productive use. But the Europeans stayed on, and as they tamed the land, the colony prospered and attracted more and more members of the aristocratic class. Social life began to take on the complexion of European court life. By 1763 yet another seasoning was added to the pot—Acadians from Nova Scotia fleeing British rule. You'll find their descendants living a little to the west of New Orleans, still engaged in farming and trapping, still speaking their unique brand of French, and proudly calling themselves "Cajuns."

French to the core from the very beginning, New Orleanians were horrified to learn in 1764 that Louis XV had secretly given their city—and them—to his cousin, Charles III of Spain. Their resentment forced the first Spanish governor to leave, and it wasn't until "Bloody O'Reilly" was dispatched by the Spanish Crown with 3,000 soldiers in 1769 that revolutionary ideas were firmly squelched (after the execution of five French patriots) and Spanish rule was accepted as a reality. With a Gallic shrug, French aristocracy mingled with Spanish nobility, intermarried, and created a new "Creole" culture.

Tragic fires struck in 1788, when more than 850 buildings were destroyed, and again in 1794 in the midst of rebuilding. From the ashes emerged a completely new city, dominated by the proud Spanish style of brick-and-plaster buildings replete with arches, courtyards, balconies, and, of course, attached slave quarters. Even today you'll see tile markers giving Spanish street names at every corner in the "French" Quarter.

The new city was much coveted by both the English and the Americans. France, recognizing its blunder in giving the city away, wanted it back. Control of the Mississippi River was at stake, and with all sorts of plots flying about, Governor Carondelet reinforced the wall around the city and armed its five forts with cannons pointing outward to fend off invaders and inward to ward off any internal uprising. France finally regained possession in 1800, with a surprisingly quiet transfer of ownership, and held on for three years while Napoleon negotiated the Louisiana Purchase with the United States for the paltry (as it turned out) sum of $15 million. To the Creole society, this was almost as appalling as Spanish rule had been to the

French settlers, for they considered all Americans barbarians who would surely bring about the end of the sophisticated Vieux Carré life-style.

Shunned by existing New Orleans society, the newly arrived Americans settled across Canal Street (so named because a drainage canal was once planned along its route, although it was never actually constructed) and set about showing the "downtown" snobs that they were no strangers to culture. Splendid mansions rose in what is now the Garden District, and a segregated social life took shape. But not for long. Yankee commercialism (which took on a boom town air "uptown") brought industry and wealth much needed by downtowners, and the vitality of warm-blooded downtown society drew uptowners like a magnet. Besides, both were forced to join forces against hurricanes, yellow fever epidemics, and floods. A spirit of unity grew between the two sections, so much so that when Andrew Jackson needed volunteers to protect New Orleans against British attack in 1814, some 5,000 citizens responded—from both sides of Canal Street. Even the infamous (but much revered in New Orleans) privateer Jean Lafitte joined in, supplying cannons and ammunition that swung the balance in favor of the Americans. Ironically the battle—which left some 2,000 British casualties as opposed to only a small number of American dead and wounded—was fought two weeks *after* a peace treaty had been signed, unbeknownst to either side at New Orleans.

From then until the Civil War, New Orleans gloried in a prosperity unmatched anywhere in the country. Wealthy cotton and sugar planters left upriver mansions from time to time to occupy luxurious town houses and to attend festivals, opera, theater, banquets, parades, and spectacular balls (including "Quadroon Balls," where beautiful mulatto girls were displayed to the gentry as possible mistresses). Hardworking Irish and German immigrants arrived in vast numbers to add their own dash of spice to the already exotic culture. Canals and levees were built to keep the city alive and a little drier; steamboats plied the river serving King Cotton and pleasure-seeking passengers; politics and gambling became passionate pastimes; and there was a lively trade in the slaves who supported the plantation economy on their oppressed backs. Federal troops put an end to all that when they marched in during 1862 to stay through a bitter Reconstruction period until 1877. New Orleans would never again be quite so flamboyant, but it was far from dead.

Like the rest of the defeated South, the city went about the business of rebuilding its economic life without the dependency on slavery that had been its downfall. By 1880 port activity had begun to pick up and industrial activity drew more and more visitors from the business world, many of whom became residents. And a new group of immigrants, Italians, came to put their special mark on the city. Through it all there survived an undiminished enthusiasm for fun. By 1880 gambling again thrived in over 80 establishments, there were almost 800 saloons, and scores of "bawdy houses" openly engaged in prostitution (illegal but uncontrolled). New Orleans was earning a reputation for open vice, and there were some who felt that something should be done to counteract such publicity. Alderman Sidney Story, in 1897, thought he had the answer. He moved all illegal (but highly profitable) activities into a restricted district along Basin Street, next door to the French Quarter. Quickly nick-named "Storyville," the district boasted fancy "sporting palaces" with elaborate décor, musical entertainment, and a variety of ladies of pleasure. Visitors and residents could purchase a directory (the "Blue Book"), which listed alphabetically the names, addresses, and races of more than 700 prostitutes, ranging from those in the "pal-aces" to the poorer inhabitants of wretched, decaying shacks called "cribs" on the blocks behind Basin Street. Black musicians came into their own when they moved from the streets into ornate bor-dellos to entertain patrons with the music we know as jazz. Although jazz itself predates Storyville, it was there that it gained the popularity that sent it upriver and into this country's musical heritage. When the secretary of the navy decreed in 1917 that our armed forces should not be exposed to so much open vice (without, it might be added, any visible support from the troops), Storyville closed down and disappeared without a trace.

IN RECENT YEARS

New Orleans has built its port into the largest in the United States and the second busiest in the world. (Amsterdam is first.) It ranks third in tourism in this country (conventions alone bring in more than 800,000 visitors each year) and is one of the top-three travel destinations for foreign visitors. (San Francisco and New York are the other two.) Drainage and epidemic problems have been con-quered by means of high levees, canals, pumping stations, and great spillways, which are opened to direct flood water away from the city.

Outside the French Quarter, the city's face has changed consid-erably over recent years. The 1984 World's Fair left a legacy of high-rise luxury hotels and a reconstructed waterfront on the Fair's site, in what was a derelict warehouse district. New Orleans's emergence as a major financial center (with more than 50 commercial banks) has brought with it the construction of soaring office buildings, mostly in the Central Business District.

Yesterday lives on in the architecture and life-style of the French Quarter, Garden District mansions, and colorful steamboats ferry-ing fun-loving passengers around the harbor—and, as always, it joins hands happily with today's Yankee entrepreneurs in a friendly, heart-warming collaboration that makes New Orleans an exciting travel experience not to be missed.

THE PRACTICALITIES

New Orleans is a gateway city, and as such has entry transportation of almost every kind available. Once you're there, its layout is fairly simple.

1. Getting There

BY AIRPLANE

No fewer than 13 airlines serve New Orleans's international airport, and among them are American, Continental, Delta, Eastern, Ozark, Pan American, Piedmont, and US Air. As we go to press, average round-trip coach fares with no advance booking and no discount are about $844 from New York, $691 from Chicago, and $994 from Los Angeles. With the current yo-yo airline fares situation, these may change, sometimes overnight. And, of course, you should *always* check for APEX fares and special promotional packages—New Orleans is a favored destination for seasonal and advance-booking discount rates with some airlines. Be sure to check on what's available when you plan your visit.

From the airport you can reach the Central Business District by bus for 90¢, by limousine for $7 per person (direct to leading hotels), and by taxi for about $20 ($8 for each additional passenger).

BY TRAIN

Amtrak trains reach New Orleans's Union Passenger Terminal, centrally located at 1001 Loyola Avenue (tel. 504/525-1179), from Los Angeles and intermediate points; New York, Washington, and points in between; and Chicago and intermediate points. Using the All Aboard America fares, you'll pay $229 from New York, $179 from Chicago, and $229 from Los Angeles. Amtrak, too, frequently offers special family rates, senior citizen discounts, and other packages, some with a rental car, so be sure to check when you reserve.

Amtrak does an especially good job with tour packages, which can be arranged through your local Amtrak Tour Desk. In 1990 options ranged from a three-night "New Orleans Special," with no-frills hotel accommodations at $95, to the three-day "Rhythm of New Orleans" package, including escorted sight-seeing tours or riverboat cruises, top-rated hotel accommodations (double occupancy), and other extras at $165. All tour prices are in addition to rail fares. Prices will change, of course, during the life of this book, but from past experience it is safe to say that Amtrak tours will be genuine moneysavers.

BY BUS

Greyhound-Trailways buses also come into the Union Passenger Terminal from points throughout the country. Round-trip fares at the time of writing are $138 from New York and $228 from Los Angeles.

BY CAR

You can drive to New Orleans via I-10, U.S. 90, and U.S. 61 and across the Lake Pontchartrain causeway on La. 25. Most hotels provide parking, and these public garages are open 24 hours a day: French Market Parking Lot, Decatur Street at St. Peter Street (tel. 529-5708); International Rivercenter, Poydras Street at the Mississippi River (tel. 561-0500); and Rivergate Convention Center, entrance on South Peter Street (tel. 529-2861). The **AAA Louisiana Division** is located at 3445 N. Causeway, Metairie, LA 70002 (tel. 504/838-7500) and will assist members with trip planning, service aids, and emergency services.

For banking services—such as foreign-money exchange, money transfers, and traveler's checks—visit the Hibernia National Bank, 313 Carondelet Street (tel. 586-5461), open from 9am to 3pm weekdays, where several foreign languages are spoken.

2. Getting Around

BY BUS

New Orleans has an excellent public bus system, and you can get complete information on which buses run where by calling 569-2700 or by picking up an excellent city map at the **Visitor Informa-**

tion Center, 529 St. Ann Street in the French Quarter. All fares at the moment are 60¢ (you must have exact change), except for expresses, which are 75¢.

A very special bus ride for your first, farewell, or "tired-feet" tour of the French Quarter is the **Vieux Carré Minibus.** Quaint little vehicles leave Canal and Bourbon streets at frequent intervals from 5am to 7:23pm. It'll cost you just 60¢ to see all of the French Quarter in comfort, although certainly not in as much detail as via the hoof-it route.

Along the riverfront, vintage streetcars, affectionately known as the "Ladies in Red," run for 1.9 miles from the Old Mint, across Canal Street, to Riverview. The fare is 60¢, there are convenient stops along the way, and there's ramp access for the handicapped—a great stepsaver as you explore this lively area of the city.

Outside the Quarter, you can park at the Louisiana Superdome and ride a **Central Business District shuttle bus,** which for 25¢ takes you down Poydras Street to the Convention Center, then back up Canal to the Superdome. If you're interested in Canal Street shopping, this is by far the most convenient and economical way to do it because you can make as many stops along the way as you want without the bother of finding that elusive parking space. It's another fare, however, each time you board. Shuttles run from 6:30am to 6pm daily except Sundays and holidays.

BY CAR

Rental cars are available from Hertz, Avis, Budget, American International Rent-a-Car, Dollar, Greyhound, Econo-Car, Holiday, and National. Driving can be difficult in New Orleans, and I've been told by locals that although traffic officers are fairly tolerant of moving violations, they're absolute murder on illegal parking, handing out tickets right and left. For that reason I strongly suggest that you put the car away for any French Quarter sight-seeing (it's more fun, anyway, on foot or by minibus) and use it only for longer jaunts out of congested areas.

A very helpful booklet, *Park Smart,* is distributed free by most hotels and all tourist offices. It details parking regulations and includes a map showing public parking facilities. On-the-street parking is metered at 25¢ per 20 minutes.

Driving within the city is relatively easy, except in the French Quarter, where several streets are blocked off at certain hours as pedestrian malls, and in the Central Business District, where congested traffic and limited parking make life difficult for the motorist. It is much smarter to park the car and use the very good public transportation provided in both areas.

ON FOOT

For my money, the *only* way to see the French Quarter and the Garden District is by foot. They're both small areas that are crammed with things you won't want to miss and easy to find your way around. Only by strolling can you really soak up the charm of both these sections. In the Quarter, look through iron gates or down alleyways for glimpses of lovely patios and courtyards and above street level for interesting façades and incredibly fragile, lacy iron railings. Along Bourbon Street, intersperse strolls with stops to listen to live jazz groups playing at open-door saloons—there's nonstop music most of the day. In the Garden District, be sure to allow enough time to drink in the beauty of the formal gardens surrounding the fine old mansions.

BY TAXI

Taxis are plentiful and respond quickly to telephone calls in New Orleans. They can be hailed easily on the street in the French Quarter and some parts of the Central Business District and are usually in place at taxi stands at the larger hotels. Otherwise, telephone and expect a cab to appear in three to five minutes. In my experience, at least two out of three drivers will get out to open doors for you at both ends of the ride. Rates are $1.15 when you enter the taxi and 25¢ for every one-tenth of a mile thereafter. Two reliable companies are **United Cabs, Inc.** (tel. 524-9606) and **Pelican Cab Service** (tel. 821-5474).

Touring tip: Most taxis can be hired for about $25 per hour for up to five passengers—a hassle-free and economical way for a small group to tour far-flung areas of the city (the lakefront, for example). Out-of-town trips cost double the amount on the meter.

BY TROLLEY

One treat you really should allow yourself is the 1½-hour ride down St. Charles Avenue on the famous old streetcar line, which has been named a National Historic Landmark. The trolleys run 24 hours a day at frequent intervals, and the fare is just 60¢ each way. Board at Canal and Carondelet streets (directly across Canal from Bourbon Street in the French Quarter), sit back, and look for landmarks in this part of town. Lafayette Square is at the 500 block of St. Charles, and across from it is Gallier Hall, built in the 1840s, which was the seat of the city's government for 100 years.

At Lee Circle, a little farther on, you'll see a huge statue of the general (Robert E., that is), which was erected in 1884—take note that he's facing *north* (that's so his back will never be to his enemies). From here on, it's fun to watch the homes that line the avenue as they change from Greek Revival to Victorian to early 1900s. The Garden District begins at Jackson Avenue, and you may want to get off the trolley to explore it fully. Even while riding by, however, you'll see many lovely homes in their garden settings. Loyola and Tulane universities are at the 6,000 block, across from Audubon Park. The park itself is worth a visit—there are huge old live oaks, a zoo, lagoons, a children's amusement park, tennis courts, and a municipal golf course. It extends all the way to the levee at the Mississippi.

The end of the line is at Palmer Park and Playground at Clairborne Avenue, but if you want to mount a shopping expedition at the interesting Riverbend Shopping Area (see Chapter X), get off at Carollton. It will cost you another 60¢ for the ride back to Canal Street, and it's a good idea to sit on the opposite side for the return to watch for things you missed going out. As a New Orleans friend once told me proudly, "The St. Charles trolley has to be the best 60¢ tour in the world!"—I'm inclined to agree with him.

A complete, detailed trolley and bus route map can be found in Chapter IX.

BY HORSE AND CARRIAGE

If you have even one romantic bone in your body, you'll find it hard to resist the authentic old horse-drawn carriages that pick up passengers at Jackson Square. Each horse is decked out with a flower-and-ribbon-trimmed straw hat, and each driver is apparently in fierce competition with all other drivers to win a "most lavishly decorated carriage" award. No matter which one you choose, you'll get a knowledgeable, nonstop monologue on historic buildings, fascinating events of the past, and a legend or two during the 2¼-mile drive through the French Quarter. They're at the Decatur Street end of Jackson Square from 9am to midnight in good weather; the charge is $8 per adult and $4 for children.

BY FERRY

One of New Orleans's nicest treats is absolutely free. It's the 25-minute (round-trip) ferry ride across the Mississippi from the foot of Canal Street, and it's a joy, whether you go by day for a view of the busy harbor or at night, when the lights of the city reflect in the mighty river. If you'd like to do some West Bank driving between trips, the ferry carries both car and foot passengers.

BY BOAT

If the horse-drawn carriages represent romance on land, they are matched on the river by several old-time steamboats that leave from the foot of Canal Street or Toulouse Street for river cruises. You'll find details of the cruises at the end of Chapter IX.

---

3. City Layout

The **French Quarter,** where the city began, is a 13-block-long area between Canal Street and Esplanade Avenue running from the Mississippi River to North Rampart Street. Because of the bend in the river, much of the city is laid out at angles that render useless such mundane directions as north, south, east, and west. New Orleans solved the geographical problem long ago by simply substituting *riverside, lakeside, uptown,* and *downtown.* It works, and you'll catch on quickly if you keep in mind that North Rampart Street is the "lakeside" boundary of the Quarter, Canal Street marks the beginning of "uptown," and the Quarter is "downtown." As for building numbers, they begin at 100 on either side of Canal. In

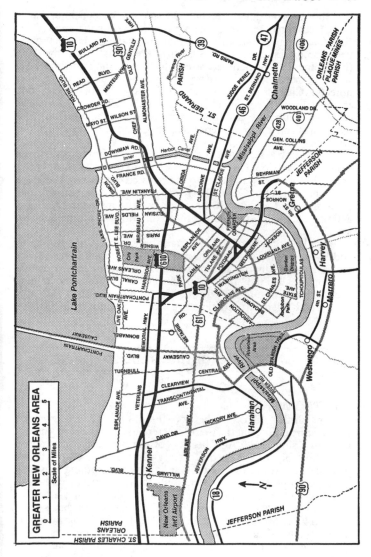

GREATER NEW ORLEANS AREA
Scale of Miles

the Quarter they begin at 400 at the river (that's because four blocks of numbered buildings were lost to the river before the levee was built). Another reminder of Canal Street's boundary role between new and old New Orleans is the fact that street names change when they cross it (that is, Bourbon Street "downtown" becomes Carondelet "uptown").

Just steps outside the French Quarter, one street behind Esplanade, **Faubourg Marigny** is one of the oldest residential areas of the city. *Fabourg* means suburb, and Marigny is the name of a prominent family in early New Orleans. For some years the area (beginning with Frenchmen Street) had been going downhill to a somewhat seedy state; these days, however, small businesses, a good hotel (see Chapter IV), several good eateries, and a popular jazz spot are revitalizing Frenchmen Street and its smaller tributaries. Because of Faubourg Marigny's proximity to the Quarter, the restaurants and entertainment there are included with those of the Quarter.

The **Central Business District** lies directly above Canal Street from the Mississippi River, stretching toward the lake to Loyola Avenue 11 blocks away and over to the elevated expressway 10 blocks from and parallel to Canal. There are pleasant plazas, squares, and parks sprinkled among all those commercial high-rise buildings, and some of the most elegant of the luxury hotels are located in this area.

The beautiful **Garden District** lies between St. Charles Avenue and Magazine Street toward the river and Jackson and Louisiana avenues. Incidentally the area past Magazine Street near the river is sometimes called the "Irish Channel" because it was home to hundreds of Irish immigrants during the 1800s. Audubon Park and Loyola and Tulane universities are a little farther out on St. Charles Avenue.

---

4. Useful Information

WHAT TO WEAR

It's a little hard to say what you should wear. The average mean temperature is 70°, but the thermometer can drop or rise several degrees in a single day. And because of the humidity, you can be uncomfortably cold or uncomfortably warm at relatively mild temperatures. However, I've found that lightweight clothing is usually enough, supplemented by a medium-weight raincoat (although from December through March it's a good idea to carry along an extra sweater). The almost subtropical climate keeps this a good place to visit almost any time of year, but July and August can be exceptionally muggy. If you do come during those months, you'll quickly learn to follow the natives' example and stay out of the noonday sun and duck from one air-conditioned building to another. And even in the rain (which averages 63 inches annually), you'll be able to get around without difficulty—to borrow a phrase from the Irish, it's a "soft rain" hereabouts.

THE LANGUAGE

The language is English, of course—but it may come in tones, accents, and pronunciations that surprise you. Don't expect to hear a lot of "you-alls" or other Deep South expressions; be prepared instead for a sort of southern Brooklynese. Unless you stick to the Garden District and university campuses, you should know before you come that *erl* means *oil*, *toin* translates to *turn*, and even the most cultured downtowner is likely to slip in a *de* or two for *the*. There are, of course, all sorts of dialects around town, as you'd expect from the ethnic backgrounds represented in New Orleans, but somehow they *all* seem to have caught a little bit of New York's Brooklyn in their speech. Various theories have been raised to explain this phenomenon: that the same ethnic groups immigrated to both cities in the 1800s, that both are seaports, or that *most* foreigners who learn English later in life adopt this kind of talk (although I have my doubts about that). Whatever the reason, it seems to be a permanent part of the New Orleans scene, and believe it or not, it actually becomes a part of the city's charm.

As for the pronunciation of certain rather ordinary street names and other commonly used words, there is simply *no* explanation—except that New Orleanians have decided (using some obscure logic, no doubt) that they should be said a certain way and that's the way they're said in New Orleans. To help you sound less like a "foreigner" as you move around town, here are some of those with the native twist:

Conti Street	*Con*-teye
Burgundy Street	Bur-*gun*-dee
Carondelet Street	Car-*onde*-let (not "lay")
Calliope Street	*Cal*-i-ope (not "Cal-*i*-opee")
Chartres Street	Charters
Dauphine Street	Daw-*feen*
Iberville Street	*Eye*-bur-vill
Bienville Street	Bee-*en*-vill
Orleans Street	Or-*leens*
	but
New Orleans	Noo *Or*-lyuns (or better yet, *Nor*-luns)
Vieux Carré	Voo Ka-*ray*

You're sure to hear others that sound peculiar—but don't question, just follow the lead of those who live there. And speaking of pronouncing words, here are a few others you should know to complete your New Orleans vocabulary:

lagniappe	lan-*yap* (a little something extra you've neither paid for nor deserve—like the 13th doughnut when you order a dozen)
bayou	*by*-u (a marshy, sluggish stream, usually feeding into a river or lake)
beignet	bin-*yea* (a cross between a doughnut and a cruller, liberally sprinkled with powdered sugar)

banquette	ban-*ket* (a French word for bench that means "sidewalk" in New Orleans, since early wooden sidewalks were elevated above muddy streets)
dressed	"served with the works"—as when ordering a sandwich
gumbo	a thick, spicy soup, always served with rice
hurricane	a local drink of rum and passion fruit punch
jambalaya	jum-bo-*lie*-ya (a jumble of yellow rice, sausage, seafood, vegetables, and spices)
muffuletta	one of the largest (and tastiest) sandwiches you'll ever see—a mountain of Italian sausage and meats with mustard, pickles, and a mess of other things piled onto thick buns
pralines	*praw*-lines (a *very* sweet confection made of brown sugar and pecans—they come in creamy and brittle styles)
crayfish	*craw*-fish (sometimes spelled "crawfish" and *always* pronounced that way—a tiny, lobster-looking creature plentiful in the waters around New Orleans and used in every conceivable way in cooking)
étouffée	ay-too-*fay* (a Cajun dish—a kind of smothered stew served with rice, which may contain crayfish and always contains *something* very good)
café brûlot	cah-*fay* brew-*low* (coffee mixed with spices and liqueurs and served flaming)

DRINKING LAWS

Alcoholic beverages are available in New Orleans around the clock, seven days a week. But be warned—although the police may look the other way if they see a pedestrian who's had a few too many (as long as he or she is peaceful and not bothering anyone else), they have no tolerance at all for those who are intoxicated behind the wheel. If you find yourself in that condition far from your hotel, you'd best take a taxi.

TOURIST INFORMATION

You'll be way ahead if, as far in advance as possible, you contact the **Greater New Orleans Tourist and Convention Center,** 1520 Sugar Bowl Drive, New Orleans, LA 70112 (tel. 504/566-5011), for their brochures on such subjects as sight-seeing, dining, entertainment, shopping, and more. If you have a special interest, rest assured they'll help you plan your visit around appropriate activities.

Once you've arrived in the city, your first order of business should be to stop by the **Visitor Information Center** at 529 St. Ann Street (tel. 504/566-5031) in the French Quarter. The center is open every day of the week (9am to 5pm from November through February, 10am to 6pm in other months) and has excellent walking and driving tour maps and booklets on restaurants, accommodations, sight-seeing, special tours, and almost anything else you might want to know about. The staff is multilingual, friendly, and a veritable fount of valuable information not only on New Orleans but also on the entire state of Louisiana.

EMERGENCIES

Should you become ill during your New Orleans visit, most major hotels have in-house staff doctors on call 24 hours a day. If there's not one available in your hotel or guesthouse, call or go to the Emergency Room at the **Touro Infirmary,** 1401 Foucher (tel. 897-7011), if you're uptown; or the **Tulane University Medical Center,** 1415 Tulane Avenue (tel. 588-5342), if you're in the Central Business District.

Other useful numbers are **Travelers Aid Society** (tel. 525-8726); **Union Passenger Terminal,** 1001 Loyola Avenue, for bus and train information (tel. 528-1610); local **transit information** (bus routes and schedules) can be obtained from the RTA Ride Line (tel. 569-2623); **time** (tel. 529-6111); and **weather** (tel. 525-8831).

SAFETY

Whenever you're traveling in an unfamiliar city, stay alert. Be aware of your immediate surroundings. Wear a money belt. Don't sling your camera or purse over your shoulder; wear the strap diagonally across your body. This will minimize the possibility of your becoming a victim of crime. Every society has its criminals, and it's your responsibility to be aware and alert even in the most heavily touristed areas.

WHEELCHAIR ACCESS

"Rollin' by the River," a guide to wheelchair-accessible restaurants and clubs is available free from the **Advocacy Center for the Elderly and Disabled,** 210 O'Keefe Ave., Suite 700, New Orleans, LA 70112 (tel. 504/522-2337).

III

THE FESTIVALS

1. MARDI GRAS
2. OTHER FESTIVALS

New Orleans means "Festival"—and if you don't believe it, try this simple little "free association" test. What's the first thing that comes to mind when someone says "New Orleans"? Mardi Gras—right? Well, that's the biggie, of course, but it's only *one* of this lively city's celebrations. There's something about the frame of mind here that just won't tolerate inhibitions—whether there's a declared celebration in progress or not! I always feel I'm celebrating something every day that I'm in the "City that Care Forgot." Actually, I don't really believe that care forgot New Orleans (there are plenty of problems to be faced and solved). It's just that New Orleanians seem to look problems in the face, shrug their shoulders, and work them out with a grin and a wink. They simply refuse to be grim!

As for officially designated festival days, a Calendar of Events issued by the Tourist Commission lists no fewer than 26 spread over the year that are observed either in the city proper or in its neighboring parishes. There's a festival of jazz and food; a celebration of spring when ladies don the costumes of long ago and shepherd an admiring public through gorgeous old mansions; there's a food festival just to celebrate the fine art of eating as it's practiced around here; there's an oyster festival, a catfish festival, and numerous crayfish festivals (which sometimes feature a crayfish race) to celebrate the generous waters of the area; there's a two-week extravaganza built around Bastille Day (the French themselves probably lack the enthusiasm that's shown here for that day); and . . . well, you get the idea. If there's any possible reason to celebrate, New Orleans throws a party.

I can't, of course, cover them all in these pages. I'll tell you about some of the most interesting, and if you take my advice, you'll write or call ahead to the **Greater New Orleans Tourist and Convention Commission,** 1520 Sugar Bowl Drive, New Orleans, LA

70112 (tel. 504/566-5011), for a current Calendar of Events to see what's going to be happening when you plan your visit. If, however, you don't see anything spectacular listed, don't worry—you'll feel festive from the moment you arrive.

---

1. Mardi Gras

Mardi Gras is the granddaddy of all New Orleans festivals, and it's been here in one form or another as long as the city itself. Volumes could be written about its history, and almost any native you encounter will have his or her own store of Mardi Gras tales. What follows here is a thumbnail sketch of its background and a quick rundown on present-day krewes, parades, and balls.

To begin with, the name *Mardi Gras* means "Fat Tuesday" in French, and that's a very appropriate name because it is always celebrated on the Tuesday before Ash Wednesday—the idea being that you have a sort of obligation to eat, drink, and be as merry as you possibly can before the Lenten season of fasting and repentance sets in. The name *Carnival* is Latin in origin (from *carnisvale*, meaning "farewell to flesh") and refers to the period from January 6 to Mardi Gras Day (in New Orleans, the Carnival season is officially opened by the Krewe of Twelfth Night Revelers ball, the only one that has a fixed date).

HISTORY

Where did the custom start? Nobody knows for certain, but some historians see a relationship to ancient tribal rites connected with the coming of spring. And a glorious, sin-filled, pagan orgy that highlighted mid-February for ancient Romans may have been an early ancestor of today's Mardi Gras. The Christian church did its best to stamp out such wild goings-on, but about all it succeeded in doing was to insist on a strict period of fasting and praying for forgiveness to follow the festive season. The point is that although New Orleans can properly claim Mardi Gras for its own in the United States, its spirit of revelry belongs to the history of the world. So, when the first French settlers arrived at the mouth of the Mississippi, what could be more natural than their bringing Mardi Gras along with them?

When Iberville, the French explorer, and his group of colonizers camped along the Mississippi in 1699, he didn't bother with keeping records, other than to note that the date was March 3. We don't know for sure, therefore, what that day's activities were in the little camp. What we *do* know is that March 3 was the day before Ash Wednesday in that year, and that Iberville named the spot, some 12 miles north of the river's mouth, "Point du Mardi Gras." It seems likely that with a centuries-long tradition of French Mardi Gras celebration behind him, Iberville celebrated the day in some sort of fashion.

It wasn't long after New Orleans was established in 1718 that the French were at it again, although their Mardi Gras consisted largely of private masked balls and parties, with street dancing limited to the poor (but lighthearted) elements of the population. When the Spanish governors took up residence, they slapped a ban on such doings, and the Americans who began arriving in 1803 continued the ban. It wasn't until 1823 that French Quarter Creoles persuaded the city government to permit the masquerade balls once more, and by 1827 it was legal to wear masks in the streets on the great day. When those street maskers started marching in processions that might—by a *big* stretch of the imagination—be called parades, is uncertain, but in 1837 the *Daily Picayune* published for the first time an account of a Mardi Gras parade.

For the next few years things began to get out of hand, with so much wildness in the streets that it seemed inevitable that the city government would have to do something to quell the disorderliness. The future of Mardi Gras in New Orleans was very much in doubt, as newspapers and citizens aroused by street violence called for a permanent end to the festival. It took six new residents of the city, who had formerly lived in Mobile, Alabama, to turn things around. Determined to save Mardi Gras and restore some semblance of order and dignity to its observance, they met with 13 friends in what was known as "the club room" over the Gem bar at 127 Royal Street. What came out of that meeting was a secret society, the Mistick Krewe of Comus, dedicated to preserving the institution of Carnival. They actually coined the "krewe" appellation, and they planned the first formal, torch-lit parade that was the pattern for all that have followed. Still adhered to, as well, is the practice of building each krewe's parade around a central theme, as did the Krewe of Comus in that first parade. It was from the Comus krewe, too, that New Orleanians took the practice of forming secret societies, ending parades with private fancy balls, always preceded by an elaborate tableau.

The Civil War put a temporary halt to things, but Comus was parading again by 1866. In 1870 a krewe known as the Twelfth Night Revelers was founded and added two new policies that still endure: They began the throwing of trinkets to onlookers (the first thrower was dressed as Santa Claus), and they were the first to have an official "Queen" reign over their ball. A royal visit in 1872 contributed something more to New Orleans's Mardi Gras traditions. The Grand Duke of Russia, Alexis Alexandrovitch Romanov, followed his ladylove, a musical-comedy star named Lydia Thompson, from New York when she came to New Orleans to star in *Bluebeard*. The city went all out to welcome him, and when it was learned that his favorite song was Lydia's favorite burlesque tune, "If Ever I Cease to Love You," every band in the Rex parade was asked to play it—that sprightly melody is now the official song of Mardi Gras. Incidentally the prestigious Krewe of Rex was born that year when a group of citizens banded together to raise money for an impressive welcome ceremony for the duke. The royal colors (purple for justice, green for faith, and gold for power) were also adopted as the festival's official colors.

Mardi Gras, despite its avowal of a "pleasure-only" basis, has served a social purpose at least once in New Orleans. During Reconstruction days following the Civil War, public unrest forced the cancellation of the festival in 1875, but in 1877 the Krewe of Momus used as its parade theme "Hades, a Dream of Momus," which held the Grant administration up to such ridicule that the entire country's attention was focused on the deplorable conditions in the South.

Today's traditional ending of Mardi Gras had its beginning in 1882, when Rex and his queen called on the Court of Comus at that krewe's ball. The Krewe of Rex also began throwing medallions instead of trinkets in 1884, and the doubloons that came many years later are an outgrowth of that substitution. The doubloons, usually of aluminum or anodized gold, show the krewe's coat of arms on one side and the parade theme of the year on the other—a marvelous, permanent souvenir of Mardi Gras if you're lucky enough to catch one. You can also purchase them at some New Orleans stores, but somehow it just isn't the same. They have become highly prized, so hold on to any you may acquire—some serious collector may someday offer a good price. The best way to come by one is to stand in the crowd and yell "Throw me something, mister" along with everyone else as the floats pass by. If your luck holds out, your pleas will be heard, and if your catch is good, you'll get the doubloon before someone else snatches it from the air.

New Orleans's blacks entered the Mardi Gras scene through a fun-filled backdoor. In 1909 a black man named William Storey mocked the elaborately garbed Rex by prancing after his float wearing a lard can for a crown. Storey was promptly dubbed "King Zulu." By 1916 his followers had grown so in numbers that they formed the Zulu Social Aid & Pleasure Club, and for years they observed Mardi Gras by wandering all over town, from one barroom to another that would extend hospitality to King Zulu. These days the Zulus get the day off to a start when His Majesty arrives by boat on the river at 7am (at the foot of Canal Street), and they follow a set parade route through the city's streets on proper floats instead of the banged-up trucks and wagons they used in their early years. They're worth getting up early to see just for their grass skirts and sometimes outrageous makeup and masks. Besides the monarch in his colorful raiment, there's a "Provident Prince" and a "Big Shot of Africa" all decked out in the-Good-Lord-only-knows-what to look for. The most notable King Zulu was probably Louis Armstrong in 1949, and in 1980 his good friend Woody Herman realized a longtime dream when he donned blackface and was crowned king of the Zulus.

Other early-morning Mardi Gras groups not to be missed are the "walking clubs," with names such as Jefferson City Buzzards, the Pete Fountain Half Fast, and Peggy Landry's Silk Stocking Strutters. To quote my good friend Arthur Hardy (author of an excellent Mardi Gras guidebook I'll tell you about later on), these clubs are "sometimes mistakenly named 'marching clubs'— actually, they *never* march; some do walk, but more than a few stumble!" You can catch these "marchers," who as much as the krewe parades embody the spirit of the day, anywhere along their St. Charles Avenue route (between Poydras and Washington).

WHAT TO SEE AND DO

What can you expect to see and take part in if you come to New Orleans for Mardi Gras? First, you must remember that this is, primarily, a party New Orleans throws for itself—those spectacular balls are private, attended only by members and their invited guests. Attendance is by invitation, not by ticket, except, that is, for the Bacchus supper dance (and even those tickets are usually hard to come by). If you should be invited to a krewe ball, there are a few things you should know. You'll be a spectator, not a participant, and unless you're a woman and have been issued a "call-out" card, you'll be seated in a separate section to view the tableau after the previous year's queen and her court have been escorted to seats of honor and masked-and-costumed krewe members have taken their reserved, up-front seats. Members, who guard their secrecy not only during Mardi Gras but also all year, are always in costumes and masks—for men it's white tie and tails if the invitation reads *de rigueur,* tuxedos if it reads only *formal.* Women, of course, are always in ballgowns. Those lucky "call-out" women will be seated separately from other guests (even their escorts) until the dancing begins and they've been called out by the krewe member who sent them the card. After a turn around the floor, they'll be given a krewe favor (a souvenir representative of that year's ball theme) and returned to their patiently waiting escorts. As members of the krewe and their ladies continue dancing, the current "royal court" will repair to the queen's supper, where friends and guests will be entertained the rest of the night—and into the morning.

One of the nicest things about New Orleans's private party is that the whole world is happily invited to come and look. And that results in a whole new cadre of not-so-private entertainments. If you think this town's restaurants and nightclubs and bars and jazz clubs are pretty special most of the time, you should see them during Carnival! You can, in fact, more or less form your own informal "krewe" of friends and have a ball that might be as much fun as those private ones, just by making the rounds in a group.

Whatever else you do or don't do, you surely won't miss seeing a Mardi Gras parade. If, that is, you come during the final 11 days of Carnival. You'll know one's coming when you hear the scream of motorcycle sirens and a herd of motorized police come into view. They'll be followed by men on horseback (sometimes mounted police, sometimes krewe members) who clear the edges of the streets for the approaching floats. The king's float is first in line, with His Majesty enthroned and waving to the mass of cheering humanity with his scepter. Then will come a float with a banner proclaiming the theme of the parade. After that, each float will illustrate some facet of the theme. And it's a grand sight—the papier-mâché lions or elephants or flowers or fanciful creatures or whatever are sometimes enormous (there are people in New Orleans who work all year designing and building Mardi Gras floats), and there's much use of silver and gold tinsel that sparkles in the sunlight or the light of torches. Those torches, or flambeaux, are carried by dancing blacks dressed in hoods and white smocks. Each float has masked krewe members who wave and throw doubloons and souvenirs. In some of the parades, the floats keep coming until you think there's no end to them—Bacchus, for instance, had 23 in 1982, and Rex had 25. Each krewe has its designated time and parade route (which makes a current Mardi Gras guidebook invaluable) and most follow some part of St. Charles Avenue, sometimes a portion of Jackson Street as well, and Canal Street, and end up at the Municipal Auditorium, where all parades disband—except the renegade Bacchus with its Rivergate terminus. Because there are more than 50 parading krewes and only 11 days in which to do the parading, the streets are seldom empty, day or night, during this period. And the rollicking, costumed crowd filling the streets is as much something to see as the parades themselves. Every conceivable manner of costume appears, and maskers made bold by their temporary anonymity carry on in the most outrageous, hilarious manner you can imagine. A great good humor envelops the whole scene, and I absolutely *defy* anyone to look on with disapproval.

On the last day of Carnival, Mardi Gras, the walking clubs are out at the crack of dawn, then King Zulu arrives around 9am, the Rex parade is mid-morning, and Comus closes the day with its evening parade (about 6:30pm). The high point of this final day is probably when Rex, the only Mardi Gras king whose identity is disclosed, arrives on his majestic float. It is a very high honor to be chosen Rex, and the selection always comes from among prominent men in the city, most well past the first blush of youth. Rex's queen, on the other hand, is always one of the current year's pack of young debutantes. Although that may make for a pretty ill-matched royal couple, there've never been any reports of incompatibility between the rulers-for-a-day. The choosing of Rex and his queen is done in the strictest secrecy, adding to the excitement that attends their first public appearance in the parade.

Another thing that's nice about Carnival in New Orleans is the fact that it doesn't cost the city one red cent except the cost of extra police for the parades and that of cleaning up the streets after Fat Tuesday. This is truly a private celebration, planned, executed, and paid for by New Orleanians themselves—and I'll wager that if not one of us dropped in for the festivities, the celebration would change not one iota.

PLANNING YOUR FESTIVAL

Now, for the practicalities—you'd like to be there for Mardi Gras, so the details have to be attended to. First, you can't really just drop in. If you do, you may find yourself sleeping in Jackson Square or on a sidewalk somewhere. Rooms are booked solid in the city itself and in the nearby suburbs, so *make your plans well ahead and book a room as soon as the plans are finalized*. It is no exaggeration to say that you should plan one year to go the next and make your reservation right then. Prices are usually a little higher during Mardi Gras, and most hotels and guesthouses impose minimum-stay requirements.

One way to eliminate many of the hassles for space during Mardi Gras is to book a package tour. Amtrak, for example, sometimes offers hotel space and some extras during Carnival, so you should check with your local Amtrak Tour Desk.

You will surely want to join the maskers with your own costume, and although it's best to plan ahead and come prepared, there are several shops in town that specialize in Mardi Gras costumes and masks (see Chapter X). One of the most reasonable is the **Mardi Gras Center**, 831 Chartres Street (tel. 524-4384). If you come early enough, they can custom-make a costume to your own design; if not, they are well stocked with new and used costumes, wigs, masks, hats, and makeup.

When you arrive, remember that while all those crowds add to the general merriment, they also make it more difficult to get in and out of restaurants in a hurry. And your progress from one part of town to another will be slowed down considerably. The point is that you should be sure to come in a relaxed frame of mind, with enough mental flexibility for the delays to be a source of enjoyment (after all, who knows *what* you may see while waiting) and not irritation.

You'll enjoy Mardi Gras more, too, if you've done a little homework before you come. Contact the **Greater New Orleans Tourist and Convention Commission**, 1520 Sugar Bowl Drive, New Orleans, LA 70112 (tel. 504/566-5011), and ask for their current Mardi Gras information. And I can't think of any one more valuable bit of preparation than the *Mardi Gras Guide* published by Arthur Hardy (4441 Iberville Street, New Orleans, LA 70119). He'll send you a copy postpaid if you send along $4.50, and credit card orders may be placed by calling 800/234-1575. If you arrive without this guide, they'll be in most bookstores and on newsstands in the city. It contains a complete history of the festival, a rundown on each krewe, parade times and routes, and a lot of other miscellaneous information that will make Mardi Gras even more fun.

Just one more thing should be said: You can figure out the future Mardi Gras date because it always falls exactly 46 days before Easter

CAJUN MARDI GRAS

For a really unique Mardi Gras experience, drive out to "Cajun Country." Lafayette, a booming but charming town in the very heart of French Acadiana, celebrates Carnival in a manner quite different from the New Orleans fête—a manner that reflects the heritage and spirit of those hardworking, fun-loving Cajuns. (For their full story, see Chapter XII.) There are three full days of parades leading up to Mardi Gras, with all sorts of attendant activities designed to *"laissez les bons temps rouler"* ("let the good times roll," an absolute creed around these parts during Carnival). This is, in fact, second in size only to New Orleans's Mardi Gras, and there's one *big* difference—the Cajuns open their final pageant and ball to the general public. That's right, you can don your costume and mask and join right in.

Instead of Rex and his queen, the Lafayette festivities are ruled by King Gabriel and Queen Evangeline. They are the fictional hero and heroine of Longfellow's epic poem *Evangeline,* which was based on real-life lovers who were separated during the British expulsion of Acadians from Nova Scotia just after the French and Indian War, and their story is still very much alive here among descendants of those who shared their wanderings. Things get off to a joyous start with the Children's Krewe and Krewe of Bonaparte parades and ball the Saturday before Mardi Gras, following a full day of celebration at Acadian Village. On Monday night Queen Evangeline is honored at the Queen's Parade. The King's Parade, held the following morning, honors King Gabriel and opens a full day of merriment. Lafayette's black community stages the Parade of King Toussaint L'Ouverture and Queen Suzanne Simonne about noon, just after the King's Parade. And following *that,* the Krewe of Lafayette invites everyone to get into the act as its parade winds through the streets. You can trot along with those on foot or ride in the vehicle of your choice (and some very imaginative modes of transportation turn up every year). If you're still up to it when this parade comes to an end in late afternoon, you can return to the hotel to get ready for the Mardi Gras climax, a brilliantly beautiful, exciting formal ball presided over by the king and queen and their royal court. Everything stops promptly at midnight, of course, as Cajuns and visitors alike depart to observe the solemnity of Lent with the fondly remembered glow of Mardi Gras to take them through to Easter.

Out in the Cajun countryside that surrounds Lafayette, there's yet another form of Mardi Gras celebration, and I'll guarantee you won't find another like it anywhere else in the world. It's very much tied to the rural life-style of these displaced people who have created a rich culture out of personal disaster. And since Cajuns firmly believe that nothing is ever quite as much fun alone as it is when shared, you're entirely welcome to come along. The rural celebration goes like this: Bands of masked men dressed in patchwork costumes and peaked hats (*capishons*) set off on Mardi Gras morning on horseback, led by their *capitaine.* They ride from farm to farm, asking at each, "Will you receive the Mardi Gras?" (*"Voulez-vous reçevoir le Mardi Gras?"*) and dismounting as the invariable "yes" comes in reply. Then each farmyard becomes a miniature festival, as they "make monkeyshines" (*faire le macaque*) with song and dance, much drinking of beer, and other antics loosely labeled as "entertainment." As payment for their show, they demand—and get—"a fat little chicken to make a big gumbo."

When each band has visited its allotted farmyards, all the bands head back to town, where everyone else has already begun the general festivities. There'll be dancing in the streets, rowdy card games, storytelling, and the like until the wee hours, and you may be sure that all those "fat little chickens" go into the "gumbo gros" pot to make a "big gumbo." It's a real "down home" sort of festival, where you can let your hair all the way down. And if you've never heard Cajun music (sort of like American country, but with a difference) or eaten gumbo cooked by real Cajuns, you're in for a treat.

You can write or call ahead for full particulars on both these Mardi Gras celebrations. Contact **Lafayette Parish Convention and Visitors Commission,** P.O. Box 52066, Lafayette, LA 70505 (tel. 318/232-3808, or toll free 800/346-1958 in the U.S. outside Louisiana, 800/543-5340 in Montreal and Quebec).

---

2. Other Festivals

JAZZ AND HERITAGE FESTIVAL

By the time mid-April rolls around, Easter has passed, the Mardi Gras is a fond memory of this year and a grand expectation for next, and New Orleanians turn to another festival celebration. Actually the Jazz and Heritage Festival combines two fêtes, as its name implies. From one weekend to another (one of the last weeks in April or the first in May), musicians, mimes, artists, craftspeople, and cooks head out to the Fair Grounds Race Track on the weekends and settle into hotel ballrooms, jazz joints, concert halls, and a special evening concert site to put on a never-ending show of what New Orleans is all about. Over 3,000 performers turn up—and that's not counting the street bands. Famous-name jazz players are drawn to this festival, and they very happily share the ten stages out at the Fair Grounds with lesser-known Cajun groups who stomp out rhythm and blues and the voices blended in sweet harmony over at the gospel music tent. You can find your favorite and stand in front of the stage all day long or make the rounds and come back to favorites or to see what new group has taken over. Remember that this is a New Orleans festival—completely unstructured with the emphasis on pure enjoyment. That's out at the Fair Grounds; on weeknights, street bands are everywhere, and if you can't find a performance of *your* kind of music going on somewhere, well, it just must not exist. If traditional jazz happens to be your preference, you'll be in heaven.

As for the "heritage" part of the festival, local craftspeople and imported artisans are there en masse with their wares (you can also see some demonstrations of just how they work), and that top-priority heritage, good food, is present in such abundance that you'll be tempted to stuff yourself way beyond the limits set by our modern health freaks. Red beans and rice, jambalaya, gumbo, crayfish, sweet-potato pie, oysters, fried chicken, andouille, boudin, poboys, crabs, and shrimp—that, believe it or not, is only a partial list of what's available. And there's plenty of cold beer to wash it down. There's just nothing quite like munching fried chicken from the Second Mount Triumph Missionary Baptist Church booth in an outdoor setting where the air is filled with strains of traditional jazz, ragtime, reggae, and the blues. There are well over 40 booths, and it's a safe bet that you'll want at least to sample each one, so come hungry.

To find out about the current dates, the artists who will be there and where they'll be performing in concert during the week, and background information, contact the Jazz and Heritage Festival, P.O. Box 53407, New Orleans, LA 70153 (tel. 504/522-4786).

SPRING FIESTA

One of the best times of the year to visit New Orleans is during the five-day-long Spring Fiesta, which has been going on since 1937. This is the one time you can get to see the inside of some of those lovely old homes. Those ordinarily closed to the public throw open their doors, and hostesses clad in antebellum dress will escort you through the premises, providing about each house or historic building all sorts of information and anecdotes that you might otherwise never know. In the French Quarter there are balcony concerts by sopranos rendering numbers sung there in the past by Jenny Lind and Adelina Patti. Out on River Road, there are plantation home tours; in the Quarter there are candlelight tours of patios; and as a highlight there is the gala "Night in Old New Orleans" parade, which features carriages bearing passengers dressed as prominent figures in the city's history and some of the best marching bands in town. Spring Fiesta always opens the first Friday after Easter. For full details, reservations, and a schedule of the modest admission fees for some of the homes, you can write to Spring Fiesta Association, 826 St. Ann Street, New Orleans, LA 70116 (tel. 504/581-1367).

LA FETE

Yes, there *is* food in every conceivable form at the Jazz and Heritage Festival in April. But by late June (sometimes early July), it's time to celebrate the local cuisine all over again, with a festival all its own. La Fête is held virtually all over town, and literally dozens of chefs set up food-tasting booths with everything from spicy Creole dishes to exotic Oriental treats to Cajun specialties to seafood in creative forms. There are also magnificent food presentations, so artistically done that it seems a shame they're made to be eaten. As one reviewer commented, La Fête adds up to "an epicure's dream, a dieter's nightmare." The whole affair is climaxed by a superb gourmet dinner. For exact dates and full details, write to La Fête, Suite 580, Oil and Gas Building, New Orleans, LA 70112 (tel. 504/525-4143).

TENNESSEE WILLIAMS FESTIVAL

In late March or early April, New Orleans honors perhaps its most illustrious writer. Tennessee Williams, although not born here, once said, "If I can be considered to have a home, it would have to be New Orleans . . . which has provided me with more material than any other city." During the three-day Tennessee Williams–New Orleans Literary Festival, many of his plays are performed, and there are symposiums on his work as well as walking tours of his favorite French Quarter haunts. For dates and details, contact the Greater New Orleans Tourist and Convention Commission, 1520 Sugar Bowl Drive, New Orleans, LA 70112 (tel. 504/566-5011).

FRENCH QUARTER FESTIVAL

In early April the three-day French Quarter Festival is a spectacular conglomeration of all the ingredients of the unique French

Quarter's rich gumbo of life. There are scads of free outdoor concerts, patio tours, a parade, a battle of jazz bands, art shows, children's activities, and talent and bartender competitions. As if that weren't enough, Jackson Square is transformed into the world's largest jazz brunch, when about 40 leading restaurants turn out to serve Cajun/Creole specialties such as jambalaya, gumbo, and crayfish fettuccine. For exact dates and other information, write to French Quarter Festival, P.O. Box 53362, New Orleans, LA 70153-3362 (tel. 504/522-5730).

CREOLE CHRISTMAS

Trust New Orleans! A few days simply are not enough for this lively city to celebrate Christmas, so the entire month of December is designated as "Creole Christmas." There are all sorts of gala events sprinkled throughout the month's calendar, including tours of impressive antebellum and postbellum homes decorated for the holiday and a great Christmas Eve cruise up the Mississippi River to view the famous levee bonfires while indulging in a gorgeous champagne dinner. Special "Papa Noël" rates are offered by hotels citywide. For full details, contact Papa Noël, 1008 N. Peters Street, New Orleans, LA 70116 (tel. 504/522-5730).

FESTIVALS ACADIENS

This is a "Cajun Country" celebration—or rather, *seven* celebrations—held during the third week of September in Lafayette. These festivals, lumped under the heading Festivals Acadiens, pay tribute to the culture and heritage of Cajun families who have been here nearly 200 years after the British expelled them from their Nova Scotia homeland. The festive week includes the Bayou Food Festival, the Cajun Music Festival, the Louisiana Native Crafts Festival, the Acadiana Fair and Trade Show, the RSVP Senior Fair and Craft Show, the Art Center for Southwestern Louisiana Festival, and the Acadian Village Festival.

At the **Bayou Food Festival,** you'll be able to taste the cuisine of more than 30 top Cajun restaurants. Specialties such as stuffed crabs, crayfish étouffée, oysters Bienville, shrimp Creole, oysters Rockefeller, shrimp de la Teche, catfish en brochette, jambalaya, chicken and sausage gumbo, smothered quail, and hot boudin are everyday eating for Cajuns, and this is a rare opportunity to try them all. It works like this: For about $6, you're given an admission ticket plus a book of coupons to be redeemed for food—a bargain in anyone's book. And if you're wondering about the quality of Lafayette's restaurant food, let me tell you that it sells more restaurant food per capita than any other American city.

The **Cajun Music Festival** (*L'Hommage à la Musique Acadienne*) got its start in 1974, when some Cajun musicians were engaged to play briefly for visiting French newspaper editors. In spite of its being a rainy night, some 12,000 Cajun residents showed up to listen. Well, the walls rang for three solid hours with old French songs, waltzes, two-steps, Cajun rock rhythms, and the special music some have dubbed "Cajun Country." Even after all that, nobody wanted to go home. Since then it has become an annual affair, and over 50,000 visitors are usually on hand. Because of the crowds, the festival is now held outdoors in Girard Park, where fans can listen in grassy comfort. Performed almost entirely in French, the music includes both traditional and modern Cajun styles (and one form, known as zydeco, combines the blues of the blacks with more traditional Cajun sounds). The music starts early and ends late, and there's no charge to come to the park and listen. Sales from food and beverage stands all go toward a fund to build a Cajun Music Preservation Hall.

You'll see native Louisiana artisans demonstrating their expertise at the **Louisiana Native Crafts Festival.** All crafts must have been practiced prior to or during the early 1900s, and all materials used must be native to Louisiana. Meeting these criteria are such arts as woodcarving of all types (with an emphasis, it seemed to me, on duck decoys), soap making, pirogue (pronounced *pee*-rogue— it's a Cajun canoe made from a dugout cypress log) making, chair caning, doll making, palmetto weaving, Indian weaving, quilting, spinning, dyeing, pottery making, jewelry making, alligator skinning, and probably a few more that I've missed.

The **Acadiana Fair and Trade Show** is put on by Lafayette merchants and businesspeople, and there's an indoor display of their goods and services, plus an outdoor carnival with rides, a midway, and games. It's sponsored by the Lafayette Jaycees, who also provide free shuttle bus service for the public from one festival to another.

The elders who have passed crafts down to many of the younger Cajuns you'll see at the Native Crafts Festival have their day in the sun at the **RSVP Senior Fair and Craft Show** (the RSVP stands for Retired Senior Volunteer Program). They're all over 60, and it's a rare treat to meet them and see their homemade articles and listen to them talk of the old days.

At the **Art Center for Southwestern Louisiana** (a big, colonial Louisiana plantation-style house), the festival features films, lectures, musical events, dance performances, and one-act plays, as well as a fine permanent collection of sketches, drawings, paintings, and sculpture by Cajuns, which capture the very essence of their unique culture. The house itself could almost qualify as an "exhibit," with its cypress-paneled library, brick flooring sealed with hot beeswax, and hand-carved wood moldings and fireplace façades. It was built entirely by local artisans.

You can visit the **Acadian Village** any time of the year, but during Festivals Acadiens, special events are often scheduled. If you have any interest at all in Acadiana's history, you'll find this little village a trip back in time. Homes and buildings here are not models or even reconstructions of originals—they're all original old Acadian homes that have been found, restored where needed, and moved to the village to create (or, as the Cajuns say, "reassemble") a typical 1800s village. It's a tranquil, charming spot.

For exact dates and full details on Festivals Acadiens, write or call the **Lafayette Parish Convention and Visitors Commission,** P.O. Box 52066, Lafayette, LA 70505 (tel. 318/232-3808, or toll free 800/346-1958).

FOR FROG FANCIERS

To prove my point that just about anything is cause for celebration in New Orleans and its environs, let me tell you about the ˇRayne Frog Festival. It's held in Cajun Country, just a few miles west of Lafayette. The Cajuns can hold their own when it comes to drumming up festivals—a harvest, a new season, a special tradition, a special talent, or just the job of being alive—and in this case they simply turn to the lowly frog as an excuse for a *fais-dodo* (dance) and a waltz contest. Not to forget the reason for it all, things get underway with frog races and frog-jumping contests—and if you arrive without *your* frog, there's a "Rent-a-Frog" service. To wind things up, there's a lively frog-eating contest. The Rayne Frog Festival is held in September. For dates and full details, contact the **Lafayette Parish Convention and Visitors Commission,** P.O. Box 52066, Lafayette, LA 70505 (tel. 318/232-3808). If this festival is not exactly your cup of tea, just glance over the list of other festivals scheduled. This is festival country!

IV

WHERE TO STAY IN THE FRENCH QUARTER

1. HOTELS
2. MOTELS
3. GUESTHOUSES
4. APARTMENT ACCOMMODATIONS

From the beginning a city that welcomed visitors with open arms and warm hospitality, New Orleans today carries on a long tradition of providing for travelers comfort that is wide-ranging in taste, style, and price. And in spite of the annual influx of hundreds of thousands in search of a place to stay, this spirited city has managed to keep historic districts, such as the French Quarter, free of the modern disease "progress," which takes the form of high-rise monstrosities that stick out like sore thumbs and deface many a formerly gracious part of the American heritage. Indeed, it is almost impossible to tell if some of the new French Quarter hotels have been built from scratch or lovingly placed inside the shell of an older building, so faithful has been the dedication to preserving the Quarter's architectural style. Even motor hotels (which eliminate the ever-present problem of off-the-street parking) have the look that is distinctly New Orleans's. Oh, you'll find those high-rises, of course, but they're uptown in more appropriate, commercial sections, where they seem to "fit" just fine. In fact the proliferation of slick new hotels brought on by the 1984 World's Fair has done a lot to ease New Orleans's chronic hotel room shortage.

As for guesthouses, they really *do* make you feel like a guest. Presided over by New Orleanians imbued with a special brand of hospitality, many are furnished with antiques and all are outstanding in terms of a homelike atmosphere. Their appeal is so great for me that I haven't even considered staying anywhere else in years.

A sort of "Open Sesame" to the lively people who live in New Orleans is **Bed & Breakfast, Inc., Reservation Service,** 1360 Moss St. (P.O. Box 52257), New Orleans, LA 70152 (tel. 504/525-

4640, or toll free 800/228-9711). Personable Hazell Boyce can put you up in luxury in 19th-century, turn-of-the-century, or modern residences. Or you can opt for an apartment in the French Quarter or Garden District. Prices range from $35 to $225, double occupancy, and she delights in arranging modest lodging for students.

But whatever your preference—be it hotel, motel, guesthouse, or bed-and-breakfast—one thing is certain: You're sure to find much more than a place to lay your head in any of the New Orleans accommodations.

One word of warning, however. In spite of the thousands of rental rooms in New Orleans, there are times when there isn't a bed to be had. Advance reservations (a good idea whatever the season) are a must during spring, fall, and winter months when the city is crowded. If you're planning your trip to coincide with Mardi Gras, it isn't an exaggeration to say that you should book as far as a year ahead. Sugar Bowl week and other festival times also flood New Orleans with visitors and require advance planning for accommodations. That's not to say that you might not run across a cancellation and get a last-minute booking, but the chance is remote, to say the least. A good time to visit New Orleans is almost anytime, but if you want to miss crowds, and hard-to-find lodging, consider coming in the month immediately following Mardi Gras (which begins soon after Christmas with the opening of Carnival season and lasts until "Fat Tuesday," the last day before Lent) or in the summer months (which can be muggy but not unbearable) when the streets are not nearly so thronged.

One more caution—the prices quoted here are those in effect as of the time of writing and, like everything else these days, are subject to change. However, even with inevitable changes, you can expect the categories to remain the same: that is, "moderate" will remain moderate even if it is at a slightly higher level.

Since I am personally convinced that the only place to stay is in the French Quarter—the very heart and soul of New Orleans—I'm listing accommodations there first. But if circumstances make another location more desirable for you, you'll find outside-the-Quarter listings in the next chapter. All rates quoted are for double occupancy.

Special note: You will almost always be asked to guarantee your reservation by either a deposit or credit-card charge, no matter what type of accommodation you decide on. Also, rates frequently jump more than a notch or two for Mardi Gras and other festival times, and in some cases there's a four- or five-night minimum requirement.

1. Hotels

THE UPPER BRACKET

Unique among New Orleans's luxury hotels is the small, European-style **Hotel Maison de Ville,** 727 Toulouse St., New Orleans, LA 70130 (tel. 504/561-5858). Dating back prior to 1742 (it appears on every early map of New Orleans), the Maison was restored several years ago to an elegance created by marble fireplaces, fine French antiques, gilt-framed mirrors, rich swagged drapes, and matching quilted bedspreads. Guest rooms surround a brick court-yard (one of the loveliest in the Quarter) with a tiered fountain and palm trees. It was here, working on one of the wrought-iron tables, that Tennessee Williams reworked *A Streetcar Named Desire* while staying in one of the converted slave quarters. Another famous tenant, John Audubon, lived in one of the seven cottages now operated by the Maison while painting the Louisiana portion of his *Birds of America*. The cottages, with brick walls, beamed ceilings, and slate or brick floors, are furnished with antiques and reflect a warm country elegance. The Maison's very personal service includes a breakfast of fresh orange juice, croissants or brioches, and steaming chicory coffee served on a silver tray in your room, in the parlor, or on the patio. Complimentary sherry and port are served in the afternoon and evening, morning and evening newspapers are delivered to your room, and that almost-vanished shoe-polishing service is available (just leave your shoes outside your door at night and notify the desk). Double-room rates start at $115 and cottages are $295 for one bedroom and $375 for two bedrooms.

Another very special small hotel right in the heart of the Quarter is the **St. Louis,** 730 Bienville St., New Orleans, LA 70130 (tel. 504/581-7300, or toll free 800/535-9706). Sophisticated elegance reminiscent of Parisian luxury hotels is the keynote here, and there's even a concierge on hand to render very specialized service. Built around a lovely courtyard that is centered by a marble fountain, the St. Louis is done in true French décor—with antique furniture, crystal chandeliers, and gilt-framed original oil paintings. Some rooms have private balconies overlooking the courtyard, and suites have *private* courtyards. This is the home of the elegant Louis XVI French restaurant (see Chapter VI). Doubles run from $125 to $170. Children under 12 stay free in their parents' room.

The **Royal Sonesta,** 300 Bourbon St., New Orleans, LA 70140 (tel. 504/586-0300, or toll free 800/343-7170), is adorned with lacy New Orleans balconies. Its 500 rooms are furnished with period pieces, and many overlook inner patios or the pool. There's a restaurant named Begue's that carries on the tradition of an older New Orleans eating spot of the same name. This is an ideal French Quarter location—within walking distance to almost everything. Doubles are $130 to $225, and there are money-saving vacation plans available from time to time.

Considered by many veteran New Orleans visitors as "the" place to stay (and certainly one of the most beautiful French Quarter hotels), the **Omni Royal Orleans,** 621 St. Louis St., New Orleans, LA 70140 (tel. 504/529-5333), is very elegant. That is as it should be, for the present-day hotel opened its doors in 1960 on the site of the 1836 St. Louis Exchange Hotel, one of this country's most splendid hostelries of that era. The St. Louis Exchange (whose rates in 1842 were an astounding $2.50 per day) was a center of New Orleans social life until the final years of the Civil War, when it became a hospital for wounded from both the North and the South, served for a time as the state capitol building and a meeting place of the carpetbagger legislature, and was finally destroyed by a 1915 hurricane. In its heyday of gala soirées and grandee visitors, it was also the innovator of the "free lunch" for noontime drinkers, creating a tradition of top-notch cuisine that survives even today. The Omni Royal Orleans has proved a worthy successor, with a lobby of marble, brass, and crystal chandeliers. Furnishings are truly sumptuous in the guest rooms, and there are extra touches such as a "good-night mint" and beds turned down at night. The classic, gourmet Rib Room is a favorite dining spot for many natives (see Chapter VI), and there's informal dining in the Café Royale's beautiful garden setting, with soft music after 8pm in the Esplanade Lounge (just right for the evening's last drink, no matter where you stay). The rooftop, poolside, palm tree–bordered La Riviera bar and restaurant is a terrific lunch spot, with unobstructed views of the French Quarter. Doubles are in the $175 to $210 range, and there are several attractive package specials available.

The **Westin Canal Place,** 100 Iberville St., New Orleans, LA 70130 (tel. 504/566-7006, or toll free 800/228-3000), has one of the most convenient locations in town—right at the river on the Canal Street edge of the French Quarter. Its window-walled 11th-floor lobby is a masterpiece of Carrara marble, fine paintings, and antiques—a lovely setting for afternoon tea. A handsome English-style pub and Le Jardin restaurant (see Chapter VI) are just steps away. Each room has a marble foyer and bath, as well as a refrigerator. Sweeping river views are part of the extras here. There's a garage for parking ($10), concierge service, a heated pool with poolside beverage service, 18-hole golf privileges, and a special elevator descending directly to Canal Place shops, a barbershop, and a beauty salon. Rates start at $205 for doubles.

MODERATE

The "Grand Old Lady" of French Quarter hotels is its largest and has been family operated by three generations of Monteleones. Covering almost an entire block, the 600-room **Monteleone Hotel,** 214 Royal St., New Orleans, LA 70140 (tel. 504/523-3341, or toll free 800/535-9595), seems to keep growing and expanding over the years without losing a trace of the charm that has been a trademark since its beginning. Room décors cover the spectrum from luxurious, antique-filled suites to more modern, very comfortable family rooms. The trellis-trimmed, green-and-white Le Café restaurant is a favorite with native New Orleanians, and the Carousel Bar, which slowly revolves under its red-and-white-striped canopy, also draws the locals. Up on top, the fabulous Sky Terrace has to be seen to be believed; there's a heated swimming pool, a putting green, the 9-to-5 Bar, and the exquisite Sky-lite Lounge, really a rooftop club that features top-notch live entertainment such as the famous Dukes of Dixieland. Rates for a double room start at $130. Ask about the attractive package deals.

The lovely **Place d'Armes Hotel,** 625 St. Ann St., New Orleans, LA 70116 (tel. 504/524-4531, or toll free 800/535-7791), has one of the most magnificent courtyards in the Quarter, as well as the largest swimming pool. The rooms are homey, many of them are wallpapered, and all of them are furnished in traditional style. Be sure that you ask, however, for a room with a window when you reserve—there are some interior rooms without windows (not all that bad, but still, a window is better). There's a breakfast room that serves a complimentary continental breakfast for guests. The location, just off Jackson Square, makes sightseeing a breeze. Guest rooms start at $89 for double occupancy.

A continental breakfast is served in your room or in the breakfast room at the **Prince Conti Hotel,** 830 Conti St., New Orleans, LA 70112 (tel. 504/529-4172, or toll free 800/877-4623), and there's free valet parking. But the nicest things here are the friendly, helpful staff and the comfortable guest rooms, many furnished with antiques and period reproductions. Prince Armand de Conti, the French nobleman who helped back Bienville's expedition to found New Orleans, would be proud of his namesake, with its small lobby beautifully furnished in the French château fashion and delicate iron grillwork lining the second-story rooms. Doubles will cost anywhere from $75 to $95.

Many rooms at the **St. Marie,** 827 Toulouse St., New Orleans, LA 70112 (tel. 504/561-8951, or toll free 800/366-2743), have private balconies overlooking the courtyard garden and pool. All are tastefully furnished with traditional pieces (although not antiques). Double-room rates are $95, which includes continental breakfast.

There's a sort of casual elegance at the **Dauphine Orleans Hotel,** 415 Dauphine St., New Orleans, LA 70112 (tel. 504/586-1800, or toll free 800/521-7111). All 109 rooms are nicely furnished with modern or period pieces (the majority have king-size beds) and wrought-iron balconies that overlook the patios and pool or Dauphine Street. Some suites are located in the former home of naturalist painter John James Audubon, which has been completely restored with private patios. There's a complimentary continental breakfast, free valet parking, cable TV with HBO, guest library, exercise room, the morning newspaper delivered to your door, and complimentary French Quarter transportation. The Bagnio Lounge was once a notorious "sporting house," and guests are given a copy of the original 1857 license, which still hangs on the wall. Double rooms start at $100.

The **Best Western Landmark—Bourbon Street,** 541 Bourbon St., New Orleans, LA 70130 (tel. 504/524-7611, or toll free 800/535-7891), sits on the site of the 1859 French Opera House, the first ever built in the United States, which burned to the ground in 1919. It's hard to tell, however, that the present building hasn't been here for just that many years, so well have the planners integrated its design into New Orleans's traditional architecture. All rooms have a Deep South décor and king-size or double beds, and some have balconies overlooking Bourbon Street. Both the Sing-a-Long piano bar and the Reunion Café (a self-service restaurant featuring Creole and Cajun cooking) are popular with guests. Prices hinge on whether or not your room faces Bourbon Street or has a balcony. Doubles without same begin at $90; those with begin at $125.

Over in the Fauborg Marigny area, **The Frenchmen,** 417 Frenchmen St., New Orleans, LA 70116 (tel. 504/948-2166, or toll free 800/831-1781), is a small inn located in two town houses built in 1860. Its Victorian-style lobby sets the tone, and although all 25 rooms differ in décor, most are furnished with antiques or period reproductions. Those in the balconied annex overlook the courtyard and pool, where there's a heated Jacuzzi. Single or double rates are $80 to $120, including breakfast, and special package rates are available.

The **Hotel Villa Convento,** 616 Ursulines St., New Orleans, LA 70116 (tel. 504/522-1793), is really a small inn and in many respects resembles a guesthouse because of the personal touch of its owner/operators, the Campo family. The building is a Creole town house, and its 24 rooms have been comfortably furnished. Some open to the tropical patio, some open to the street; many have balconies; and the lovely "loft" rooms are unique family quarters, each with a queen-size bed on the entry level and twin beds in the loft. A continental breakfast is served just off the lobby in a small, cheerful breakfast room or on the patio. Doubles run from $49, two-bedroom suites begin $95.

---

2. Motels

THE UPPER BRACKET

A friend urged me to inspect the **Holiday Inn—Château LeMoyne,** 301 Dauphine St., New Orleans, LA 70112 (tel. 504/581-1303, or toll free 800/HOLIDAY), saying that "it's not like any Holiday Inn you've ever seen." She was right: Although it is, in fact, a member of that chain, it is so distinctly French Quarter that you'd never associate it with any of those highway stopover hostelries. Housed in buildings over a century old, with arched colonnades and winding staircases, the place exudes character and charm. Patios and converted slave-quarter suites add to the Old New Orleans flavor, and bedrooms are furnished in a comfortable traditional style. There's a restaurant on the premises and free off-street parking. If you plan to do much sight-seeing or business outside the French Quarter, the Château LeMoyne's location is ideal—only minutes away from the Central Business District and the trolley that takes you to the Garden District. And, of course, anything in the Quarter is within easy walking distance. Double rooms here cost $90 to $110.

Right in the heart of the Quarter is the **de la Poste Motor Hotel,** 316 Chartres St., New Orleans, LA 70130 (tel. 504/581-1200, or toll free 800/448-4927). Its 100 rooms are spacious and comfortable, and most either overlook the Grande Patio and pool or face onto one of the more interesting French Quarter streets. The courtyard, incidentally, has a magnificent staircase leading up to a second-level outdoor patio. Parking is free, there's a baby-sitting service, and children under 12 stay free in the same room with their parents. Double-occupancy rooms begin at $85; location, accommodations, and service all qualify as deluxe.

MODERATE

Another restoration is **Le Richelieu Motor Hotel,** 1234 Chartres St., New Orleans, LA 70116 (tel. 504/529-2492, or toll free 800/535-9653), which is housed in what was once a row mansion and then a macaroni factory. They're proudest here of their VIP suite, which has three bedrooms, a super kitchen, and even a steamroom (and rents for a whopping $375 a night), but the "ordinary" guest rooms I saw were all exceptionally nice and much less expensive (doubles are $80 to $95). Most have brass ceiling fans, many have a refrigerator, and there are one- and two-bedroom suites for as little as $110. There's a pool in the large courtyard and lunch service poolside. Most rooms have a balcony, and all overlook either the French Quarter or the courtyard. Le Richelieu is the only French Quarter motel with a free self-park on the premises—you keep your car keys, so there's no wait for an attendant to bring your car.

There are no fewer than five patios—and each a jewel—at the family-owned **Provincial Hotel,** 1024 Chartres St., New Orleans, LA 70116 (tel. 504/581-4995, or toll free 800/535-7922). Rooms in the 1830s building are high-ceilinged, and each is decorated in a distinct style with imported French and authentic Creole antiques. My own favorite holds a huge carved mahogany double bed with a high overhanging canopy topped by a carved tiara. Gaslights on the patios and the overall feeling of graciousness make this one a real delight, a tranquil refuge from the rigors of sight-seeing or nighttime revelry. The pleasant restaurant serves breakfast, lunch, and dinner at moderate prices. Rates for double-occupancy rooms range from $75 to $95. There is free parking, and bargain package rates are available during summer months.

Not much elegance, but a good deal of charm and just plain comfort, can be found at the **Château Motor Hotel,** 1001 Chartres St., New Orleans, LA 70116 (tel. 504/524-9636), one of the best buys in town pricewise. Its flagstone-paved courtyard is bordered by an awning-covered café, where breakfast and lunch are served outdoors. There are a few four-poster beds, as well as bed/living room combinations. Parking is free. Doubles run $60 to $75, and there is a 10% discount for seniors.

3. Guesthouses

My personal "home" is with Mrs. Junius Underwood at the **French Quarter Maisonnettes,** 1130 Chartres St., New Orleans, LA 70116 (tel. 504/524-9918). If for no other reason, it would be my choice because of Mrs. Underwood's gracious personality and dedication to the welfare and happiness of her guests. Manager Bud

Godley, a recent addition to the staff, is equally welcoming and caring. There are, however, many other attractions. The Maisonnettes are in an 1825 mansion entered through a lovely iron gateway leading to the arched carriage drive and flagstone courtyard in the rear. A wrought-iron balcony rings the second story, overlooking that courtyard and its three-tiered, 17th-century French cast-iron fountain, tropical plants, and vines. Guest units on the ground floor open through wide French doors onto the courtyard or carriage drive, and second-floor rooms overlook the courtyard. All have modern, very comfortable furnishings, and Jesse, who is a delightful part of your stay here, keeps them impeccably clean (he's also always on hand to lend cheerful assistance with luggage). Each has a private bath and air conditioning and heat (individually controlled), and the morning newspaper is delivered to your door every morning.

The location is a sightseer's dream—across the street is the historic Beauregard House; next door is the Ursuline Convent built in 1734 and said to be the oldest building in the Mississippi Valley; and just a few blocks away is the old French Market, so handy for coffee and beignets to begin or end the day. Best of all, there's Mrs. Underwood, whose thoughtfulness extends to furnishing a privately printed brochure of tips on dining, sight-seeing, shopping, and almost anything else to make your visit more entertaining and comfortable, all gleaned from her intimate, longtime association with New Orleans. Children over 12 are welcomed as are "well-behaved" pets. Rates of $45 to $55 make this one of the best bargains in New Orleans, and it is very popular, making advance booking an absolute must. There's private parking at an additional charge.

At **623 Ursulines St.,** New Orleans, LA 70116 (tel. 504/529-5489), Jim Weirich and his partner, Don Heil, have created four suites in old slave quarters, leaving some in near-original state and making all thoroughly modern as far as comfort goes. Each has a living room, bedroom, and private bath and opens onto a courtyard that holds azaleas, towering crepe myrtle trees, and magnolias. Three suites of comparable size are in the main house, and rates range from $50 to $80. A decided plus here is the warm hospitality —Jim and Don know New Orleans intimately and are a gold mine of tips on how to make your stay more fun. Jim and Don don't give their guesthouse a name, but simply use the street number. If you plan to visit New Orleans and are a guesthouse devotee, I heartily recommend that you call in advance for reservations—this is a very popular spot. Garage parking is available at an additional charge.

If you think a Bourbon Street address automatically means a noisy, honky-tonk environment, think again. The **Lafitte Guest House,** 1003 Bourbon St., New Orleans, LA 70116 (tel. 504/581-2678, or toll free 800/331-7971), is far enough down to be in a quiet, pleasant residential neighborhood, yet close enough for you to walk anywhere in the Quarter. The three-story brick building, with its typical New Orleans wrought-iron balconies on the second and third floors, was constructed in 1849 and restored in the last few years. There are marble fireplaces, exposed brick walls, and 14-foot-high ceilings, and 13 of the guest rooms are furnished with a blend of modern upholstered pieces and massive Victorian antiques. The 14th, on the top floor, is huge, with four dormer windows affording a splendid French Quarter view and modern furnishings. All guest rooms have a telephone (unusual for most guesthouses). There's a continental breakfast of fresh juice, croissants, jam and butter, and coffee or tea; wine and cheese in the parlor during the "happy hour"; and the daily newspaper—all included in the room rate. Doubles here run $65 to $135, and there's a charge of $15 for each extra person in a room.

Grenoble House, 329 Dauphine St., New Orleans, LA 70112 (tel. 504/522-1331), is truly an elegant home-away-from-home. The 17 suites here are beautifully furnished with a mix of fine antiques and the best of modern fittings—all have a fully equipped kitchen—and each one is different. This is an old French Quarter town house built around a courtyard that features a swimming pool with heated whirlpool spa and a barbecue pit. Suites all have king- or queen-size beds, there's a sofa bed in each living room, and a continental breakfast is included in the rate. A very special "extra" here is the concierge service—they'll book theater tickets, restaurants, and sight-seeing tours and even arrange a gourmet dinner brought to your suite or a private cocktail party in the patio if you want to entertain friends. Rates begin at $125 for a one-bedroom suite with queen-size bed, a one-bedroom with king-size bed goes for $165, and two-bedroom suites start at $230 (weekly rates also are available).

Over on the outer limit of the French Quarter, **Melrose Mansion,** 937 Esplanade Ave., New Orleans, LA 70116 (tel. 504/944-2255), ranks as probably the most splendid guesthouse in the city. Rosemary and Melvin Jones have lovingly restored this three-story 1884 Victorian mansion, with its square turret set at a jaunty angle in one corner, to combine the utmost in luxury with the warm, personal hospitality of a private home. Its architectural style is hard to pin down—in Rosemary's words, it is "a bit of Victorian Gothic, Victorian Italiante, along with a suggestion of the baroque and the classic, as seen in the upper-level Corinthian capitals." The old house has a rich and varied history (ask about Miss Kitty—she was an ex-stripper with a seagoing lover—who lived out her last years here).

Guest rooms are furnished with marvelous antiques, and the crème de la crème has to be the Donecio Suite, with a magnificent four-poster bed, a marble bathroom complete with Jacuzzi and separate dressing room, and a wide balcony on which breakfast often is served. (Lady Bird Johnson was its first tenant and went away with raves.) The mansion's elegant drawing room is the focal point for gatherings for afternoon tea or wine-and-cheese trays. Breakfast comes with silver coffee service, beautiful china and crystal, fresh-baked muffins, and fresh fruit and can be served in your room, on the balcony, or poolside. The Parc Henry Suite, atop the original carriage house and overlooking the pool, sleeps three or four. But the best feature of this pampering place may well be its staff. Rosemary and Melvin are always on hand; Willy is everyone's dream of a doorman; and the Jones' right-hand man, Terry, looks after each guest and every visitor as if he or she were his personal houseguest. The rates at Melrose Mansion run from $195 to $395; be advised to book as far in advance as possible.

---

4. Apartment Accommodations

If you'd like to experience French Quarter living as a temporary "local," I can't think of a better place to do it than in the one apartment that Joe Impastato—owner of the historic **Napoleon House,** 500 Chartres St., New Orleans, LA 70130 (tel. 504/524-9752)—has made available. The three-room upstairs flat, with two balconies, was the longtime residence of his uncle, and its furnishings are what might be called "New Orleans homey"—several antique pieces intermingle happily with rather well-worn furnishings of indeterminate age but definite comfort. The apartment is right in the heart of the Quarter, with one of the city's best pubs and light-meal restaurants downstairs. The only danger is that you might find yourself joining the throngs of other visitors who have come to New Orleans and never gone back home. The rates are $125 for two people and $175 for four.

WHERE TO STAY OUTSIDE THE QUARTER

1. HOTELS
2. MOTELS
3. GUESTHOUSES
4. CAMPGROUNDS

There are many considerations that could lead you to find accommodations outside the French Quarter, and you will find a wide price range of hotels and motels in almost any section, whether you wish to be near the universities, in the Central Business District, or on the outskirts of town. There are also several superior guesthouses outside the Quarter.

One thing I should add: With the advent of the 1984 Louisiana World Exposition came a flood of new hotels outside the French Quarter. In fact the bulk of the city's 20,000 hotel rooms are now outside the French Quarter. To their credit, most of the new establishments reflect a distinct New Orleans flavor. However, even with all these additional rooms, there will be times when booking could be a problem—so the sooner you reserve, the better.

1. Hotels

THE UPPER BRACKET

The **New Orleans Hilton Riverside & Towers Hotel,** 2 Poydras St. at the Mississippi River, New Orleans, LA 70140 (tel. 504/561-0500, or toll free 800/445-8667), has perhaps integrated itself most successfully into the life-style of the city. Located in what some are coming to call the "River Quarter," the Hilton sits right at the riverfront, adjacent to the World Trade Center of New Orleans, the Rivergate Convention Center, and the New Orleans

Convention Center, yet it somehow manages to avoid the sterile impersonality projected by so many large hotels. Maybe it has to do with a décor that makes use of warm colors such as tea rose and emerald green; Italian oak and mahogany paneling; travertine marble; and deep-pile, handwoven carpeting. The 90-foot, nine-story, multilevel atrium creates a feeling of space, but it is so well designed that there is none of that rattle-around boxiness that always makes me a little nervous. Although no one could describe it as "cozy," it is broken up into attractive centers such as the English Bar, Le Café Bromeliad, the French Garden Bar and Oyster Bar, Le Croissant Coffee Shoppe, and Winston's. There are in fact ten restaurants and lounges within the 1,600-room complex (see "Dining Outside the Quarter," Chapter VII). You will know without doubt that the Hilton has won New Orleans's approval when you learn that Pete Fountain moved his jazz club from the Quarter to a third-floor replica here. There's also a swinging dance club, the Rainforest—on the 29th floor, with glass walls, gnarled cypress trees, and lush greenery (as well as a simulated "rainstorm")—which serves a very nice weekday luncheon.

Guest rooms are, of course, the primary concern of travelers, and those at the New Orleans Hilton are spacious; most have fabulous views of the river or the city; and all are furnished in a country French manner, using muted colors and French treatment draperies keyed to the etched toile of the wall coverings. Light-softening sheer-glass curtains let you take full advantage of those gorgeous views. The epitome of luxury is to be found on the 25th, 26th, and 27th tower floors, which hold 132 guest rooms, including 13 sumptuous suites, and boast a bevy of "concierge" people ready to take care of the nitty-gritty details of your stay, as well as a private club and honor bar. The newest Hilton addition is its 456-room, low-rise Riverside complex perched on the edge of the Mississippi. There are six luxurious suites and eight courtyards with fountains and lush tropical foliage, open to the river.

Rates range from $145 to $184 for doubles, with suites running $375 to $1,300, and guests are eligible for membership in the Rivercenter Tennis and Racquetball Club, which includes the use of a gym, saunas, whirlpools, a jogging track, squash court, tanning booths, aerobics classes, and massage.

Elegant is the word for the **Pontchartrain Hotel,** 2031 St. Charles Ave., New Orleans, LA 70140 (tel. 504/524-0581, or toll free 800/777-1700), located in the Garden District. Rooms are beautifully furnished, and the service will make you feel like a pampered favorite within minutes of your arrival. Everything in this New Orleans institution is in the continental tradition at its finest, and the gourmet cuisine of the Caribbean Room (see Chapter VII) is internationally known. Special low-salt, low-cholesterol menus are available on request. Other extras include free limousine service to the French Quarter and a "Staying With Safety" package for senior citizens (with doorman and elevator operator on duty around the clock). Double-room rates are in the $110 to $200 range.

New Orleanians remember it as the Roosevelt, and today's **Fairmont Hotel,** on University Place, New Orleans, LA 70140 (tel.

504/529-7111, or toll free 800/527-4727), upholds the tradition of elegance left by its predecessor. There's the feel of luxury from the moment you enter the lobby, with its deep carpeting, dark-red velvet chairs and sofas, magnificent chandeliers, and impressive oil paintings. The rooms are spacious, with marvelous high ceilings and such extras as an electric shoe buffer and evening maid service. On the rooftop recreation area there's a swimming pool, two tennis courts, and a cozy bar that serves beverages and sandwiches. For many years, the sophisticated Blue Room presented headliner entertainers. (Remember those old radio broadcasts "from the Blue Room of the Hotel Roosevelt in downtown New Orleans"?) I'm happy to report that although it was redecorated in recent years, that lovely décor of blue and gold and French period furnishings has changed very little since the days of my visits years ago. These days, the Blue Room is used for private functions only, except for Sundays, when there's a sumptuous brunch (see Chapter VII). An addition is Bailey's, a casual, 24-hour Irish bar that serves a full food menu and drinks. For fine dining, there's the romantic Sazerac Restaurant. In short, the Fairmont is a "grand hotel" in the old manner that offers midtown convenience as a bonus. Double rooms range from $150 to $225.

Of the newer hotels, one of the loveliest is the high-rise **Windsor Court,** 300 Gravier St., New Orleans, LA 70140 (tel. 504/523-6000). Centrally located between Poydras and Canal streets, the hotel has some 330 accommodations, of which 280 are deluxe suites that go for amazingly moderate prices. Two nice touches are the English tea served in a pretty lobby lounge and two corridors that are minigalleries displaying works of art. Italian marble and antique furnishings distinguish the two lobbies. The Windsor Court Bar is a clubby sort of gathering place, and the restaurant overlooks the courtyard. Among the guest facilities are a health club sporting a resort-size pool, sauna, and steamroom. Numerous conveniences are available for business travelers, who might want to conduct business conferences in the privacy of their own suites or in the especially planned meeting spaces.

As for those suites, each features its own individual décor, large bay windows looking out over the river or the city, a private foyer, a large living room, a bedroom entered through french doors, a marble bath, separate his-and-her dressing rooms, a "petite kitchen," and a wet bar. They, as well as the guest rooms (all of which come with a wet bar), are exceptionally spacious and beautifully furnished. The rates range from $155 to $250. Children under 18 stay free with their parents. This one is truly a standout.

The **Hotel Inter-Continental,** 444 St. Charles Ave., New Orleans, LA 70130 (tel. 504/525-5566), rises in red granite splendor within walking distance of Canal Street shopping and the Central Business District. Its 500 deluxe rooms and suites feature separate conversation seating, dressing areas, minirefrigerators and bars, built-in hairdryers, and even safes. The furnishings in the guest rooms as well as the public areas are a nice blend of classic and contemporary styling, and the large marble lobby holds a lounge that serves afternoon tea as well as drinks. Gourmet meals are served in

Les Continents Restaurant, and Pete's Pub combines rich paneling with art deco touches. Other facilities include a health club, pool, and several services for business travelers. Rates are in the $147 to $190 range for doubles and $240 to $1,200 for suites.

The **Hotel Le Meridien,** 614 Canal St., New Orleans, LA 70130 (tel. 504/522-1456), is one of the city's most dramatic new hotels, with lots of marble and a spectacular inside waterfall. Among its services are a pool with poolside beverage service, health club, a shopping arcade, and some rooms that come with a refrigerator and/or private patio. There are some 497 rooms and suites, plus valet parking ($8), a brasserie serving continuously from 7am to 11pm, a gourmet restaurant, and cocktail lounges with entertainment. Rates run from $140 to $180 for doubles.

MODERATE

The **St. Charles Inn,** 3636 St. Charles Ave., New Orleans, LA 70115 (tel. 504/899-8888), is only five minutes away from Tulane and Loyola universities and ten minutes from the French Quarter or Louisiana Superdome via the trolley. All rooms have either two double beds or a king-size bed. There's a lounge and restaurant, and extras include a complimentary continental breakfast served in your room and the morning newspaper. Doubles start at $75.

The gracious mahogany-paneled drawing room (complete with comfortable sofas and chairs and a large fireplace) of the **Avenue Plaza Hotel,** 2111 St. Charles Ave., New Orleans, LA 70130 (tel. 504/566-1212), sets the tone at this small hotel that was once an apartment building. All rooms are nicely furnished and have a wet bar, coffee maker, and refrigerator. There are excellent health-club facilities; a courtyard swimming pool; a rooftop sundeck; and a lovely, window-lined dining room overlooking St. Charles Avenue. Doubles run $95 to $300.

It's hard to know whether to label the **Prytania Park Hotel,** 1525 Prytania St., New Orleans, LA 70130 (tel. 504/524-0427, or toll free 800/862-1984), a hotel or a guesthouse. Centrally located in the historic Garden District, owned and enthusiastically operated by Mr. and Mrs. Alvin Halpern, the small hotel has a unique combination of atmospheres. The Victorian Building, which dates back to 1834, is beautifully restored and furnished in period hand-carved English pine. The 49 streamlined rooms in the modern addition retain the New Orleans architectural ambience, opening onto landscaped courtyards, and feature the conveniences of microwave oven and refrigerator. The St. Charles Avenue Streetcar Line is half a block away, providing quick and easy access to the French Quarter and all the major attractions. Dining out is a pleasure because the hotel is situated in the heart of the uptown restaurant district, with innovative cuisines and price ranges to fit all budgets. A complimentary continental breakfast is served each morning, and off-street parking is free. With a choice of contemporary or old-world setting, and a friendly, well-trained staff, the Prytania Park is a charming hotel run with the same personal attention as a guesthouse. Rates for double rooms range from $79 to $99, but as with most New Orleans accommodations, rates increase during special events.

You'll find convenience and comfort at budget prices only half a block outside the French Quarter at the **Hotel La Salle,** 1113 Canal St., New Orleans, LA 70112 (tel. 504/523-5831, or toll free 800/521-9450 in the United States; Freephone in the United Kingdom, 08/00-0089-1001). There are no frills here, but there are plainly furnished, clean, and comfortable rooms that come with or without private bath. There's an old-fashioned air to the small lobby with its high ceilings, overhead fans, carved Austrian wall clock, and an old-time wooden reception desk. Free coffee is always available in the lobby, and a continental breakfast can be served in your room for a small additional charge. Roland and Pat Bahan own and operate the La Salle, and they have been known to arrange such extras as practice rooms for out-of-town musicians who come to audition for the New Orleans Symphony. This is a favorite with European visitors who appreciate bathroom-down-the-hall savings as well as with jazz musicians just arriving in the city. Doubles run from $42 to $47 with private bath and $32 to $37 without.

2. Motels

THE UPPER BRACKET

The **Holiday Inn Crowne Plaza,** 300 Poydras St., New Orleans, LA 70130 (tel. 504/525-9444), has 441 units, plus suites, a Concierge Floor, and a restaurant and lounge with entertainment. It's an attractive hotel that includes among its many amenities a pool with poolside beverage service, an exercise room, cable TV, and free in-room movies. There's valet parking at a small additional charge. Suites and the 22 rooms on the luxury-level Concierge Floor come with a complimentary continental breakfast and refreshments, refrigerators, and a private cocktail lounge—all at higher rates than the standard $100 to $135 for doubles.

MODERATE

For motel convenience and comfort, you simply cannot beat the **Days Inn Canal** 1630 Canal St., New Orleans, LA 70112 (tel. 504/586-0110, or toll free 800/232-3297). The French Quarter is only five blocks away; Poydras Plaza shopping mall, only one block; the Superdome, five blocks; the Rivergate shopping mall, 16 blocks; and the Rivergate Convention Center, 21 blocks. The motel's 216 comfortably furnished and nicely decorated rooms all have double beds and the spaciousness typical of this dependable chain. There's a pool with cabaña, same-day dry-cleaning service, guest laundry, free parking, and a good restaurant. Double rooms range seasonally from $50 to $140. *Special note:* If you're 55 or older, be sure to look into Days Inn's September Days Club membership, which offers discount room rates.

The **Quality Inn Midtown,** 3900 Tulane Ave., New Orleans, LA 70119 (tel. 504/486-5541, or toll free 800/827-5541), is not quite as centrally located, but it is still only about five minutes from the Central Business District. All the rooms have balconies, many facing the courtyard and swimming pool; are spacious; and have double beds. There's free parking, in-room movies, a health club, a restaurant, and a lounge with live entertainment. Doubles are in the $49 to $99 range.

The 17-story **Holiday Inn Downtown—Superdome,** 330 Loyola Ave., New Orleans, LA 70112 (tel. 504/581-1600), is centrally located, with easy access to New Orleans's business and financial centers, as well as the Louisiana Superdome and the French Quarter. Each of the 300 rooms has recently been renovated and has a balcony and city view. Guest rooms are large enough for a "sitting room" area and are furnished with modern, comfortable fittings. The dining room boasts some of the renowned Audubon prints, and there's a rooftop pool and Jacuzzi. Rates for double rooms are in the $85 to $110 range.

3. Guesthouses

If you're in New Orleans to visit Tulane University or Loyola University or Newcomb College, you'll want to know about these nicely located guesthouses.

On the far edge of Audubon Park, the **Parkview Guest House,** 7004 St. Charles Ave., New Orleans, LA 70118 (tel. 504/861-7564), is a rambling Victorian structure built in 1884 as a hotel for the Cotton Exposition. It has been in the National Register of Historic Places since 1981. You get a feeling of another era from the minute you enter the wide central hall with its gleaming crystal chandeliers through a front door that sparkles with etched-glass panels. A lovely stained-glass window is the focal point of the large lounge, with its comfortable sofas and chairs, and all the rooms are furnished in antiques. I immediately fell in love with the room on the first floor just to the right of the front door—it has floor-length windows and a carved walnut bed and dresser that made a strong appeal to the romantic in my soul. All the rooms, however, reflect an old-fashioned comfort that's hard to resist. Some have a balcony. There's a large dining room, with windows overlooking the park, where a complimentary continental breakfast is served daily—a pleasant way to start the day. All guests have the use of a refrigerator and ice machine anytime. Most of the 25 rooms have a private bath, although three have a bath connecting with another room, and there's individually controlled heat and air conditioning in all. Double rooms go for $65 to $75. At this time they don't allow pets, but this policy may be relaxed, and it wouldn't hurt to check when you book.

Just off St. Charles Avenue, the **Josephine Guest House,** 1450 Josephine St., New Orleans, LA 70130 (tel. 504/524-6361), is a lovely 1870 Italianate-style home presided over by Mary Ann Weilbaecher. Much attention to detail has assured that its restoration has been faithful to the era in which it was built, and the rooms are beautifully furnished with antiques. All the guest rooms have a private bath (with marvelous original fixtures). Rates here run from $65 to $100, with the one suite at $135.

The **St. Charles Guest House,** 1748 Prytania St., New Orleans, LA 70130 (tel. 504/523-6556), is a small, cozy place with simple, comfortable guest rooms and lots of personal attention from Joanne Hilton and her friendly staff. Guests are given a front-door key so that they can come and go as they please, and there are often impromptu poolside snacks or New Orleans–style meals of jambalaya or red beans and rice. The rooms are basic, with no telephone or television, but there's always plenty of activity around the pool and patio, where guests gather in the morning for juice, rolls, tea, and coffee. In addition to single and double rooms with private baths, there are rooms with double beds and shared baths in the main buildings and "Cajun cabins" and backpack rooms with shared baths that open onto the pool and patio area. The rates for rooms with private baths are $45 to $60 and for rooms with shared baths are $30 to $45.

---

4. Campgrounds

There are two KOA campgrounds, one on each side of town. The **KOA New Orleans West,** 219 S. Starrett Rd. (La. 48), River Ridge, LA 70123 (tel. 504/467-1792), is the closest campground to the west of the city and welcomes tenters as well as vehicles, for which there are full hookups. The lounge provides games, and you can swim in the pool as well as buy provisions in the on-site store. City and boat tours are available, and if you want to "do" the French Quarter on your own, there's city transportation to and from as well as rental cars available. The **KOA New Orleans East,** Rte. 16, Box 100, Slidell, LA 70461 (tel. 504/643-3850), is a half mile east of I-10 on La. 433. Full hookups are here, too, in a country setting that includes two pools, a recreation room, and miniature golf. Riverboat, nightclub, swamp, and city tours are available. The rates at both campgrounds are $19 for two, $3 for each additional person, and $15 for tenters.

DINING IN THE FRENCH QUARTER

If New Orleans's population is an exciting "stew" of nationalities and cultures, its cuisine is a rich, tasty "gumbo" of French provincial, Spanish, Italian, West Indian, African, and Native American cooking flavored with a liberal dash of full-fledged southern. Those who return time after time do so as much for the food as for the jazz, the Mardi Gras, and the sight-seeing. Indeed, dining out in New Orleans rightly falls under the heading of entertainment.

Provincial French recipes brought to the New World by early settlers fast acquired a subtle change with the use of native herbs and filé (ground sassafras leaves) from Native Americans. Saffron and peppers arrived somewhat later along with the Spanish. From the West Indies came new vegetables, spices, and sugarcane, and when slave boats arrived, landing many a black woman in a white kitchen, an African influence was added. Out of all this came the distinctive "Creole" culinary style unique to New Orleans. Italian touches later on added yet another dimension to the city's tables, and through it all, traditional Old South dishes were retained virtually intact.

CUISINE

Both *Cajun* and *Creole* have come to mean "New Orleans." What's the difference in the two cuisines? Chiefly it lies in their origins. Cajun cooking came from country folk, those Acadians who left France for Nova Scotia in the 1600s and made their way to the swamps and bayous of rural Louisiana after being expelled by the British in the 1700s. Their much-loved French dishes traveled with them, but along the way the recipes were adapted to ingredients available locally. Their cuisine tends to be quite robust and hearty, with sausage, duck, poultry, pork, and seafood prepared in a rich roux (a seasoned mixture of fat and flour) to lend a distinctive flavor and served over rice. Creole dishes, on the other hand, were developed by French and Spanish city dwellers. Delicate sauces and attention to presentation are characteristic of "haute Creole," while "low Creole" favorites, such as red beans and rice, are likely to come to table with as little fanfare as Cajun food.

In practice, however, the two cuisines have effected such a happy marriage in New Orleans that it's often difficult to distinguish between them—even the city's leading chefs can't always draw the line. Internationally famed Paul Prudhomme, of K-Paul's Louisiana Kitchen, says simply that what has emerged is "Louisiana food." He goes on to say, "Nowhere else have all the ethnic groups merged to combine all these different tastes, and the only way you'll know the difference, honey, is to live 'em!" Suffice it to say that no matter *how* a New Orleans restaurant classifies its culinary offerings, you're bound to find one or two examples of Cajun and Creole cooking on the menu.

As a rule of thumb (but remember, rules are made to have exceptions), when it comes to New Orleans food, *Creole* means hot and *Cajun* will be spicy. But both can mean hot *and* spicy. The much-loved spices are onions (both green and regular), bay leaf, thyme, parsley, cloves, allspice, cayenne pepper, filé, and Tabasco (a red-hot sauce made of red peppers fermented in brine and vinegar). There is a whole family of sausages: boudin (boo-dan), which contains onions, spices, pork, and rice and comes in white or red; chaurice (cho-reece), which is a hard sausage used chiefly for flavoring beans or soups; andouille (ahn-dwe-ye), which is also hard and a bit saltier than chaurice; and delicious smoked sausages. Seafood is everywhere—in fact, I find it next to impossible to order anything else when I'm in town. Oysters on the half shell (usually simply called "raw oysters" in New Orleans) are just the beginning of an oyster feast that includes soups, stews, pies, baked specialties such as oysters Rockefeller (on the half shell in a creamy sauce and spinach —so named because that was the only name rich enough for the taste), an oyster loaf (which elevates "sandwich" into the realm of a delicacy), and a host of other creations. Crabs, shrimp, and crayfish are used in imaginative recipes or served plain, hot or cold. Gumbo is a thick soup, always served with rice, usually containing crab, shrimp (sometimes oysters), and okra in a tomato base. Jambalaya is made with meat and seafood combined with rice and seasonings. Beef and veal (you may see either on a menu as *daube,* pronounced "dohb") take on added luster in New Orleans restaurants, as do classic French and Italian dishes. There's also a special quality to the French bread, with its crisp, flaky crust and its insides as light as a feather. Two mainstays of any native's diet are red beans and rice and "poboy" sandwiches (they once cost a nickle; are made with a long, skinny bread loaf; and can contain anything from roast beef and gravy to ham and cheese to fried fish, shrimp, soft-shell crabs, or oysters, in which case they become an "oyster loaf"). One of the largest (and tastiest) sandwiches you'll ever see is the muffuletta—a mountain of Italian sausage and meats with mustard, pickles, and many other things piled onto a thick bun.

And never let it be said that New Orleanians neglect the libations that precede, accompany, and follow a proper meal. As a matter of fact, they lay claim to adding the word *cocktail* to our modern vocabulary (that came about when a Monsieur Peychaud, who presided over the bar at 437 Rue Royale, took to serving small drinks in egg cups—*couquetiers* in French—and Americans took to ordering them by a mangled version of the word). Since then more than a few inspired concoctions have appeared on the scene, among them the Sazerac (bourbon or rye with bitters), the Ramos gin fizz (gin, egg whites, and orange flower water), and the Hurricane (rum and passionfruit punch). If you're a cocktail drinker, take my advice and try the local fare. *One note of caution:* Alcoholic drinks are available around the clock, and it's easy to overindulge. If you do, just be sure to walk back to your hotel or take a taxi. The police take a very dim view of drivers who've had one too many, and they are *very* vigilant.

As for coffee, you'll find it strong, hot, and black, with or without chicory (which adds a slightly bitter flavor—it was first used to stretch scarce coffee beans during the Civil War). Chicory coffee just might be what the Turks had in mind when they declared that the beverage should be "black as hell, strong as death, and sweet as love." Stouthearted purists drink it black, most natives mix it half-and-half with hot milk for café au lait. And at least once during your stay, do end a meal with café brûlot (cah-*fay* brew-*low*), a lovely mixture of coffee, spices, and liqueurs served in special cups, with ladle and chafing dish, and flamed at your table.

Restaurants pride themselves on their wine lists. If you are doubtful as to what to order with your entree, do not worry—your waiter will know.

DINING TIPS

Along with their love of exciting combinations of international cooking, the people of New Orleans have inherited an appreciation for fine service in elegant surroundings as well as a sense of fun that delights in gourmet dishes that appear in the plainest of settings and the plainest of meals (such as boiled crayfish or red beans and rice) that show up in the fanciest of eateries. Many New Orleanians eat out at least three times a week, and with their native sense of festivity, they may stretch out an evening to include cocktails at a favorite spot, an appetizer (such as oysters Rockefeller) at another, an entree at still another, and a dessert perhaps in a favorite courtyard setting. And for many, the evening is not complete without a stop by the Café du Monde for café au lait. In other words, dining out is an occasion, no matter how often it occurs. Incidentally you can follow their example and double the number of restaurants you get to sample during even a short stay. Keep in mind, however, that if your evening's itinerary includes the upper-bracket restaurants, men will be required to wear jackets and ties. Another tip for sampling the better spots with an eye to the budget is to plan your main meals at lunch, when prices are lower and menus are often identical to those at dinner.

A few last words about New Orleans restaurants: They number

in the hundreds; service will almost always be efficient, friendly, and relaxed; and if your budget keeps you out of the most famous, you'll have no trouble at all finding very good samples of New Orleans specialties in less formal (many times, very inexpensive) places that are just as much fun. I might add that no matter how many restaurants I list in this book, you will surely find at least one on your own that is so great you'll wonder how I missed it.

And because it really doesn't fit any "restaurant" category, I'd like to spotlight right up front one of my favorites—the **Café du Monde** in the French Market, an indispensable part of the New Orleans food scene. Across from Jackson Square and absolutely habit-forming, this delightful spot has been a favorite with New Orleanians for years. There are only four items on the menu— coffee (black or au lait), milk, hot chocolate, and beignets (three to a serving)—and each item costs 80¢. Beignets (bin-*yeas*) are square, doughnutlike confections that come hot, crisp, and covered with confectioner's sugar. One order and a cup of café au lait have served as breakfast, lunch, or a light dinner (after one of those "splurge" lunches) for me at one time or another, for the incredible price of $1.60. There's an indoor dining room, but I wouldn't miss sitting outside under the awning to take advantage of the Mississippi River breeze and unexcelled people-watching. Besides your fellow diners, there's all of Jackson Square, with horse carriages lined up across from the café, as well as shoppers headed for the French Market a little farther along Decatur Street. The café is open around the clock every day but Christmas, and you'll find many a native as your neighbor if you show up in the dawn or predawn hours.

Because New Orleans has such a great number of really terrific places to eat, because space limitations make it impossible for me to tell you about more than a few, and because I know many of our readers believe the food in this city to be perhaps its greatest attraction, I am going to suggest another source of restaurant recommendations. Tom Fitzmorris, longtime restaurant reviewer in the city, publishes an excellent reference, *The New Orleans Eat Book*. In its pages you'll find critiques of more than 300 eateries, as well as an index that tells you just where to find exactly the type of cuisine you're looking for. Tom knows the food and has followed the ups and downs of restaurants for many years. He shares his expertise in a lively, often witty manner—his reviews are, in fact, a minicourse in New Orleans culinary history and make a good read anytime. He'll ship the book to you for just $8.95 (including postage). Contact Tom Fitzmorris, c/o New Orleans Big Bend and Pacific Company, P.O. Box 51831, New Orleans, LA 70151 (tel. 504/821-3100). By the time you read this, the book may also be for sale at newsstands and in bookshops around the city.

The wheelchair-bound will want to send for the helpful booklet "Rollin' by the River," which lists French Quarter and Central Business District restaurant and entertainment spots that provide access for their wheels. Contact the **Advocacy for the Elderly & Disabled,** 210 O'Keefe, Suite 700, New Orleans, LA 70112 (tel. 504/522-2337).

As in the case of hotel rates, it must be said that the restaurant prices quoted here are those in effect at the time of this writing. In these uncertain times, they will probably differ to some degree by the time you visit New Orleans. The categories, however, should remain the same: that is, budget will still be budget, even if the dollar amounts are a little higher.

---

1. Top Restaurants

Any preferential listing of New Orleans's top restaurants is bound to be subjective, so let's start with my favorite. And there's a bit of history that goes with it. Some 20 or more years ago, when I was a frequent visitor to the city, I always headed straight for **Arnaud's,** 813 Bienville St. (tel. 523-5433), for some of the finest dining to be found anywhere. Housed in historic old buildings dating back to the 1700s, the restaurant was opened in 1918 by "Count" Arnaud Cazenave (the fictitious title was bestowed by locals in recognition of his grand manner and great love of life), and after his death in 1948 the old traditions were carried on for many years by his daughter. Then a decline set in that eventually led to the restaurant's desertion by even the most loyal of its wide clientele. But in late 1978 an Egyptian-born "newcomer" to the city (he arrived in 1966) fell in love with the old restaurant as he had with the New Orleans woman who became his wife. Archie and Jane Casbarian bought Arnaud's and set about a restoration that would have gladdened the old count's heart. The lovely mosaic tile floors were patched and polished; the lighting fixtures, dark-wood paneling, original ceiling medallions, and antique ceiling fans were refurbished; Le Richelieu Bar was restored; a delightful Grill Bar was added; and when wood was stripped from interior columns, beautiful fluted iron posts were revealed. Flickering gaslights now welcome you into the large dining room where potted palms, beveled-glass windows, and crystal chandeliers re-create the turn-of-the-century air that has always been Arnaud's. There is also the upstairs Germaine Wells Mardi Gras Museum, which holds an extensive private collection of Mardi Gras gowns owned by the late Mrs. Wells, the count's daughter and previous owner of Arnaud's.

Best of all, of course, is what has happened in the kitchen and with the dining service itself. The food is once more something to dream of in far-away places, and formally dressed waiters who are as knowledgeable, efficient, and friendly as they are stylish see to your needs at tables laid with classic linen cloths and set with sterling silver, original Arnaud china, fine crystal, and original water decanters. Executive chef Guy Petit has retained old specialties such as shrimp Arnaud, trout meunière, and a superb caramel custard, and he is constantly creating exciting new dishes. The menu is à la carte, with prices that range from $16 to $27. At lunch there's an inexpensive table d'hôte selection along with an à la carte menu; lunch is served from 11:30am to 2:30pm Monday through Friday. Dinner hours are 6 to 10pm seven days a week (until 10:30pm on Friday and Saturday). Le Richelieu Bar is open from 11am to

2:30pm and 5:30pm to closing Sunday through Friday, 5:30pm to closing on Saturday and Sunday. There's a terrific Sunday brunch featuring eggs Benedict, eggs Arnaud, omelets in several versions, and other specialties, along with the jazz of Sal Alcorn, Jr.'s Trio. Hours are 10am to 2:30pm, and prices range from $18 to $28 for a complete meal. If you're dining, reservations are recommended (but are not necessary at the bar). This has been a favored place to eat, especially during Carnival season, with New Orleanians over the years, and I rejoice to report that now it has reclaimed their devotion.

Who hasn't heard of **Antoine's,** 713 St. Louis St. (tel. 581-4422), and dreamed of at least one meal in this legendary restaurant that has been run by the same family for more than 150 years? Once inside the ironwork-adorned building, you're in a world of white tile floors, slowly turning antique ceiling fans, and 15 separate rooms that run the gamut from plainness to grandeur. As for the food, choose from such classics as oysters Rockefeller, pompano en papillot, chicken Rochambeau, and filet de boeuf marchand de vin; or settle for something simpler from a menu that lists more than 150 selections. To accompany your choice you have at your disposal one of the richest wine cellars in America. Be sure to bone up on your French before you come, for there's not a word of English on the à la carte menu. Prices are à la carte, and complete dinners run upward of $30 per person. Lunch hours are noon to 2pm, and dinner is from 5:30 to 9:30pm Monday through Saturday; the restaurant is closed on Sunday. Be sure to make reservations, and even then be prepared for a wait at peak hours. If you want to dine with locals, try for a table in the Annex.

Don't worry about reservations at **Galatoire's,** 209 Bourbon St. (tel. 525-2021)—it doesn't accept them (even the visiting Duke and Duchess of Windsor had to wait in line). So unless you take a tip from the natives and go to lunch before noon or dinner before 6pm, you'll line up with everyone else. But, believe me, it's worth the wait. This is another family-run restaurant (since 1905), and one critic describes it as one of the most magical eating experiences in town. With its mirrored walls and gleaming brass fixtures, it is certainly one of the loveliest. The seafood dishes simply have no match: Try trout amandine, trout Marguéry, or the perfectly broiled pompano meunière. At lunch, you might opt for oysters en brochette, eggs Sardou, or stuffed eggplant. All come to table in a state of perfection. This is a restaurant that draws its charm from a comfortable sense of its age; good, unfussy service; and a way with seafood that will leave you beaming. The à la carte menu is the same at lunch and dinner, and hours are 11:30am to 9pm (from noon on Sunday); it's closed on Monday and holidays. (*Tip:* If you go on a Sunday afternoon, you'll find yourself in the company of New Orleans family groups who have made Sunday dinner here a ritual for generations.) Prices are in the $10 to $20 range.

One of the most famous New Orleans restaurants is **Brennan's,** 417 Royal St. (tel. 525-9711). It occupies a 1795 building that was once the home of Paul Morphy, international chess champion, and although the restaurant has been here only since

1946, it has from the start won a place in the hearts of residents and visitors alike. The Brennan family seems dedicated to providing fine food, good service, and exceptional atmosphere. Be prepared, however, for a long wait at busy periods, even if you have a reservation— if that's a problem, come at dinner, when it's less crowded. The lush tropical patio here has to be seen to be believed, and there's a view of it from any table in the downstairs rooms. *Elegance* is the only word for the interiors, but it is warm elegance, not the cold, sterile kind. "Breakfast at Brennan's" has, of course, become internationally famous, and you can breakfast here even in the evening. But if that's what you have in mind, take heed and don't plan another meal that day—you'll want to be able to do justice to the sumptuous dishes listed on a menu that tempts you with items such as eggs Hussarde (poached eggs atop Holland rusks, Canadian bacon, and marchand de vin sauce, topped with hollandaise sauce and accompanied by grilled tomato) or trout Nancy (filet of fresh trout sautéed and topped with lump crabmeat sprinkled with capers and lemon-butter sauce). Even their omelets are spectacular. This is not your typical bacon-and-eggs breakfast, but breakfast in the tradition of antebellum days in the Quarter, so if you really want to do it right, order one of their complete breakfast suggestions. A typical one begins with eggs Sardou (poached eggs atop creamed spinach and artichoke bottoms, served with hollandaise sauce), followed by grillades and grits, sautéed baby veal (served in a spicy Creole sauce with fines herbes and freshly cracked black pepper), and topped off by crêpes Fitzgerald (served with a sauce of crushed strawberries flamed in maraschino) and hot chicory coffee. A marvelous eye-opener to begin the whole thing with is an absinthe Suissesse (a legendary Brennan's drink that has the faint flavor of anisette). Well, you get the idea—this is a very special restaurant serving very special meals. Breakfast and lunch prices will run about $18 to $35, and dinner will run $28 to $46, depending on whether your selections come from the table d'hôte or à la carte menu. Brennan's is open every day except Christmas from 8am to 2:30pm and 6 to 10pm, and it's best to reserve ahead.

Reserve ahead also—and as far in advance as possible—at **Broussard's**, 819 Conti St. (tel. 581-3866). This venerable old (it's been here more than 70 years) New Orleans restaurant has three dining rooms that vary from opulent elegance in the largest (the Napoleon Room) to Italian rustic in a smaller room overlooking the courtyard (the Garibaldi Room). The third (the Josephine Room) has a delightful French country provincial décor. And you'll find some of the city's best French-Creole cooking in these surroundings. Along with old standbys, you might choose an innovative creation such as the superb shrimp and crabmeat Jean Lafitte (gulf shrimp and lump crabmeat sautéed and delicately flavored with parsley, a hint of garlic, white wine, and shallots). The flaming desserts are simply glorious, with absolutely perfect crêpes and perfectly blended fillings, and the bananas Foster have a marvelous caramelized syrup. Broussard's is open for dinner only, every day from 5:30 to 11pm, and prices range from $16 to $22 à la carte. There's a strict dress code.

Ask almost any New Orleans native for a list of favorite restaurants and chances are that the Omni Royal Orleans Hotel's **Rib Room,** 621 St. Louis St. (tel. 529-7045), will be at or very near the top. It's a pretty room, with arched windows, high ceilings, natural brick, lots of wood, and open rôtisserie ovens in the back of the room. As you might guess, the specialties are beef, and the Rib Room has raised its cooking to an art. Roasts are exceptional and served piping hot. Prime ribs rank highest in most patrons' esteem, but there are also filets, sirloins, brochettes, tournedos, and steak au poivre. Veal, lamb, and duckling also appear on the menu, as do trout, crab, oysters, and shrimp. At lunch, a variety of egg dishes and salads are also offered. The Rib Room is open every day for lunch from 11:30am to 3pm (prices from $10 to $15) and for dinner from 6:30 to 10:30pm (prices from $19 to $30). At least one meal at the Rib Room is a *must* for any New Orleans visit.

K-Paul's Louisiana Kitchen, 416 Chartres St. (tel. 524-7394), is the place that started all the hoopla about Cajun cooking when chef Paul Prudhomme spread its virtues across the entire country. This is also where you'll find the *hottest* interpretation of that cuisine —lots of pepper and other hot seasonings—as well as probably the best. Known for its blackened redfish and Cajun martini (only for the very brave or those with cast-iron innards), K-Paul's also specializes in fiery gumbo, chicken and rabbit from its own farm, and Cajun popcorn (fried crayfish tails). You'll have to decide if you really are prepared to wait in line as much as an hour before gaining admittance to the plain, cafélike interior, where harried waitresses will serve you on wooden tables sans tablecloths that you'll share with other dinners unless your party numbers four or more. Prices have soared to *very* expensive heights, so expect to pay about $40. K-Paul's is open 5:30 to 10pm Monday to Friday only; it does not accept reservations.

---

2. Next-Best Restaurants

Set in the small, stylish St. Louis hotel, the **Louis XVI,** 829 Toulouse St. (tel. 581-7000), is a fine French restaurant. The elegantly appointed dining room looks onto a lush courtyard complete with a sparkling fountain. Crystal chandeliers and wall sconces bathe diners in a soft, relaxing glow, and everything seems designed to put you in a proper mood for the excellent cuisine.

Rack of lamb and trout Louis XVI are among the stars of the menu, as are beef Wellington, lamb en croûte, and delicious creamed soups. Dinner is served every day of the week from 6:30 to 11pm and will average about $35 (vegetables included). Reservations are a good idea although not always necessary.

The **Palm Court Café,** 1204 Decatur St. (tel. 525-0200) is not only a delightful place to enjoy Creole and French culinary specialties but also the repository of a collection of jazz records that will probably contain any of the classics you might be looking for. Owners Nina and George Buck have a long history in the recording business, as well as a passionate love of good eating, and the Palm Court is a perfect blending of those two loves—exceptional food comes to table accompanied by top-line jazz performers. At some point during the evening, there's usually a "second-line" march led by the talented dancing waiters, with diners happily jumping up to join in. As for the food, gumbo, shrimp Creole, oysters bordelaise, Creole beef indienne, and jambalaya are just a few of the à la carte menu specials, with entree prices running between $8 and $14. The hours are noon to 11pm Wednesday through Sunday, with music every night and at Sunday brunch. It is best to book ahead at this popular spot.

One of the loveliest and most atmospheric of French Quarter restaurants is the **Court of Two Sisters,** 613 Royal St. (tel. 522-7261). There are entrances from both Royal and Bourbon streets into a huge courtyard filled with flowers, fountains, and low-hanging willows, with a wishing well at its center. The building and its grounds were designed by an early French territorial governor of Louisiana to create the atmosphere of his homeland, and the unusual name comes from a Shop of the Two Sisters that was operated here in the late 1800s by two maiden ladies (sisters, of course). You can dine outside amid all that lush planting or in the Creole Patio Room. Creole and French cuisines are specialties. You'll know you've found a friendly establishment from the very first, because a sign just outside the door lists their hours as "Buffet Brunch 9am to 3pm, Dinner 5:30 to 11pm. Visiting and browsing allowed 3:30 to 5pm. Have a nice day." You can accept that invitation to browse and enjoy a cocktail in the courtyard. An innovation here that is gaining increasing popularity is the daily Jazz Brunch Buffet (from 9am to 3pm), which features over 50 dishes (meat, fowl, fish, vegetables, fresh fruits, homemade bread, and pastries) and strolling jazz musicians. Reservations are necessary for dinner, where delicacies such as shrimp Toulouse, crabmeat Rector, and chicken Michelle are good bets. Prices run from $17 to $25 à la carte and $28 for a complete meal table d'hôte. (The Jazz Brunch Buffet is $18.)

For some of the finest French cooking in New Orleans, go to **Le Bistro,** in the Hotel Maison de Ville, 733 Toulouse St. (tel. 528-9206). This restaurant has a marvelous filet mignon stuffed with herbed cheese and served with a garlicky bordelaise sauce; a great local favorite are the sweetbreads, which come sautéed, with lemon butter and capers. The hours are 11:30am to 2:30pm on Monday through Saturday, and 6 to 10pm daily. Expect to pay around $30.

The enormous success of Le Bistro is due almost entirely to its first chef, Susan Spicer. She has now gone on to open a place of her own, **Bayona,** 430 Dauphine St. (tel. 525-4455), in a century-old Creole cottage. Her French soul shines through there in such specialties as garlic soup, coriander shrimp with black bean cake, and duck breast with pepper jelly glaze. Dinner prices run about $25, but lunch is a bit less. The hours are 11:30am to 2:30pm Monday through Friday and 6 to 10pm every day except Friday and Saturday, when Bayona closes at 11pm.

You may have to look a bit for **Moran's Riverside Restaurant,** 44 French Market Pl. (tel. 529-1583). It's hidden away on the second floor of the Bazaar Building of the renovated market complex. The site is just opposite the crescent bend of the river, and Moran's makes full use of it by providing an outdoor terrace with a sweeping view of the French Market and the Mississippi River. It's a terrific place for a before- or after-dinner drink. The dining room is done in low-key elegance, with a window wall that lets you enjoy the river view during dinner (incidentally there's no need to insist on a window table—the view's great from any position in the room). It's French-Italian cooking here, with all sorts of pasta offerings (they make their own and even operate on the main floor a "pastaficcio" where you can make purchases to take home), seafood, steak, chicken, lamb, and veal. I found seafood sauces—such as the lemon-butter sauce on shrimp scampi "Don Josey"—light and well seasoned, and the salad with house dressing was exceptional. Another favorite is chicken majestic (chicken in a sauce of chives, mushrooms, shallots, and sprinkled with cognac). And if you've any room left, try the delicious amaretto parfait for dessert. Moran's is open every day but Sunday, from 6 to 11pm (later on weekends), and reservations are advisable. The menu is à la carte, with prices ranging from $15 to $30 for entrees.

3. Moderately Priced Restaurants

One of the delights of exploring New Orleans is discovering the many small, inexpensive places to eat, some just as exciting as the better-known restaurants. What you'll find here is a sort of thumbnail sketch of some of my own favorites—it simply isn't possible to list them all or to tell you all I'd like to about these in this limited space. But do explore on your own—you'll be certain to find others.

Across from the French Market at the **Café Sbisa,** 1011 Decatur St. (tel. 561-8354), you're likely to run into some of New Orleans's best artists and writers, along with other natives entertaining guests from all over the world. It's an old building, and the interior is casual, with mirrors reflecting ceiling fans and potted greenery and the tile floor reminding you of its humble beginnings. Seafood here is freshness itself, with such specialties as swordfish, smoked fish, salmon, mussels, clams, and an excellent bouillabaisse. Steak, lamb, and duckling round out the menu. Prices are in the moderate range ($12 to $25). Dinner hours are 6 to 11pm Monday through Thursday and until midnight on Friday and Saturday. Lunch is served from noon to 3pm Monday through Friday, and on Sunday there's a champagne brunch from 11am to 3pm and dinner from 6 to 11pm.

Ralph & Kacoo's, 519 Toulouse St. (tel. 522-5226), may well be crowded no matter when you go. Although your wait for a table here will be at the bar, surrounded by a lively crowd of other waitees, it will seldom be for more than 15 to 20 minutes. Once seated at a table, you'll be rewarded by quite good Creole dishes, mostly seafood, at very reasonable prices. You might try the crayfish platter or a platter of crab cooked in three different ways. Everything is fresh, and the portions are ample. The hours are 11:30am to 10:30pm seven days a week, with prices in the $15 to $20 range.

The **Olde N' Awlins Cookery,** 729 Conti St. (tel. 529-3663), symbolizes several of the city's food traditions. First, it's located in an 1849 building whose history includes having begun as two private residences, a later resurrection as a large rooming house that combined the two, a probable short stint as a brothel, and service for a time as bistro bars, then a disco, before lying idle nearly two years prior to becoming a restaurant. Since its opening in mid-1983, the family-operated restaurant has dished up traditional Cajun and Creole favorites and attracted a loyal clientele from the ranks of city residents. Using the freshest of Louisiana seafood and local seasonings, the kitchen turns out specialties such as Cajun jambalaya, blackened redfish, and shrimp Creole, as well as soups, salads, and great desserts. Its blackboard menu changes daily, featuring whatever is freshest each day. In a rather plain setting that makes use of the original old brick and a delightful courtyard, informality is the keynote. The restaurant does not accept reservations, but with hours of 11am to 11pm seven days a week, with entrees topping at $16, and a lively, distinctly New Orleans ambience, this is one place where you won't mind a short wait to be seated.

Mr. B's Bistro and Bar, 201 Royal St. (tel. 523-2078), is owned and operated by Ralph and Cindy Brennan and is one of the most attractive restaurants in town. The décor is one of polished oak floors, warm wood paneling, marble-topped tables, and large bay windows that look out onto Royal Street. In keeping with the bistro spirit, you can drop in for appetizers and a salad or a casual glass of wine or enjoy a full meal. Traditional New Orleans dishes are featured, and a treat here is the charcoal-grilled fish (grilled over hickory and pecan logs) or pasta jambalaya. Dinner entrees are priced from $10 to $20; complete dinners are from $18 to $25. All prices are a little lower at lunch. Lunch hours are 11:30am to 3pm weekdays; dinner hours are 5 to 10pm daily; and weekend brunch is 11:30am to 3pm (jazz brunch on Sunday). Besides being a great place for a moderately priced meal, this is a superb "rest-the-feet" break when wandering about the Quarter.

Tujague's ("Two-jacks"), at 823 Decatur St. (tel. 525-8676), is the second restaurant to occupy this site. The first was run by Madame Bergue, who began in 1856 cooking huge "second breakfasts" for the butchers who worked in the French Market across the way. So well loved were her elaborate, leisurely meals that even today her name lives on in a modern eatery in the Royal Sonesta Hotel. Today Tujague's serves only lunch and dinner, but continues the original cook's tradition of simply serving whatever she was cooking up that day. This is a favorite with New Orleanians, who seem to mind not at all that there's a very limited menu. At lunch, you have a choice of three entrees (which might include a traditional specialty here such as brisket of beef with horseradish sauce, their terrific shrimp rémoulade, and the freshest fish available that day), but the five-course meal will consist of soup, salad, entree, vegetable, dessert, and beverage for no more than a modest $7.50 to $10.50. If something lighter appeals to you, choose gumbo served with a side dish of shrimp salad at just $6. Six courses at dinner will run about $18 to $20. The hours are 11am to 3pm and 5 to 10:30 pm daily.

The **Royal Café,** 700 Royal St. (tel. 528-9086), is a delightfully casual eatery, with dining rooms on both the ground and the second floors. But it is the upstairs balcony that appeals to most who come here to eat. That's the balcony so often photographed by tourists, and when you dine there, along with your food you enjoy a superb view of the French Quarter itself. There's also the Mardi Gras Room for private parties. No matter where you dine, however, the food will be top-notch. Try New Orleans "lost bread" for breakfast (it's listed as "French Quarter toast" on the menu), a spicy shrimp Creole at lunch, and pompano Mardi Gras at dinner. Should you have a bit of difficulty choosing, there's a terrific "Taste of New Orleans" sampler that gives you a cup of gumbo; a green salad; a small bowl of red beans, sausage, and rice; followed by the aforementioned shrimp Creole—served with fresh-baked French bread at the amazing price of $13.

Mike Anderson's Seafood, 215 Bourbon St. (tel. 524-3884), is an offshoot of the popular restaurant by that same name in Baton Rouge. As the name implies, seafood is the specialty here, and it comes in all varieties—fried, baked, boiled, or charbroiled. Especially good are the crayfish bisque and the crayfish étouffée. It's a busy, casual place; the portions are large; and the prices are low (under $17 for a full dinner). The hours are 11am to 10pm Sunday through Thursday and 11:30am to 11pm on Friday and Saturday.

Early on during your New Orleans visit, you're likely to develop an itch to duplicate some of these great dishes in your own home. Well, you can scratch that itch by signing up for lunch that comes with a liberal dash of learning at the **New Orleans School of Cooking,** 620 Decatur St., in the Jackson Brewery (tel. 525-2665). It's a great way to learn the secrets of Creole cooking as local Louisiana cooks and chefs conduct entertaining and informative demonstrations of basic techniques, then serve the dishes you've just seen prepared. Groups are limited in number, so reserve as far in advance as possible; if classes are full, inquire about the possibility of special evening courses. The school is in the back of the Louisiana General Store, which is crammed full of cookbooks, Cajun and Creole seasonings, and a host of other New Orleans gift items. The cost is $15, and the session hours are 10am to 1pm Monday through Saturday. The school also has a free Louisiana gift catalog.

In one of the only five buildings to survive the disastrous fire of 1788, the **Gumbo Shop,** 630 St. Peter St. (tel. 525-1486), is just one block off Jackson Square. There's a lovely informal atmosphere in both the small patio and the warm indoor dining room. Murals of Old New Orleans, ceiling fans, lots of brass, and a fireplace with an antique mirror hung above the mantel create a charm that seems to make the excellent Creole food taste even better. Their seafood gumbo is a meal in itself, and if you haven't yet tried jambalaya, this is the place. Red beans and rice are also featured (there's a marvelous combination plate with red beans and rice, shrimp Creole, and jambalaya), and there are salads, po-boys, sandwiches, and homemade desserts. Lunch and dinner are served from 11am to 11pm at prices that range, à la carte, from $9 to $17.

I have New Orleans friends to thank for introducing me to **Port of Call,** 838 Esplanade Ave. (tel. 523-0120). With my strong penchant for seafood when I get anywhere near this city, I didn't feel especially drawn to a hamburger place. Not, that is, until I stepped inside the cozy wooden interior, met some of the friendliest people in the city, and feasted on mushrooms in wine, as well as one of the best hamburgers I've ever had. Now I understand my friends' enthusiasm and why this place stays so packed at lunch and dinnertime. Other times, the bar stays busy with neighborhood people who make this their "local." There are pizzas as well as hamburgers and those wonderful mushrooms in the front room, and excellent filet mignon, rib eye, and New York strip steaks in the back dining room. Your food tab can run anywhere from $5 to $18, depending on whether you're eating hamburger or steak (which is aged prime beef). Because businesspeople come from all over the city to eat here, it's often jammed at regular eating times—so try it at off-hours or after 7pm, when people who work in the Quarter gather here to relax. The hours are 11am to 1am daily. Port of Call is open every day of the year except the Fourth of July, when the entire staff packs up and goes off on a picnic. *Note:* They also have a take-out service.

Running parallel to and one block behind Esplanade Avenue, Frenchmen Street is home to two very good eateries. **Alberto's,** 611 Frenchmen St. (tel. 949-5952), is a small Italian eatery above the Apple Bar, with one of the friendliest staffs in the city. Alberto Gonzalez, owner and chef, holds sway in a setting of bare wooden tables, lots of hanging greenery, and a whimsical stuffed parrot. The food here is New Orleans with a touch of Italy—fettucine with shrimp, pasta with clam sauce, cannelloni, and soft-shell crabs with crayfish tails (in season, of course) are a few of Alberto's specialties. The prices are amazingly low: $6 to $9, with an occasional special that may run up to $13. Locals flock to this charming little place, so you may have a wait (not such a chore, with the 24-hour bar just downstairs). The hours are 6 to 11pm every day but Sunday.

The **Santa Fe,** 801 Frenchmen St. (tel. 944-6854), has Mexican cuisine with a huge dash of pure Creole. It has tortillas that come with seafood fillings, a "Mexican gumbo" (a contradiction in terms?), and seafood burritos. If you hanker for traditional Mexican, order enchiladas or tostados with meat and cheese. The Santa Fe is open 11am to 11pm Tuesday through Friday and 5 to 11pm on Saturday, but it is closed Sunday and Monday.

Farther out on Esplanade, not really in the French Quarter but not far away, the **Mystery Street Café,** 3201 Esplanade Ave. (tel. 947-6117), sits at the junction of Esplanade and Mystery Street. It is the epitome of a neighborhood bistro, but New Orleanians (who know good food when they find it) come here in droves for a basically French and Mediterranean cuisine. At lunch, the Salad Marseillaise—with grilled fish, scallops, and shrimp—hints of a Creole influence, as do several dinner selections. Deluxe sandwiches are also served at lunch, and a standout at dinner is the roast leg of lamb stuffed with feta cheese and spinach. It's a delightful mix of food in a delightful little eatery. You won't pay more than $7 or $8 at lunch (11:30am to 2:30pm Tuesday through Friday) and $10 to $13 at dinner (5:30 to 10:30pm Tuesday through Sunday). The excellent Sunday brunch is a mere $7.50 and is served from 10:30am to 3pm.

4. Budget Restaurants

"Budget" in the French Quarter can often mean "very, very good." That's due, I think, to two things: first, there are many favorite dishes here that aren't made of costly ingredients (red beans and rice, for example); second, there are so many good cooks in this city who can make almost anything taste delicious. So whatever preconceived notions you bring with you about luncheonette-style eateries, be ready to revise them after trying one or two of the following.

If you're an oyster lover, there's nothing quite like standing at the oyster bar in the **Acme Oyster House,** 724 Iberville St. (tel. 522-5973), eating a dozen or so freshly shucked oysters on the half shell. (You can have them at a table, but somehow they taste better at the bar.) If you can't quite go them raw, try the oyster loaf here. There's also a sandwich menu, with beer, of course, as the perfect accompaniment. This is a New Orleans institution and a fun place to eat—the shuckers behind the bar are as much a treat as those lovely oysters. The Acme is open from 11am to "about 10pm," and the cost of your meal will depend on your appetite, but you'd have to be *very* hungry to run up a tab above $6 or $7.

Of course, if you get a yen for oysters after 9pm, there's always **Felix,** 739 Iberville St. (tel. 522-4440), right across the street. It's also almost legendary among New Orleanians, and it stays open into the wee hours. In addition to raw oysters, there's a selection of fried or grilled fish, chicken, steaks, spaghetti, and omelets, and the Creole cooking is quite good. It's a bit untidy, sometimes crowded and noisy, and almost always looks disorganized, but if you pass it by on those grounds you'll be missing a real eating experience. The prices are a bit higher than those at the Acme, and the hours are 10:30am to midnight weekdays, until 2am Friday and Saturday, and 10pm on Sunday.

Captain Al's Seafood & Oyster Bar, 635 Bourbon St. (tel. 524-3817), adjoins the Maison Bourbon, home of some of the street's best jazz, and is open from 11am to 2am daily. The very moderately priced menu ($4.50 to $12) offers—in addition, of course, to oysters—traditional New Orleans dishes such as red beans and rice, shrimp étouffée, barbecued shrimp, and Cajun jambalaya. There's also a wide range of specialty drinks, as well as 16 brands of beer. Eat inside or in the small courtyard out back; in either, you'll dine to the sound of jazz.

On the corner of Royal and St. Ann streets, the **Père Antoine Restaurant** (tel. 581-4478) is an attractive European-style place with huge mirrors in back and flowers out front. Cajun and Creole cookery are specialties here, with Cajun snapper (cooked in a rich tomato sauce, a nice change from "blackened"), shrimp, or crayfish étouffée featured. The seafood platter, with catfish, shrimp, scallops, crab, and Cajun popcorn (that's deep-fried seasoned shrimp), is a real bargain at $13. For lighter meals, there are soups and salads; sandwiches and burgers; omelets; and New Orleans favorites such as red beans and rice, jambalaya, and chicken Creole. The prices range from as low as $5 up to $15, and the hours are 9am to midnight daily.

Petunia's, 817 St. Louis St. (tel. 522-6440), has settled into an old house between Toulouse and Conti streets and dishes up enormous portions of New Orleans specialties at prices that can only be called budget. Breakfast and Sunday brunch are popular here, with a large selection of crêpes that are billed as the world's largest, and probably are. Creole and Cajun cuisines are featured on the menu, with prices ranging from $10 to $18 for complete dinners. The hours are 8am to midnight, seven days a week.

For a fun way to sample most of New Orleans's legendary dishes, head for the third level of the Jackson Brewery, St. Peter and Decatur streets, any day of the week between 10am and 10pm. Given the umbrella name of **Jaxfest,** the entire level consists of take-out stands for such specialties as red beans and rice, fried chicken, and barbecued ribs; Cajun fried oysters and shrimps, Cajun shrimp salad, and gumbo from **Patout's Cajun** (a branch of one of the western Louisiana Cajun country's leading restaurants); calzone and other Italian treats from **Café Sbarro;** Creole seafood gumbo from **Greco's Fish Market;** and cannoli, spumoni, ice cream, espresso, and so on from **James Brocatto Italian Ice Cream.** "Take-out" here means bringing your food to a pleasant tiled dining area over on the river side or on the wide outside terrace. If you're lucky, you'll do your sampling to the strains of live jazz sporadically performed on the ground level. The prices are unbelievably low at all stands.

One of the French Quarter's most charming casual eateries is **La Madeleine,** 547 St. Ann St., at Chartres St. (tel. 568-9950). One of a chain of French bakeries, La Madeleine has a brick, wood-burning oven that turns out a wide variety of breads, croissants, and brioches. A glass case up front holds marvelous pastries to take out or eat in the cafeteria section, where quiches, salads, soups, sandwiches, and other light entrees are available. This restaurant is delightful for a continental breakfast or light lunch. You can eat well for $5 to $10, 7am to 9pm daily.

I first found **Molly's Irish Pub,** 732 Toulouse St. (tel. 568-1915), on a rainy day in the heart of the Quarter when I ducked in for an Irish coffee to ward off the chill and stayed to enjoy a platter of fried oysters, french fries, and salad for just $5.50. And I never had better anywhere else in the city. That says a lot for the kitchen here, especially since there is a very wide variety on the menu. It's open 24 hours a day and is a great place to watch all sorts of New Orleans types as well as tourists who find it as I did. Breakfast is served at any hour, making this pub a special favorite of night owls who have a taste for bacon and eggs after a night on the town.

Jim Monaghan, who originated Molly's, now devotes full time

to his establishment over on Decatur Street across from the French Market. One of the prime movers in the upgrading of what was once a run-down, rather seedy part of the Quarter, Jim has brought his own brand of enthusiasm to this part of town. His warm personality is reflected by staff members who make every visitor feel welcome and, on a return visit, like a valued member of a special club. There's the best Irish coffee in New Orleans at **Molly's at the Market,** 1107 Decatur St. (tel. 525-5169). For a bit of fun, drop by Molly's on Thursday, when "Media Night" finds a local celebrity behind the bar and a lively crowd of locals in front. Open Monday through Thursday 10am to 2am, and Friday, Saturday, and Sunday 8:30am to 2pm.

Napoleon House, at the corner of Chartres and St. Louis streets, is so named because at the time of the "Little Corporal's" death there was actually a plot hatching in this 1797 National Landmark house to snatch him from his island exile and bring him to New Orleans. The third floor was added expressly for the purpose of providing him with a home after the rescue. It wears its history well and with dignity. There's a limited menu of po-boys, Italian muffuletta sandwiches, and pastries ($4.50 to $8.75); the jukebox plays only classical music. This is a very popular spot with residents and many visiting celebrities. The hours are daily 11am to 1 or 2 am.

The **Café Maspero,** 601 Decatur St. (tel. 523-6250), is open from 11am to 11pm Sunday through Thursday and to midnight (and often later) Friday and Saturday and serves the largest portions I've run into—burgers, barbecue, steaks, and so on—as well as an impressive list of wines, beers, and cocktails, all at low, low prices. This is a lively spot, especially following a concert, the opera, or the theater, when locals drop by in droves, and it's not unusual to see patrons lined up for tables. Be assured, however, that it's worth your time to wait—the quality is as good as the portions are large, and the prices are in the $5 to $10 range.

The bright, charming **Honfleur Restaurant** in the Provincial Hotel, 1024 Chartres St. (tel. 581-4995), serves exceptional food at reasonable cost. Breakfast is especially good here, at prices that range from $3 to $7. Lunch specialties include red beans and rice, southern fried chicken, and an open-face roast beef sandwich that is excellent. The prices begin at $5. At dinner, choose from Creole gumbo, shrimp, trout, or pahee veal at prices from $6 to $10. The waitresses are among the friendliest in town, and Evelyn Revertiga, the lovely manager, gives personal attention to every guest. It's open from 7am to 9pm every day of the week.

---

5. For the Sweet Tooth

The tiny **La Marquise,** 625 Chartres St., serves pastries (French) on the premises, either in a crowded front room that also holds the display counter or outside in a small but delightful patio. Maurice Delechelle is the master baker and guiding hand here, and I promise you, you've never had more delectable goodies. There are galettes bretonnes (butter cookies), pain au chocolat (chocolate bread), cygne swan (an éclair in the shape of a swan filled with whipped cream), choux à la crème (cream puff), and mille feuilles (napoleons), as well as croissants, brioches, and a wide assortment of strudels and Danish pastries. Prices are minimal (some as low as 50¢), and you can buy coffee in paper cups if you decide to buy your sweet here and take it elsewhere. La Marquise is almost always crowded, and if the patio has no seats available, there's always Jackson Square just a few steps away for a dessert picnic. The hours are 8am to 5:30pm on weekdays and 7:30am to 8:30pm on Saturday and Sunday.

There's a larger La Marquise at 617 Ursulines St., so you can indulge that sweet tooth even when you're not in the Jackson Square vicinity.

There's been an **Angelo Brocato's Original Italian Ice Cream Parlor** in New Orleans since 1905, and except for a brief interruption, Brocato's has been in the French Quarter. This is the family on whom the city's most demanding hostesses have depended for three generations to cater those occasions for friends and special guests when sweets must reach the heights of sheer perfection. Happily you'll now find the Brocatos back in new quarters at 537 St. Ann St. (tel. 486-1465), serving their fabulous ice cream, Italian ices, cannolis, and a whole feast of other pastries from 10am to 6pm Monday through Friday, until 11pm on Saturday, and until 8pm on Sunday.

VII

DINING OUTSIDE THE QUARTER

1. DOWNTOWN

2. CENTRAL BUSINESS DISTRICT

3. UPTOWN (INCLUDING THE GARDEN DISTRICT)

4. METAIRIE

5. LAKE PONTCHARTRAIN

6. OUT OF TOWN

Good eating in New Orleans is by no means confined to the French Quarter—you'll find it all over town. To make life easier for you as you move around the city, I'm listing restaurants in this chapter by area, however, not by price category. You'll find the most expensive listed first, then moderate places, and budget places last. Area boundaries for this purpose are rather broad: "downtown" (remember, that's *downriver* from Canal Street) is outside the French Quarter, but on the same side of Canal Street; the Central Business District is roughly the area upriver from Canal, extending to the elevated expressway (U.S. 90); "uptown" includes everything upriver from Canal and as far as Carrollton toward the lake, including the Garden District; "lake," of course, means the area along the shores of Lake Pontchartrain; and "out of town" means across the Mississippi River or Lake Pontchartrain. If all that sounds a little confusing, turn back to the Greater New Orleans map in Chapter II and you'll get the general idea.

Because it can't be repeated too often, let me remind you again that price ranges quoted are those in effect at press time. Any differences that you encounter will be due to our ever-present nemesis, inflation.

1. Downtown

Ever eaten in a church? Well, it's a unique experience at **Christian's,** 3835 Iberville St. (tel. 482-4924). Started by a grandson of the Galatoire clan, this lovely restaurant serves French and Creole cuisines, with lots of seafood specialties, some of which are prepared with the most delicate of French sauces. Try the oysters Roland, the broiled fish filet, or the marvelous bouillabaisse. The little church building remains unaltered on the exterior, and inside it's been beautifully restored. Only about ten minutes from the French Quarter, it's open for dinner from 5:30 to 10pm Monday through Saturday, but closed Sunday and certain holidays. Menus are à la carte, with a price range of $17 to $27.

Mention "Creole with Soul" in New Orleans, and every native will know you're referring to **Chez Hélène,** 1530 W. Robertson St. (tel. 947-9155). This small, unfancy restaurant is run by a great chef, Austin Leslie, whose Aunt Hélène started things with the help of Austin's mother. Both women have since retired, but Austin learned his trade well from them. Fried chicken here is the sort that will turn the stoniest Yankee into a confirmed southerner—brown, crispy, and in a word, perfect. Red beans and rice come with remarkable chaurice, or hot sausage, and Austin's oysters Rockefeller rival those at you-know-where (where they originated). As one food critic noted, Chez Hélène proves beyond a shadow of a doubt that Creole cooking has always had soul.

Because this place is so popular, you'd better make reservations if you have a large party—if there's only one or two, it's fun just to come along and wait at the bar over a drink. The hours are 11am to 1am seven days a week. As for prices, they're the same at lunch and dinner, and a meal will cost anywhere from $6 to $16. *Note:* The neighborhood is such that it's best to go by cab after dark.

If you prefer staying in the French Quarter, go along to the new branch of Chez Hélène at 316 Chartres St., in the de la Poste Motor Hotel (tel. 525-6130). The hours are 7am to 10pm Monday through Thursday, until 10pm Friday and Saturday, and 10am to noon Sunday.

You won't get an argument locally that "the best steak in town" is served at **Ruth's Chris Steak House,** 711 N. Broad St. (tel. 486-0810). It is, in fact, prime beef, well aged and beautifully prepared. Cuts include filets, strips, rib eyes, porterhouses (for two or more), and probably a few more. Pork chops and one or two other meats appear on the menu, but this is primarily a steak house—and one that will not disappoint. There's another Ruth's Chris at 3633 Veterans Blvd. in Metairie (tel. 888-3600). Prices at both run $18 to $30, and both are open from 11:30am to 11:30pm, seven days. It is best to make reservations. (There are also branches in Baton Rouge and Lafayette—see Chapter XII.)

Locals will tell you that **Dooky Chase,** 2301 Orleans Ave. (tel. 821-2294), is where you'll find some of the city's best soul food. And it's soul food with distinctive New Orleans touches—such as shrimp Dooky with its spicy rémoulade sauce and superb stuffed shrimp. The fried chicken here is terrific, and steaks are also on the menu. If hunger pangs strike you'll find Dooky's filled with kindred souls. Prices run $12 to $20, and hours are 11:20am to midnight seven days a week. *Note:* It is best to go by cab after dark.

2. Central Business District

Kabby's Seafood Restaurant, 2 Poydras St. at the Mississippi River (tel. 584-3880), looks out over the river through a 200-foot-wide, 14-foot-high window. It's a spectacular setting, and the décor in earth tones of green, beige, and brown is a charming blend of traditional and art deco styles. You enter through a New Orleans courtyard foyer that features a bubbling fountain, custom-designed lampposts, and tropical plantings. The adjacent bar features a large stained-glass canopy, with live entertainment and dancing in the evening. At lunch, salads, sandwiches (oyster loaf, muffuletta, and so on), and other specialties run $8 to $15. At night seafood is the thing to order, and there's a sumptuous seafood combo that's a real feast and costs $30. Beef, chicken, and veal are also on the menu, but remember that this *is* a seafood restaurant. An excellent Sunday brunch is $18. The hours are 10:30am to 2:30pm and 6 to 11pm daily. Reservations are advised.

You'll find the **Bon Ton Café,** 401 Magazine St. (tel. 524-3386), absolutely mobbed at lunch with New Orleans business-people and their guests, and at dinner you'll be seated *only* if you have reservations. Such popularity is largely due to its owner, Al Pierce. He grew up on the banks of Bayou Lafourche; learned Cajun cooking from his mother; came to New Orleans in 1936; bought the Bon Ton in 1953; and since then has been serving up seafood gumbo, crayfish bisque, jambalaya, crayfish omelet, and other Cajun dishes in a manner that would make his mother proud. This is a small, utterly charming place, and one not to be missed if you want to sample true Cajun cooking at its best (more subtle than Creole, making much use of shallots, parsley, bell peppers, and garlic). It's open from 11am to 2pm for lunch ($9 to $15) and 5 to 9:30pm for dinner ($17 to $21). It is closed Saturday and Sunday. The lunch menu is semi–à la carte; at dinner the menu is table d'hôte.

One of New Orleans's most elegant Sunday brunches is served in the **Blue Room** of the Fairmont Hotel, University Place (tel. 529-7111). There are three seatings (10am, noon, and 2pm), for which you must make reservations. The price is $20 for adults and $12.95 for children.

Although space does not permit full write-ups, you really should know about these two Central Business District restaurants —each is very good, and is as different from the other as night is different from day. **Isadora,** 1100 Poydras St. (tel. 585-7787), serves Nouvelle Creole food in a spectacular art deco setting, is a great lunch favorite with local businesspeople, and is in the expensive price range. At the other end of the spectrum, **Uglesich's,** 1238

Barrone St. (tel. 523-8571) at Erato Street near Lee Circle, is old and more than a little rundown in appearance, but it is well loved locally for its outstanding sandwiches of fried food (leave your jacket behind or you'll carry the fried smell all day), at prices that seldom reach $10.

You should also know that in 1991 three Brennan family cousins will open **Cousin's City Café** in a Canal Street location. The prices are to be in the moderate range, and if they follow family tradition, the dining should be terrific.

You owe it to yourself to make at least one pilgrimage to **Mother's,** 401 Poydras St. (tel. 523-9656), which is within walking distance of the Louisiana Superdome and major hotels. When you go, be sure to allow time to stand in line—bankers queue up with warehouse workers, dockworkers, and just about everybody else from this part of town for *the* best po-boy sandwiches in New Orleans. Made on crisp French bread so fresh that it's just cooled down from the oven, the po-boys here are real creations, many of them served with a rich thick gravy that may leak, but the sandwich is so good that you won't mind. Try the roast beef or ham. There are plate lunches, too, such as the excellent gumbo, red beans, Jerry's award-winning jambalaya, and spaghetti pie. Mother's is always crowded, but don't let that throw you off—by the time you make your way through the line, there'll be room at a table. The hours are 5am (with one of the best breakfasts in the city) to 10pm Monday through Saturday and 7am to 10pm on Sunday, the dress is casual, and your meal will be under $5.

If you're winding up a late evening in this part of town, there are two inexpensive 24-hour places worth a stop before heading home. **Bailey's,** in the Fairmont Hotel on University Place, is a cozy spot softly lit by Tiffany-style lamps and decorated with antiques. At any hour of the day you can order breakfast items such as waffles, pancakes, and omelets or New Orleans specialties such as red beans and rice with hot sausage and a seafood platter. There are also sandwiches and burgers, as well as a nice selection of po-boys. In the Hilton, 2 Poydras St. at the Mississippi River, **Le Croissant,** a coffee shop, serves light, moderately priced meals and snacks. On the lobby level, it's a pleasant place to begin or end a day.

There's been a lounge run by the same family in the old brick building that now houses **Ernst's Café,** 600 S. Peters St. (tel. 525-8544), since 1902. Its brick walls, high ceilings, and heavy timbered bar make it an interesting and attractive setting for excellent sandwiches, sausage and eggs, red beans and rice, and po-boys at prices that won't top $10. If the weather is fine, eat outside on the long balcony that gives a good view of the river. The hours are 8am to 2:30pm Monday through Saturday.

---

3. Uptown (Including the Garden District)

Since it opened in 1948, the **Caribbean Room** in the elegant Pontchartrain Hotel, 2031 St. Charles Ave. (tel. 524-0581), has won a list of culinary awards as long as your arm, and it really epito-mizes New Orleans cuisine at its finest. The décor, like that of the rest of the hotel, is refined (almost understated) luxury. As for service—well, "impeccable" and "solicitous" come to mind. The French and Creole kitchen turns out specialties such as shrimp saki and backfin crabmeat with a lovely creamy, rather tart house dress-ing (actually, it's a combination of two, mustard and French) that have made fans of a host of celebrities—including Arthur Rubin-stein, Gerald Ford, and Mary Martin. Lunch is served from 11:30am to 2pm (semi–à la carte prices from $9 to $15); dinner is served from 6 to 10pm (à la carte entrees from $18 to $30); and there's a Sunday Brûlot Brunch from 11:45am to 2pm for $20. It is best to make reservations.

The unusual, rather grand blue-and-white building at the cor-ner of Washington Avenue and Coliseum Street was built as a restaurant in 1880 by Emile Commander and is now owned by members of the Brennan family of French Quarter fame. **Commander's Palace** (tel. 899-8221) is a consistent favorite of locals and visitors alike. The patio, fountains, lush tropical plantings, and soft colors are a perfect backdrop for mouthwatering Creole special-ties. Outstanding are dishes such as trout with pecans and a spicy crabmeat topping, veal chop tchoupitoulas (with Creole season-ings), and sauté of crayfish. If you're a jazz buff, don't miss their famous Jazz Brunch (Saturday and Sunday, 10am to 12:30pm), where Dixieland is played by jazz greats. Brunch prices start at $16, lunch runs from $9 to $15, and dinner is $25 to $34. Command-er's, in addition to serving some of the best food in town, is a fun place and quite a social center—reservations are a must, sometimes days in advance.

For dining in the continental manner, you just can't equal the **Versailles,** 2100 St. Charles Ave. (tel. 524-2535). The lovely St. Charles Room looks out on tree-shaded St. Charles Avenue through glass walls; the warm, red-walled Marie Antoinette Room is lit with huge, cut-glass chandeliers; and the Trianon Room provides elegant seclusion. But what makes the Versailles really special is its food—specialties such as bouillabaisse marseillaise, escalope de veau Prin-cess, and veal Madagascar are a gourmet's delight. They do their own baking, and the wine cellar is outstanding. Dinner hours are 6 to 10pm every day except Sunday, when it's closed. Reservations are required. If you're driving, an added plus is free valet parking. Prices on the semi–à la carte menu are in the $17 to $26 range.

If you have New Orleans friends, chances are they'll take you at least once to **Pascal's Manale,** 1838 Napoleon Ave. (tel. 895-4877), for barbecued shrimp—if you don't have local friends, by all means go out on your own. It's crowded, noisy, and is in the upper reaches of the moderate price range, but you'll leave as much a fan as any native. Don't expect fancy décor or artificial "atmosphere"—the emphasis is on food and conviviality. (Sunday nights are actually more like social gatherings than those of a commercial nature.) Pascal's bills itself as an Italian–New Orleans steak house, but for my money, it's specialties such as spaghettini Collins (with a butter sauce topped by chopped raw scallions), tiny buster crabs sautéed in butter and lemon, and snapper Catherine that account for its popularity (after, of course, those marvelous barbecued shrimp, a house creation). A la carte prices run from $7 to $10 at lunch and to $10 to $20 at dinner, and hours are 11am to 10pm Monday through Friday, from 4pm on Saturday and Sunday.

A short trolley ride from the Quarter, the **Delmonico Restaurant**, 1300 St. Charles Ave. (tel. 525-4937), was founded in 1895 and has been run by the La Franca family since 1911. It is essentially a comfortable, family-style eatery, with just a touch of elegance and one of the most varied menus in New Orleans. As a dedicated seafood lover, I favor the soft-shell crab Delmonico, but steaks are very good, and the fresh vegetable salad is a wonder. It's open daily from 11:30am to 9:30pm, and prices are in the $14 to $25 range.

In the Riverbend area, **Brigtsen's**, 723 Dante St. (tel. 861-7610), occupies a small house and is presided over by Frank Brigtsen, a former chef at K-Paul's. The only "blackened" item you'll find on his menu here, however, is an excellent prime rib, and he has a magic touch with seafood. Outstanding are the sautéed trout with pecans and crabmeat, the grilled chicken with hot and sweet peppers, and the grilled tuna. The prices are high ($35 to $40), and the hours are 5:30 to 10pm Tuesday through Saturday. Reservations are absolutely necessary (call a day or two in advance if possible).

Gautreau's, 1728 Soniat St. (tel. 899-7397), is a charming little bistro not far off Saint Charles Avenue on the edge of the Loyola and Tulane university section of New Orleans. It's an elegant, intimate place, (which can, however, be a little noisy), and marvelous old wood display cases that held medications back in the days when this was an apothecary shop now hold wine. The menu changes daily, at both lunch and dinner, and you'll be in luck if eggplant Eloise (stuffed with crabmeat, shrimp, and diced carrots, celery, and green pepper) or redfish Key West (cooked with pistachio nuts and lime) are on offer when you're there. Outstanding among desserts is the coffee-toffee pie. Lunch prices are in the $8 to $20 range; dinner prices are from $15 to $25. Lunch hours are 11am to 2:15pm Monday through Friday; dinner hours are from 6 to 10pm Tuesday through Thursday, until 11pm on Friday and Saturday. Gautreau's is closed Sunday and Monday evenings.

P.J.'s Coffee & Tea Company, 5432 Magazine St., (tel. 895-0273), is just the place if you're mad about tea or coffee—some 30 different teas and 21 types of coffee are sold here, and you can taste as many as 18 teas and 3 or 4 coffees on any given day. They do their own roasting, and their iced coffee is very special, made by a cold-water process that entails 12 hours of brewing. Assorted pastries are available to go with the brew you choose. The hours are 7am to 11pm Monday through Friday and 8am to 11pm Saturday and Sunday.

Copeland's, uptown at 4338 St. Charles Ave. (tel. 897-2325), operates on a near-fast-food basis, yet its Cajun and Creole dishes are so authentic that it has gained a loyal local following. The setting is attractive, all the ingredients are fresh, and the recipes have been collected from some of New Orleans's leading chefs. Blackened redfish here is excellent; less spicy are redfish Lacombe and redfish Copeland. Veal, steaks, and barbecued lamb ribs are outstanding on the extensive menu. Prices are in the $15 to $22 range, and it's open every day from 11am to midnight.

Stephen & Martin's, 4141 St. Charles Ave. (tel. 897-0781), is a lively part of New Orleans's "in" scene. It's a large, pleasant eatery serving good Creole dishes, as well as Italian pastas (try the stuffed shells), and delicious barbecued shrimp. The prices are in the $15 to $22 range, and the hours are 11am to 11pm (until midnight on Friday and Saturday) daily.

Upperline, 1413 Upperline, between St. Charles Avenue and Prytania Street (tel. 891-9822), is a small, popular uptown place that specializes in charcoal-grilled foods, chief among them pompano and shrimp. In addition to chicken, a terrific seafood boudin, and filet of redfish, there's a good selection of pasta dishes (try fettuccine with crabmeat). À la carte will run $25 and up at dinner, and the hours are 5:30 to 10pm Sunday through Thursday and 5:30 to 10:30pm on Friday and Saturday. Reservations are required.

The **Home Furnishings Café,** uptown at 1600 Prytania St. (tel. 566-1707), has a unique setting—it's in a furniture store. Following the example of European shops, the owners of the store have installed an attractive, bright little cafeteria on the second floor. The light-lunch menu varies but always includes salads (chicken, spinach, tuna, and so on), sandwiches, hamburgers, and quiche, with hot dishes such as red bean soup, chicken curry noodle soup, shrimp Creole, and other local favorites. Everything is freshly made. The desserts are yummy: cheesecake, mousse, and Gloria's chocolate-chip cookies. You can lunch here for about $5, from 11:30am to 2pm Monday through Saturday.

Another of the inexpensive, homey places so loved by people who live in New Orleans is **Casamento's,** 4330 Magazine St. (tel. 895-9761). The plain exterior holds a warm, friendly restaurant decorated in Spanish tiles and lots of plants. Almost always crowded (mostly with locals), Casamento's has an excellent oyster bar and some of the best seafood plates in town at unbelievably low prices. Their oyster loaf is especially good, but then so are the fried softshell crabs and anything else that you might order here. Incidentally, don't confuse the oyster *loaf* with the oyster sandwich—the loaf is made with a large loaf of white bread toasted and buttered and filled with fried oysters and large enough for two; the sandwich comes on regular toast. The hours here are 11:30am to 1:30pm and 5:30 to 9pm every day except Monday. Sad to say, Casamento's closes from mid-June to mid-September. The average cost for a meal runs $10 to $17.

Flagon's Wine Bar and Bistro, 3222 Magazine St. (tel. 899-6471), is a pleasant, lighthearted spot for a simple glass of wine, a light repast of sandwiches and/or desserts, or a full meal of such delicacies as redfish in parchment or duck breast in cabernet sauce. Pastas are delicious (try the pasta with crabmeat, dill, and fried buster crab). There are more than 40 fine wines available by the glass, with as many as 350 good vintages to buy by the bottle. The prices are moderate, the ambience is great, and the hours are 11:30am to

2:30pm and 6 to 10pm weekdays but to 11pm Friday and Saturday. The wine bar is open 11:30am to 1am daily.

If you're out in the Riverbend area, don't bypass the **Camellia Grill,** 626 S. Carrollton Ave. (tel. 866-9573). It's right on the trolley line and serves a great variety of sandwiches, omelets, salads, and desserts at low-to-moderate prices. The hamburgers are really special; the sandwiches are stuffed to overflowing with corned beef, ham, or whatever, and the omelets are enormous. This is one place in which you can count on having a filling meal at low cost, and although it's counter service and you may have a short wait for a seat, surprisingly, you'll be given a real linen napkin. That counter service is actually a bonus feature—it provides a front-row contact with the friendly, entertaining waiters on the other side. Hours are 9am to 1am Monday through Thursday but to 3am Friday and Saturday and to 1am Sunday. You can walk away full for $5 to $9.

A young lady with whom I shared my Amtrak ride to New Orleans told me to be sure and stop in at **Ye Olde College Inn,** 3016 S. Carrollton Ave. (tel. 866-3683). You could, she told me, have marvelous red beans and rice, a good oyster loaf, or really good po-boys for prices under $6. She was right. Not only that, I found their fried chicken and many of the daily dinner plates to be well above par. The College Inn is rightly popular with locals, and it's open from 11am to 10pm (to 1am on Friday and Saturday).

Just across from City Park, within sight of the famous "dueling oaks," the **Tavern on the Park,** 900 City Park Ave. (tel. 486-3333), is a delightful re-creation of art deco eateries of the Prohibition era. The historic building is a marvelous setting for the restaurant's steak and seafood specialties, with broiled cold-water lobster, fresh trout, and superb steaks high on the list of local favorites. The prices are low to moderate, and the hours are 11:30am to 10pm Sunday through Thursday but to 11pm on Friday and Saturday.

4. Metairie

Crozier's Restaurant Français, 3216 W. Esplanade, N. Metairie (833-8108), which has moved to Metairie from its lakeside location of many years, has retained its charming European flavor, with fresh flowers and candles on the tables. Authentic French cooking accounts for this restaurant's long-standing popularity, with specialties that include onion soup, escargots, coq au vin, escalope de veau, and lovely desserts. The wine list is limited but good and moderately priced. At lunch (11:30am to 2pm Tuesday through Friday) prices run $6 to $15; at dinner (6 to 10pm Tuesday through Saturday) prices run $14 to $20. Reservations are recommended.

Bozo's, 3117 21st St., Metairie (tel. 831-8666), has been run by the Vodonovich family for more than 50 years, and you'll find one of the present generation on duty every time the doors open. New Orleanians have much affection for this plain, unpretentious fish house, and it's easy to see why when heaping plates of seafood appear cooked to perfection and served by friendly and efficient waitresses. Fried catfish—crisp and utterly delectable—is lightly breaded with cornmeal. Shrimp, oysters, crawfish, crabs, and—well, almost anything that swims or lives in nearby waters—make up the bulk of the menu, which also includes a great chicken andouille gumbo; a few steak, chicken, and veal selections; and a good list of sandwiches. The prices are unbelievably low, starting at $4.90 for the gumbo and topping out at $14 for a rib-eye steak. The hours are 11am to 3pm and 5 to 10pm Tuesday through Saturday but to 11pm Friday and Saturday. Bozo's is worth the trip out to Metairie.

You'd need a personal New Orleans friend to tell you about **Lido Gardens,** 4415 Airline Hwy. (tel. 834-8233). That's how I learned about the unpretentious roadside Italian restaurant that very quickly became one of my favorite places to eat. Run by the friendly Mongiat family, the place has a warm, homey décor sparked by red-checked tablecloths and a wishing well draped with wine bottles in the center of the dining room. Pasta dishes are outstanding here, and veal appears in a wide variety of traditional recipes (piccata, milanese, scaloppine, parmigiana, saltimbocca, and so on). If you've never tried involtini (prosciutto and cheese rolled in veal and simmered in butter, wine, and rosemary), you'll be in for a real treat. The prices are in the moderate $10 to $18 range, and the hours are 11am to 2pm every day except Saturday for lunch, 5 to 9pm for dinner Monday through Thursday but until 10pm on Friday and Saturday. It is closed Sunday.

5. Lake Pontchartrain

Bruning's Seafood on the Lake, 1924 West End Parkway (tel. 282-9359), has been serving a classic New Orleans seafood menu since 1859. There's a beautiful view of Lake Pontchartrain, and you'll dine over the water. The boiled seafood here is especially good, as is the seafood gumbo, and fried dishes show up grease-free. A good buy, if you can't make up your mind, is the generous seafood platter. An average meal from the moderately priced menu will run approximately $10 to $18. Bruning's is open from 11am to 9:30pm daily, and it stays open until 10:30pm on Friday and Saturday.

6. Out of Town

About 30 minutes' drive on U.S. 90 west of the city, 4½ miles west of Avondale, there's a plain plywood building with a shell front painted white that holds one of this area's best restaurants. **Mosca's** (tel. 436-9942) is well worth the drive. It was begun in 1946 by Provino and Lisa Mosca, and their son, Johnny, and daughter, Mary, have carried on the unique style of cooking that combines elements of Italian and local Creole cuisine. If an evening out of the city appeals to you, by all means make the trip and sample dishes you won't find anywhere else. I can especially recommend the Italian crab salad (they use vinegar to flavor the crab and pickle the vegetables), and Mosca's Italian oysters are a treat. Other specialties are quail with wild rice; squab and Cornish hen, also with wild rice; and chicken cacciatore (you get the entire chicken). Everything is prepared to order, and you can wait as long as 40 minutes. À la carte prices run $25 to $35, Mosca's accepts no credit cards or checks—and no reservations on weekends (they're absolutely essential at other times). Mosca's closes on Sunday and Monday, but it is open 5:30 to 9:30pm other evenings *usually,* but since these hours can vary, it's safer to call ahead, even on weekends when you can't reserve.

In the other direction, across the Lake Pontchartrain causeway in Lacombe (between Slidell and Mandeville) is another French restaurant that rates a rave. **La Provence,** on I-90 (the Mandeville–Slidell Road) at I-12 in Lacombe (tel. 626-7662), is a jewel of a place that could be bodily transported from the countryside of Louisiana to that of France and be perfectly at home. Founded by a Frenchman with the unlikely name of Chris Kerageorgiou (there's a Greek lurking somewhere in his ancestry, but he was born in Provence in France), the rustic country-inn atmosphere envelops you the minute you step inside.

There's a great fireplace, waitresses dressed in Provençal dress (they're local ladies, friendly and efficient), and fragrances from the kitchen that tell you in advance you're in for a great meal. Chris and his Cajun wife, Charlotte, run things, and his creations combine classic French dishes with marvelous Greek, Creole, and south-of-France touches. If I had to pick a favorite, it would probably be poulet au fromage, which enhances chicken with vermouth, shallots, cream, and Swiss and bleu cheeses. The duck à l'orange is positively magnificent, the rack of lamb is superb, the pompano is unique. I adore this place. The portions are large, and the wine list is extensive (with a nice moderately priced selection as well as rare vintages). La Provence is so popular that you'd best reserve way in advance. An average meal from the à la carte menu will run about $35, and dress is semicasual (jacket optional). It's closed Monday and Tuesday, open for dinner from 5 to 11pm every other day except Sunday, when hours are 1 to 9pm. This one's a "don't miss" if you have wheels.

VIII

SIGHT-SEEING IN THE FRENCH QUARTER

1. A STREET-BY-STREET GUIDE
2. MUSEUMS
3. TOURS

In many respects the French Quarter *is* New Orleans, and many visitors never leave its confines. I think that's a mistake, and I'll tell you why in the next chapter. Be that as it may, the French Quarter is where it all began, and in its 90 or so square blocks, there's more sight-seeing excitement per square foot than many entire cities—or even states—can boast.

The narrow old streets are lined with ancient buildings (many of them a century and a half old) whose fronts are embellished with that distinctive lacy ironwork. Their carriage drives or alleyways are often guarded by more of the ironwork in the form of massive gates and offer glimpses of backyard enchantment in some of the loveliest courtyards in the world. Secluded from street noises and nosy neighbors, the courtyards provide the beauty, relaxation, and privacy so dear to Creole souls, as well as the very important ventilation for their homes. Of course, many of these venerable buildings now serve as entertainment centers that often ring with merriment that is anything but restful; and many more house shops of every description. But above ground level most also have apartments (many of them quite luxurious) in the time-honored custom of combining commercial ventures with living space. A diminishing few are still in the hands of original-owner families. Whatever its present use, almost every building in the Quarter could tell tales of romance and history that would enthrall the dullest soul.

Thanks to the Vieux Carré Commission, not even "progress" is allowed to intrude on a heritage that blends gaiety with graciousness, the rowdiness of Bourbon Street with the quiet residential areas, and the "busyness" of commerce with the sense of leisure and goodwill. Progress is here, all right, with all its attendant benefits, but New Orleans *insists* that it conform to this special life-style, not the other way around. There's not even a traffic light within the whole of the French Quarter—they're relegated to fringe streets—and street lights are of the old gaslight style. Do not worry about those absent traffic lights—automobiles are banned from Royal and Bourbon streets during a good part of the day, making these streets pedestrian malls, and the area around Jackson Square is a permanent haven for foot traffic because no vehicles are allowed.

Laid out in an almost perfect square back in 1718 by a French royal engineer named Adrien de Pauger, the French Quarter is easy to get around in. And even in these high-crime days, you're relatively safe wandering its streets during daylight hours. After dark, as in most metropolitan areas, it's best to exercise caution when walking alone outside the centers of activity—in New Orleans, that means Bourbon, Royal, and Chartres streets and the streets that connect them (there's safety as well as fun in the numbers that throng those streets all night long).

Those driving into the French Quarter should know that all streets are one-way, and on weekdays during daylight hours, Royal and Bourbon streets are closed to automobiles between the 300 and 700 blocks.

It won't take you long to learn how the streets run, especially if you have armed yourself with the excellent walking-tour map passed out by the **Tourist Commission,** 529 St. Ann Street (tel. 566-5031). In fact, no one should set out to explore this city—inside or outside the French Quarter—without first stopping by the commission. Both the walking and the driving tours they suggest are circular in route, easy to follow, and so informative that they're minicourses in New Orleans history and culture. They provide the best possible introduction to this grand old city.

There is so much to see in the French Quarter that the following can, at best, be only a very subjective list. One thing is certain: No matter how carefully you plan your time, you're bound to get back home and discover that you've missed at least one sight-seeing highlight. People who live here will tell you that the only thing to do is move down and settle in to a lifetime of exploration! Because you and I can't do that, I'll do my best to give you a rundown on the things I think shouldn't be missed. I've arranged them by streets, rather than in a suggested route, so that no matter where you find yourself, you'll have easy reference to what you're seeing. *(For a prescribed walking tour—on which I could not hope to improve—stick to the aforementioned Tourist Commission route.)* As I said, this is a very subjective list—by the time you leave for home, you'll have one of your own.

1. A Street-by-Street Guide

JACKSON SQUARE

Jackson Square lies at the very heart of the French Quarter, facing Decatur Street "riverside" and Chartres Street "lakeside,"

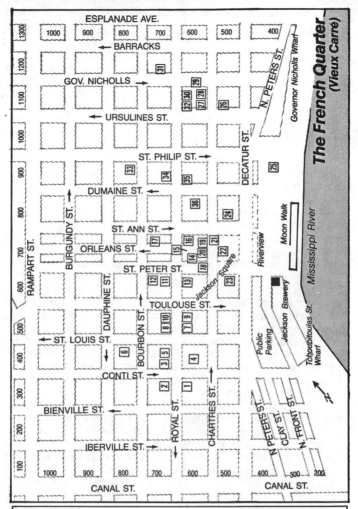

The French Quarter (Vieux Carré)

KEY TO THE NUMBERED REFERENCES: 1. Old Bank of Louisiana; 2. Old Bank of the U.S.; 3. Old La. State Bank; 4. New Orleans Court Building; 5. Casa Faurie; 6. The Hermann House; 7. Maison Seignouret; 8. Merieult House; 9. Casa de Comercio; 10. Court of Two Lions; 11. LeMonnier House; 12. Maison de Fléchier; 13. Maison LeMonnier; 14. Spanish Arsenal; 15. LaBranche House; 16. St. Anthony's Garden; 17. Salle d'Orléans; 18. Père Antoine's Alley; 19. The Presbytère; 20. St. Louis Cathedral; 21. The Cabildo; 22. Pirates Alley; 23. Pontalba Buildings; 24. 1850 House; 25. Court of the Two Sisters; 26. Old Ursulines Convent; 27. Beauregard House; 28. Soniat House; 29. Clay House; 30. LaLaurie House; 31. Thierry House; 32. The Gallier House; 33. Lafitte's Blacksmith Shop; 34. cornstalk fence; 35. Miltenberger Houses; 36. "Madame John's Legacy."

bounded on the "downriver" side by St. Ann Street and by St. Peter Street "upriver." Since 1721 (when it was called Place d'Armes), it has served as a military parade ground; the flags fluttering from its flagpole have changed no fewer than seven times; it has witnessed ceremonies transferring the Louisiana Territory from French to U.S. control (perhaps the greatest real estate deal in history, since the land Pres. Thomas Jefferson bought from Napoleon for a mere $15 million was large enough to contain all or a part of 13 of our present states); there have been public hangings on its grounds; it has acquired its new name (in the 1850s, when New Orleans changed the name to honor its hero of the 1815 battle fought out at Chalmette Battleground); and it has seen the erection of a giant bronze statue of its namesake, Gen. Andrew Jackson. (Incidentally that inscription on the statue's base, "The Union Must and Shall Be Preserved," is the work of a hated Union general, Ben Butler, during his occupation of the city during the Civil War, and is his very *loose* interpretation of an Andrew Jackson remark made years before.) During all those years it has been a focal point for New Orleanians' daily lives, functioning as a sort of city courtyard or patio. Today you can enter through its lamp-topped iron gates for a brief respite from whatever your day's activities may be or wander around the outside of its iron fence, making the sidewalk artists and their sketches and musicians and performers of all descriptions a part of those activities. It's a pleasant garden spot set aside as a pedestrian mall, with one side looking toward the Mississippi River and historic buildings lining all three of its remaining sides. The most famous and *the* one most instantly recognizable New Orleans landmark is the cathedral directly facing you if you view the square from the Decatur Street side.

The **St. Louis Cathedral** is across from the Chartres Street entrance to Jackson Square, and the one you see today is the third to stand in this spot. A hurricane destroyed the first in 1722. Then, on Good Friday of 1788, the bells of its replacement were kept silent for religious reasons rather than ringing out the alarm for a fire that eventually went out of control and burned down over 850 buildings, and the cathedral was once again destroyed. Rebuilt in 1794, largely through the generosity of a Don Almonester (who is buried in front of St. Joseph's shrine on the right as you face the altar), it is of Spanish design, with a tower at each end and a higher central tower, and its construction is of brick covered with stucco to protect the mortar from dampness. Inside, look for the six stained-glass windows depicting St. Louis (French King Louis IX) at various stages of his life and canonization. There's also a spectacular painting on the wall above and behind the main altar, showing St. Louis (the cathedral's patron saint) proclaiming the Seventh Crusade from the steps of Notre Dame. You're welcome to poke around inside from 9am to 5pm Monday through Saturday and 1:30 to 5pm on Sunday.

On the right side of the cathedral (as you face the Mississippi River), also facing Jackson Square, is the **Cabildo,** on the corner of Chartres and St. Peter streets. It has been, in turn, a French police station and guardhouse, the statehouse of the Spanish governing body (the Very Illustrious Cabildo), New Orleans's City Hall, and the Louisiana State Supreme Court. Since 1911 it has been the permanent home of the Louisiana State Museum. Badly damaged by fire in 1988, the Cabildo is closed, but it is expected to reopen in late 1992.

One further note: If you think those old Civil War cannons out front look pitifully small and ineffective by modern standards, you might like to know that in 1921, in a not-so-funny prank, one was loaded with powder, an iron ball was rammed down its muzzle, and it was fired in the dead of night. That lethal missile traveled from the Cabildo's portico across the wide expanse of the Mississippi and some six blocks inland before landing in a house in Algiers, narrowly missing its occupants!

Incidentally that's **Pirates Alley** that runs between the Cabildo and the cathedral from Chartres Street to Royal Street. There's absolutely *no* evidence to support the story that pirates once transported their stolen goods along this pathway, but it holds onto the name with tenacity, despite its official tag of Orleans Alley. You'll usually find artists displaying their paintings here, as well as outside the railing of **St. Anthony's Garden,** directly in back of the cathedral (it is said that back in dueling days many a gentleman defended his honor in this little garden). The garden is named for a beloved Capuchin priest affectionately called Père Antoine, and the walkway between Chartres and Royal streets on the downtown side of the cathedral is given the name of Père Antoine's Alley, in his honor.

On the left side of the cathedral (facing the Mississippi), on the corner of Chartres Street and Jackson Square, the **Presbytère** is very similar to the Cabildo and was originally intended to be used as a home for the cathedral priests. Ironically it has never served that purpose, but the name still sticks. It was begun in 1794 but was not actually completed until 1813, when the government took it over. Since then it has been used as a courthouse, and since 1910 it has been the property of the Louisiana State Museum. You'll be fascinated even before you go inside, for over to the extreme right of the colonnade, that cigar-shaped iron object is the first iron submarine ever built—by the Confederate Navy, no less. It was launched in 1861, could travel all of four miles an hour, and was powered by a crew of four with hand cranks. Take a close look—it's a far cry from the atomic submarines of today. Inside the Presbytère you'll find all sorts of historical exhibits, including antique pianos, Newcomb pottery, Louisiana portraits, and changing exhibition galleries. Hours are 10am to 5pm Wednesday through Sunday. Adults pay $3, students over 12 and seniors pay $1.50, and those under 12 are free.

On both the St. Peter and the St. Ann streets sides of Jackson Square, those twin, four-story, red-brick buildings are the **Pontalba Buildings,** with some of the most beautiful cast-iron balcony railings in the Quarter and a history that reflects the determination of a plucky New Orleans woman to compete with those upstart American "uptowners" and keep business concerns in the Quarter by providing elite-address shops and living quarters on the square. Indeed, these are said to be the first apartment buildings in the country—they were designed by Baroness Micaela Almonester Pontalba (she was the daughter of the Don Almonester responsible for rebuilding the cathedral) to accommodate shops on the ground level, with elegant living quarters (as well as servants' quarters) on the upper floors. They were begun in 1849 and built under her direct supervision; you can see her mark today in the entwined initials "A-P" in that lovely ironwork. The 16 row houses on St. Peter Street were completed in 1850, and those on St. Ann Street were completed in 1851. The luxury apartments have enormous rooms, high ceilings, and long windows that open onto the balconies. From the first they have attracted prestige tenants (Jenny Lind was one of the first, and William Faulkner once lived here), and they are much sought-after even now, with a long waiting list. Those on St. Peter Street now belong to the city of New Orleans, and the State of Louisiana owns those on St. Ann Street.

The shops in both rows make marvelous browsing. When you're on the St. Peter Street side, stop by the **Puppetorium** at no. 514, where *The Legend of Jean Lafitte* is presented with 50 giant marionettes. It's open every day except Christmas and Mardi Gras from 10am to 6pm. The **Café Pontalba,** on the corner of Chartres and St. Peter streets, is a good spot to tarry for a light snack, a refreshing drink, or just people-watching. Over on the other side, the **1850 House,** 523 St. Anne Street, is owned by the Louisiana State Museum and restored just as it might have been in 1850, with Louisiana-French-Victorian furnishings that include a great tester canopied bed, authentic utensils, toys of the period, and even servants' quarters up on the third floor. You can step back in history Wednesday through Sunday from 10am to 5pm for a $3 charge for adults; $1.50 for seniors and students over 12, and free for children under 12.

DECATUR STREET

Before the levees were built, Decatur Street was right on the riverfront. Over the years, however, the mighty Mississippi has deposited silt that gradually built up the land mass now housing wharves and warehouses. Starting at Canal Street, the entire 100 block on the lakeside is occupied by the massive **Custom House,** which was begun in 1848 and not completed until 1880. It's worth a few minutes to go up to its second floor to see the handsome "Marble Hall" in the very center of the building. Across the street toward the river stands **Canal Place,** where you'll find branches of some of this country's leading fine stores.

Some 13 acres of the riverfront, from Canal Street to St. Peter Street, have been landscaped as the **Woldenberg River Park.** This oasis of greenery in the heart of the city is centered by a large lawn, with a brick promenade leading to the Mississippi and more than 600 trees—oaks, magnolias, willows, and crape myrtles—and 1,400 shrubs to beautify this tranquil spot. The park will also be the setting for the Aquarium of the Americas, scheduled for a late 1990 opening.

Farther along, directly across from Jackson Square where St. Peter Street ends at Decatur, rises a big six-story Romanesque Revival building. From 1891 until just a few years ago this was the brewhouse of Jax beer, a regional brew still very popular in these parts. What you see from Decatur Street is the rear of the building, which is not too exciting. A group of enthusiastic, energetic native sons has, however, transformed the old landmark into an exciting food, entertainment, and shopping complex with a riverfront promenade to open up a long stretch of the Mississippi after years of being obscured from pedestrian view. You could literally spend an entire day in the **Jackson Brewery.** Its first two levels hold specialty retail shops featuring local and imported foods, crafts, furniture, clothing, and so forth. But it's the third floor you're likely to head for time and again between explorations of the building: Something they've dubbed the Jaxfest holds forth 12 hours a day, seven days a week, and I guarantee that you won't go just once. In a rip-roaring celebration of New Orleans fine food, kiosks, booths, wine bars, international beer bars, and the like will be dishing up examples of the cooking that has made this city famous the world over. It's a place to sit down, relax, and indulge in good eating.

Just past the Jackson Brewery, pretty riverside **Washington Artillery Park,** with its splashing fountain, has always been a "promenade" for New Orleanians, and now the elevated area has been renamed the **Moon Walk** (for Mayor "Moon" Landrieu). There are attractive plantings and benches from which to view the city's main industry, its busy port (second only to Amsterdam for tonnage handled each year). To your right you can see the Greater New Orleans Bridge and World Trade Center of New Orleans (formerly the International Trade Mart) skyscraper, as well as the Toulouse Street wharf, departure point for excursion steamboats.

Continuing "downriver," you will reach the upper edge of the **Old French Market,** which runs for about six blocks along the Mississippi. By all means stop at the outdoor **Café du Monde** for café au lait and beignets to fortify you for serious sight-seeing, to lift your spirits, or just on general principles (personally, I can never pass this place without at least one order's worth of people-watching). As for the market itself, there's been one here since Native American days (when Choctaws traded with the French), and the first building was constructed by the Spanish about 1791. Gradually other buildings were added—a meat market, open-air vegetable stalls, and spice stands—and three of the present buildings were put up in 1912. Since then there have been two restorations—one by the WPA in 1937 and more recently a $2½-million effort in 1975 that has resulted in the old colonnaded buildings having their innards gussied up for all kinds of shops and candy and pralines bakeries. There are several good eateries in the market (see Chapter VI), and there's still a Farmers' Market in the outdoor sheds back of the renovated buildings. Even if you're staying in a hotel room and are not in the market for fruits and vegetables, don't miss this section just for the lively conversation as vendors and customers continue the sort of trade that brought the French Market into being. Of course, there's good "take-back-home" shopping all through the market, and you'll hardly escape without a souvenir purchase or two. In back of the French Market, near Barracks Street, there's an open-air flea market every Saturday and Sunday that's one of the neatest free attractions in the city.

Across the street from the Old French Market, from Jackson Street all the way over to Esplanade, Decatur Street was, not too long ago, a seedy, run-down area of wild bars and cheap rooming houses. No more. An exciting renaissance resulted in all sorts of interesting shops (such as Santa's Quarters at 1025–1027 Decatur, and the Bombay Company at Ursuline and Decatur, 1 French Market Place), and oldtime eateries such as Tujague's (823 Decatur). Decatur Street is far from "finished"—it's already drawing a local clientele with a slightly bohemian flavor, and as more casual/smart bars open and nightlife assumes a relaxed "respectability," it will no doubt attract even larger crowds. At any rate, it's a fun street, so allow enough time to stroll, browse, and perhaps bend an elbow or two. And as you pass 919 and 923 Decatur Street, let your imagination conjure up the Café des Refugiés and Hôtel de la Marine that were here in the 1700s and early 1800s, gathering places for pirates, smugglers, and European refugees (some of them outlaws), a far cry from today's scene.

CHARTRES STREET

Pronounced "Charters," this street was named for a family of the French nobility. It runs along one end of Jackson Square and its most prominent buildings are those that face the square, described above. There are, however, several other points of interest on the street.

At the corner of St. Louis and Chartres is what was once a coffee house and exchange (where slaves once were bought and sold along with other "commodities"). The original Pierre Maspero's Exchange was a popular meeting place in 19th-century New Orleans, and when Gen. Andrew Jackson was in dire need of support (both men and supplies) for the defense of the city, it is said that he huddled here with the privateer Jean Lafitte to enlist his aid. He got it, and the Battle of New Orleans ended successfully for the Americans. Now, don't be surprised when you hear that these two plotted at other locations as well—apparently these two drank and schemed a lot, at several locations in the Quarter.

The **Napoleon House,** 500 Chartres Street, was also the center of intrigue as far back as the late 1700s. There are actually *two* Napoleon Houses on Chartres Street, and both have interesting legends as to how they became associated with the "Little Corporal's" name. The house at 514 Chartres was, in 1815, the home of New Orlean's mayor, Nicholas Girod. He was attending a play at the St. Philip Theatre when news came of Napoleon's escape from Elba, and he immediately took the stage to proclaim publicly that if the beloved emperor came to New Orleans (as everyone was certain he would—where else, after all, would he meet with such affection?), the mayor's residence would be placed entirely at his disposal. Napoleon, of course, never came, then or later. But during his later exile on St. Helena, a plot was hatched at *this* Napoleon House (500 Chartres Street) to rescue him from the island and bring him back to live here (indeed, the third floor was added expressly for that purpose). A ship was being outfitted with funds supplied by that same Nicholas Girod and manned by a crew recruited by Dominique You (one of Lafitte's pirate leaders) for the mission when news arrived of Napoleon's death. The other Napoleon House (514 Chartres Street) was, during its long history, the shop and residence of a local druggist, Louis Dufilho.

Tradition says it was at the 538 Chartres Street site that wind from an open window blew a candle flame against flimsy curtains and set off on Good Friday, March 21, 1788, a fire that eventually wiped out more than 850 buildings. Because the cathedral bells were stilled in honor of the religious date, the fire was completely out of control before most of the townspeople even knew about it.

That fine old Spanish-style house at 617 Chartres Street was built in 1795 for Bartolomé Bosque. In the rear of the carriageway, there are three separate patios opening one into the other.

The **Beauregard-Keyes House,** 1113 Chartres Street, has more than one claim to fame. The "raised cottage" with its Doric columns and handsome twin staircases was built by a wealthy New Orleans auctioneer back in 1826 as a residence, and a world-famous chess champion, Paul Morphy, was born to his daughter in one of its rooms in 1837. Then, in the winter of 1866–67, a defeated and financially broke Confederate, Gen. P.G.T. Beauregard, lived in a rented room here while he tried to find work. From 1944 until 1970 it was the residence of Frances Parkinson Keyes, who wrote many novels about this region. One of them, *Madame Castel's Lodger,* is directly concerned with the general's stay in the house. *Dinner at Antoine's,* perhaps her most famous novel, was also written here. Mrs. Keyes left the house to a foundation, and the house, rear buildings, and garden are now open to the public. The gift shop has a wide selection of Frances Parkinson Keyes novels. There's a $4 admission for adults and discounts for seniors, students, AAA members, and preservation groups. Viewing hours are 10am to 3pm Monday through Saturday.

Across the street is the Archbishop Antoine Blanc Memorial, which includes the **Old Ursuline Convent,** Archiepiscopal Residence, 1114 Chartres Street, completed in 1752, with the founder of the city, Sieur de Bienville, on hand for its opening. The Sisters of Ursula were, for years, the only teachers and nurses in New Orleans —they established the first schools for Catholic girls, for blacks, and for Native Americans, and they set up the first orphanage in Louisiana. The nuns moved out of the convent in 1824 (they're in an uptown location these days), and in 1831 the state legislature met here. It now houses Catholic archives dating back to 1718. Especially noteworthy is the fact that this is the oldest building of record not only in New Orleans but also in the entire Mississippi Valley, and it is the only surviving building of the French Colonial Period in the United States. Included in the complex is the beautifully restored old Chapel of the Archbishops, erected in 1845 and still used as a house of worship. There are public tours in part of the complex on Wednesday at 2pm, with fees of $2.50 for adults, $1.50 for students, and $1 for children under 12.

ROYAL STREET

Royal Street is perhaps best known for its concentration of antiques shops. Not so well known is the fact that this is the street once traveled by the *Streetcar Named Desire,* a name made famous by New Orleans's adopted son, playwright Tennessee Williams. You'll find that streetcar parked at the Old Mint in the 400 block of Esplanade, but with or without streetcars, Royal Street is a sightseeing tour in itself.

In 1857 the four-story building at 127 Royal Street held a popular bar, the Gem, on the ground floor that is occupied these days by commercial shops. The Gem was where many duels were arranged as well as the meeting place for New Orleanians of all ilk, from governors to soldiers of fortune. But it was the meeting held in January of 1857 that proved so momentous for the city. You see, the heart of New Orleans revelry—Mardi Gras, itself—stood in danger of being abolished permanently because of so many attendant episodes of violence, and had not a small group formed a secret society (in the club rooms above the Gem) to restore order to the celebration, it might have perished in the very city with whose name it has since become synonymous. It was the Mistick Krewe of Comus that sprang to life that day, and it remains a Mardi Gras leader (see Chapter III). The building is not much to see these days, but give it at least a token nod as you walk past in recognition of the very real part that it played in keeping Mardi Gras on the New Orleans scene.

Three important banks once operated on corners of the Royal and Conti streets intersection. The **Bank of Louisiana,** 334 Royal Street, was erected in 1827. This handsome old building now houses the French Quarter police station. At 339 Royal, the old **Bank of the United States** was built in 1800—notice its fine handforged ironwork. The structure at 401 Royal was designed by Benjamin H. Latrobe, one of the architects of the Capitol in Washington, and it opened in 1821 as home of the **Louisiana State Bank.**

The entire 400 block of Royal Street (on the river side) once held beautiful Spanish-style Creole town houses, all of which were demolished in 1907 in favor of the massive marble civil courts building, which was completed in 1910.

A dedicated missionary, Fr. Adrien Rouquette, was born at 413 Royal Street in 1813. Intensely interested in local Native Americans when no one else was, Father Rouquette not only ministered to the tribes across Lake Pontchartrain but also actually moved in with them and adopted their dress and many of their customs.

Brennan's Restaurant, at 417 Royal Street (of those well-known breakfasts; see Chapter VI), is housed in a mansion built in 1795 for the maternal grandfather of Edgar Degas, the French painter. It later served as a bank (those initials in the balcony railings, *BL,* were for Banque de la Louisiane) and the family home of chess champion Paul Morphy (he died in a second-floor bathroom in this house). It became a center of much entertaining, however, in the 1820s and 1830s, when its then owner, Martin Gordon, welcomed guests—such as Gen. Andrew Jackson—to lavish banquets and balls. It seems fitting, somehow, that the tradition of gracious hospitality survives today in the famous restaurant.

Masonic Lodge meetings were held regularly in a drugstore at 437 Royal Street back in the early 1800s. But something more important to American culture also happened there, when the druggist, Antoine A. Peychard, served after-meeting drinks to lodge members in small egg cups, whose French name *(coquetier)* was Americanized to *cocktail.*

The **Brulatour Court** you'll hear mentioned from time to time in New Orleans is at 520 Royal Street, and it is a splendid home built in 1816 for wine merchant François Seignouret. WDSU-TV now lives here, but you're welcome to walk into the courtyard, one of the few four-walled courtyards in the French Quarter. Notice the elaborate, fan-shaped ironwork on the right end of the third-floor balcony. Incidentally the wine merchant is virtually revered today for the fine furniture he produced (with a graceful S worked into the ornamentation of every piece).

The **Merieult House,** at 533 Royal Street, built in 1792, was one of the few French Quarter structures to escape that disastrous 1794 fire. The first owner's wife very nearly became the mistress of a French castle when Napoleon offered one in exchange for her hair, which was flaming red in color (he wanted it for a wig to present to a Turkish sultan). This dignified and beautiful New Orleans residence must have been quite enough for Madame Merieult, however, for she flatly refused the emperor. Nowadays this is home to the **Historic New Orleans Collection—Museum/Research Center,** 533 Royal Street (tel. 523-4662), which is housed in five buildings that consist of a museum, gift shop, and comprehensive research center for state and local history. The Williams Gallery, free to the public, presents changing exhibitions that focus on Louisiana history and culture. Guided tours are available of both the founders' elegant residence and the Louisiana history galleries. The residence of Gen. and Mrs. L. Kemper Williams is a charming, eclectically furnished home that reflects the gracious mid-20th-century life-style of its owners. A tour of the history galleries, located in the 1792 Merieult House, brings to life some 200 years of the state's past through original maps, paintings, photographs, documents, and rare books. Tour hours are 10am, 11am, 2:10pm, and 3pm Tuesday through Saturday, and admission is $2 for each tour. No children under 12 are permitted in the Williams residence. Hours for the research center and gallery (both free) are 10am to 4:45pm Tuesday through Saturday.

One of the best-known landmarks in the Quarter is the **Court of the Two Sisters,** at 613 Royal Street. It was built in 1832 for a local bank president, on the site of the home of an earlier French governor in the 1700s. The two sisters were Emma and Bertha Camors (whose father owned the building), and from 1886 to 1906 they ran a curio store here. If you don't plan to have at least one meal in the restaurant now on the premises (see Chapter VI), do stop by for a cool drink in the beautiful patio, which has a charming wishing well in the center.

When you spot the **Old Town Praline Shop** at 627 Royal Street (tel. 525-1413), turn and walk through the carriage drive to see another of New Orleans's beautiful patios. This 1777 building is where Adelina Patti, the noted opera singer, came for a visit and stayed to become something of a local heroine in 1860. Only 17 at the time, Adelina saved the local opera company from financial ruin when she stepped in as a last-minute replacement for an ailing lead soprano in *Lucia di Lammermoor*—she was a tremendous hit, and the season was an assured success. This building is also one of the only two that survived the great fire of 1794. (I can personally recommend the fresh pralines sold there today by the family who has owned the place since 1934—they sweeten the rest of your sightseeing considerably.) The shop is open from 10am to 5:30pm Monday through Saturday.

On the southeast corner of Royal and St. Peter streets, **Le Monnier Mansion,** at 640 Royal Street, once towered above every other French Quarter building as the city's first "skyscraper," all of three stories high when it was built in 1811. A fourth story was added in 1876 (perhaps to help it keep its skyline supremacy).

At this same intersection, the **LaBranche House,** 700 Royal Street, is probably the most photographed building in the Quarter—and no wonder. Take a look at the lacy iron grillwork, with its delicate oak-leaf-and-acorn design, that fairly drips from all three floors. Actually there are 11 LaBranch buildings, three-story brick row houses built between 1835 and 1840 by wealthy sugar planter Jean Baptiste LaBranch. Eight face St. Peter Street, one faces Royal, and two face Pirates Alley, and it was only when wrought-iron balconies came into vogue about 1850 that they were added to the St. Peter and Royal street façades. If you plan to preserve them on film, the best vantage point is diagonally across Royal Street so that both street exposures will show in your picture. The lovely old building now houses the Royal Café (see Chapter VI).

The three houses at 900, 906, and 910 Royal Street are the **Miltenberger Mansions,** built by a wealthy widow in 1838 for her three sons. Her great-granddaughter, Alice Heine, was born in 1910 and moved into the ranks of European royalty when she married first a duke and then the Prince of Monaco.

The house at **915 Royal Street** is not the original building on the site, but there is a survivor of that earlier home—the unusual cast-iron fence in a pattern of cornstalks, complete with shucked ears, intertwined with morning glory vines and blossoms. It came by sea to New Orleans in 1834, when a Dr. Biamenti is said to have ordered it for his young midwestern bride, who yearned for the waving cornfields of her home farmland.

The **Gallier House Museum** at 1132 Royal Street (tel. 523-6722) was built by James Gallier, Jr., as his residence in 1857. The carefully restored town house contains an early working bathroom, a passive ventilation system, and furnishings of the period. The adjoining building houses historical exhibits, as well as films on decorative plasterwork, ornamental ironwork, wood-graining, and marbling. The hours are 10am to 4:30pm (last tour begins at 3:45pm) Monday through Saturday and noon to 4:30pm Sunday. Admission is $4 for adults, $3 for senior citizens and students, and $1 for ages 5 to 11 (children under 5 are free). There is plenty of free parking at the museum.

Go by to see the **LaLaurie Home** at 1140 Royal Street in broad daylight—after dark you might be disturbed by ghostly moans or the savage hissing of a whip or might even catch a glimpse of a small black child walking on the balcony. This is the Quarter's haunted house. Its story is a New Orleans tale of horror. It seems the very beautiful and socially prominent Delphine LaLaurie lived here and entertained lavishly, until one night in 1834 when a fire broke out and neighbors crashed through a locked door to find seven starving slaves chained in painful positions, unable to move. The rescuers were appalled and highly incensed. When the next day's newspapers suggested that the dazzling hostess might have set the fire herself, a mob assembled outside the house. Madame LaLaurie and her family escaped their neighbors' wrath, however, when they dashed out the carriage drive in a closed carriage and fled the city, eventually to Europe. The heartless woman did not return to New Orleans until several years later, after she died on the continent—and even then her body had to be buried in secrecy. This unhappy house has now been renovated and turned into luxury apartments—I wonder how its tenants sleep at night.

BOURBON STREET

No, it's *not* named for the whisky, but for the royal family of France. Still, sometimes you might wonder about that, especially when the sun goes down and Bourbon Street releases whatever inhibitions it might have during daylight hours to become one of the "naughtiest ladies" anywhere. The nine or so blocks of bars, jazz clubs, strip joints, and restaurants (which vary from the sleaziest to the grandest) are alive with the sound of music, street dancers, and hundreds of visitors intent on just one thing—having a good time. It is, of course, lively enough during the day, but after dark there's no place else quite like it. Down toward Esplanade things are a bit quieter, and it is very much like other streets in the Quarter—it's those *other* nine blocks that have made this street an instantly recognized name around the world.

Two blocks from Canal Street, the **Old Absinthe House,** at 238 Bourbon Street, was built in 1806 by two Spaniards and is still owned by their descendants (although they live in Spain and have nothing to do with running the place). The drink for which it was named is outlawed in this country now, but with a little imagination you can sip a modern-day libation and visualize Andrew Jackson and the Lafitte brothers plotting the desperate defense of New Orleans in 1815. It's the custom here to put your calling card on the wall, and the hundreds and hundreds of browning cards form a covering not unlike tattered wallpaper. It was, of course, a speakeasy during Prohibition, and when federal officers closed it down in 1924, the interior was mysteriously stripped of its antique fixtures, including the long marble-topped bar and the old water dripper (used to drip water into absinthe), all of which just as mysteriously reappeared down the street at a corner establishment called, oddly enough, the **Old Absinthe House Bar** (400 Bourbon). It, too, follows the calling-card custom. If you can't keep all that straight, just remember that if you're in an Old Absinthe House that doesn't have entertainment, you're in the original *house*—and if you see that grand brass water dripper on a marble-topped bar, you're in the new home of the original bar and fixtures.

Give a nod to the hotel that now occupies 541 Bourbon Street, in memory of the great old French Opera House that stood on this site from 1859 until it burned down in 1919. It was designed by Gallier and was the first structure designed just for opera to be built in the United States.

The **Fortin House,** 624 Bourbon Street, was built in 1834 by a doctor for his young bride. Walk back into the patio and you'll see how neighbors often built connecting doorways between their courtyards.

At the corner of Bourbon and St. Peter streets (700 Bourbon Street) once stood the Bourbon House bar and restaurant, which was so beloved of writers and artists (Tennessee Williams was one who dropped in from time to time) that when it closed during the 1960s, they gave it a brass band funeral, and it lives on in the fond memory of many a native.

That little cottagelike building on the corner of Bourbon and St. Philip streets is **Lafitte's Blacksmith Shop,** at 941 Bourbon Street. For many years now it has been a bar (for the full story, see Chapter XI), but the legend is that Jean Lafitte and his pirates posed as blacksmiths here while using it as headquarters for selling goods they'd plundered on the high seas. It has survived (thanks to the loving care of owners in recent years) in its original condition, and you can still see the brick-between-posts construction. That simply means that bricks were used only to fill in a wooden frame (locally made bricks were too soft to be the primary building material). Step inside and the dusky interior will kindle your imagination—it's a tribute to its modern-day owners that they haven't let the age of chrome and plastic come anywhere near this old place.

DAUPHINE STREET

The farther Dauphine Street (pronounced "daw-*feen*") gets from Canal Street, the more attractive it becomes. You will, however, see buildings typical of the Quarter along its entire length.

Look for the **Pierre Cottage,** 430 Dauphine Street, another example of the brick-between-posts construction of the 1700s. Bricks for this house were made right in the courtyard, and the mortar was strengthened with shells from Lake Pontchartrain. It was built in 1780, was only partially damaged in the great fire of 1788, and is one of the oldest cottages in the Quarter.

When John James Audubon was working on his 435-plate *Birds of America,* he did 167 of them in Louisiana. He sketched a good many upriver near St. Francisville, but he spent a year in the French Quarter (1821–22) at **511 Dauphine Street.** The ornithologist and his family lived in the little cottage at a time when his fortunes were meager and the times were hard.

No one has ever reported the presence of ghosts at the **LePrete Mansion,** 716 Dauphine Street, but they may well be there. As in the LaLaurie house over on Royal Street, these walls could tell a tale of horror. Back in 1792 there arrived in New Orleans a wealthy Turk, the brother of a sultan. That he was enormously wealthy was immediately apparent, and his entourage included many servants, as well as a "family" of five beautiful young girls. They all landed in the Crescent City in the *Youseff Bey,* a Turkish freighter that had evidently been hired for their exclusive passage. The rumor quickly spread that his wealth had been stolen from his brother and that the girls were also the sultan's "property," a part of his harem. Be that as it may, the Turk rented the LePrete house for the summer when its owner left to spend the season on his downriver plantation, and the palatial home very quickly became the scene of lavish entertainments with guest lists that included the cream of society. On one fateful night, however, shrieks were heard by neighbors, followed by complete silence the next morning, with no signs of activity. Eventually neighbors entered the house and found the summer tenant's body lying in a pool of blood surrounded by the bodies of the five young beauties. There was no sign of his servants. To this day no one knows if they were responsible for the murders or if the freighter crew, with a late-found loyalty to the sultan, decided to return the ruler's stolen goods to win his favor (or, as seems more likely, they may have stolen the gold and embarked on a career of piracy at sea). Another explanation put forth was that members of the sultan's court followed his brother to avenge the sultan and return the gold. Whoever was responsible, the murder victims have never returned to haunt the premises, which are now apartments. In 1968 this tale of terror was the Mardi Gras theme of the Krewe of Niobe.

BURGUNDY STREET

In one of those New Orleans pronunciation quirks, this street is called "bur-*gundy,*" after the French duke of Burgundy. It is primarily residential in nature. It is interesting to stroll along this street, if just to see another facet of the French Quarter's eclectic architecture. The houses are not as elegant as those on other streets, but the small cottages are very much a part of the city's architectural mix. For years this street went by the inelegant name of Craps Street on the downriver side of Esplanade—real estate developer Bernard de Marigny so christened it after his favorite game of chance.

RAMPART STREET

The mud ramparts that were early New Orleans's only protection ran along this street, then the city's outer boundary.

On the corner of Rampart and Conti streets, **Our Lady of Guadaloupe Chapel/International Shrine of St. Jude,** 411 N. Rampart Street, was put up in 1826 as a chapel convenient to the St. Louis Cemetery No. 1—funeral services were held here rather than in St. Louis Cathedral so as not to spread disease within the confines of the Quarter, and it became known as "The Burial Chapel." In the intervening years it has been renovated, and it now houses an International Shrine of St. Jude (the saint of impossible causes who is often thanked publicly for favors in the "Personals" column of the *Times-Picayune*). Another saint is honored here by a statue next to the main altar. His name is St. Expedite, a name that legend says was given to the statue when it arrived at the church in a packing crate with no identification but stamped "Expedite."

The 700 block of Rampart Street faces what was once Congo Square, which then became Beauregard Square (after the Confederate general), and is now **Louis Armstrong Park** (after that beloved son, Satchmo). It is the site of the **Civic Cultural Center** (for more details, see Chapter IX).

IBERVILLE STREET

Pronounced "*Eye*-bur-ville," this street is named, of course, for the French-Canadian explorer. Its main distinction (in my very subjective view) lies in the two marvelous oyster bars within a block of each other: the Acme, at 724 Iberville Street, and Felix's, at no. 739. When an oyster appetite strikes during the day, I usually head for the Acme (along with the rest of New Orleans, it sometimes seems), and Felix's is a sort of oyster security blanket for a late-night yen, because it stays open until 2am. As an aside: That old adage about eating oysters only during months that have an *R* in their names may have held true in the days before refrigeration when the hot months were *R*-less and seafood spoiled quickly, but nowadays you can enjoy them virtually any time of the year. For more complete information on these two oyster meccas, see Chapter VI.

BIENVILLE STREET

This street, too, is lacking in scenic attractions (mostly commercial institutions of the more mundane sort), with one notable exception. **Arnaud's Restaurant,** 813 Bienville Street, is an attraction in itself, as you'll see from my rave comments in Chapter VI. The building is ancient, the food is magnificent, and the loving restoration of both by Archie and Jane Casbarian is enough to give Bienville Street a secure place in my affections. Go by to look, if not to eat, or have a drink in either of the two lovely old bars. Upstairs at Arnaud's, the **Germaine Wells Mardi Gras Museum** is a uniquely "New Orleans" spot. Ask to see this impressive and dazzling collection of Mardi Gras costumes that were worn by one of the city's legendary figures, daughter of the "Count" Arnaud who founded the restaurant. There's no admission charge, and this is an exhibit that brings home the extravagant spirit of Carnival in New Orleans.

CONTI STREET

This is another street named for a family of the French nobility, and its New Orleans pronunciation is *"Con*-teye."

Between Chartres and Royal streets, in the 600 block of Conti, there's a little alley called **Exchange Alley.** Back in the 1830s it went all the way to St. Louis Street and the old St. Louis Hotel (where the Royal Orleans Hotel now stands), and the houses at the corner of Conti and Exchange were devoted to a practice much revered in New Orleans—dueling. These were the houses of the fencing masters, who specialized in assuring their clients of emerging victorious on the field of honor.

Farther up Conti, between Dauphine and Burgundy, you'll find the **Musée Conti Wax Museum,** at 917 Conti Street (tel. 525-2605). New Orleans history is depicted here in marvelously lifelike tableaux of costumed wax figures in authentic settings using antique furniture. Almost every scrap of history (carefully researched for authenticity) and many of the city's legends are represented—the time span is three centuries. There are 32 different scenes of legends surrounding the likes of Andrew Jackson, Jean Lafitte, Marie Laveau and her voodoo dancers, Mardi Gras Indian Chief Montana, and even a modern jazz figure—so don't imagine that this is a "quickie." And at the very end of all that serious history is a display of Mardi Gras costumes worn by the Knights of Sparta, as well as a strictly-for-fun haunted dungeon, with all the villains of literature shown going about their dastardly deeds. The whole family will love this place, which is open every day (except Christmas and Mardi Gras Day) from 10am to 5pm. The admission is $5 for adults, $4.50 for senior citizens, $3 for children ages 4 to 17. Those under 4 are admitted free with their parents. You'll leave with directions for an excellent self-guided Louisiana Legends Walking Tour to Jackson Square ($1.50 with admission).

ST. LOUIS STREET

It's too bad you and I have arrived in New Orleans too late to visit the old St. Louis Hotel—it must have been something to see. Of course, its replacement, the **Royal Orleans Hotel,** 621 St. Louis Street, does its best to keep alive the old hostelry's traditions of grandeur (and it even retains one of the original walls on the Chartres Street side of the building), but it takes some imagination to visualize the great building, with stores and business offices on the first floor and an auction block in the central rotunda. It was, without doubt, the grandest gathering spot in the Quarter in its earliest days (the mid-1800s), although it fared rather poorly after the turn of the century. Magnificent balls were held in the domed, marble-floored ballroom. Notables such as Henry Clay, who made his only speech in the state here, were guests, as were carpetbagger legislators during Reconstruction years when the hotel served as the state capitol from 1874 to 1882. By 1915 it had deteriorated so badly (the English writer John Galsworthy was inspired to write "The Old Time Place" after finding a horse wandering around loose inside) that it was torn down during a campaign to rid the French Quarter of rats. (There was a near-panic at the time because of the danger of bubonic plague.) Despite a great public hue and cry, down it came.

The world-famous **Antoine's Restaurant** is at 713 St. Louis Street, and it has been at this location since 1870. The original Antoine (Alciatoire) operated over on Royal Street a boarding house that became so well known for its food that he moved into this 1850s building, which has been expanded to include five others to house 15 dining rooms. You'll find a complete description of the restaurant in Chapter VI.

If you're a "states' righter" in these days of big government, take a good look at 720 St. Louis Street—Pierre Soulé, a prominent New Orleans attorney who spent his life fighting for "the cause" until his death in 1870, lived here.

At 820 St. Louis Street, the **Hermann-Grima House** (tel. 525-5661) dates from 1831, when it was built by a wealthy merchant, Samuel Hermann. He sold it in 1844 to Felix Grima, a noted attorney, and these days it offers a look back into New Orleans's golden era, 1830–60. The house has period furnishings and two courtyards. The original slave quarters are in the rear courtyard, and you can visit the old carriage house and stable (which still has stalls and feeders). From October through May on Thursdays you can witness a demonstration of Creole cooking in the restored 1830s kitchen. The house is open Monday through Saturday from 10am to 4pm (closed Sunday) for an admission fee of $3 for adults and $2 for senior citizens, students, and children 8 years and older. It is closed on major holidays.

TOULOUSE STREET

You might call Toulouse a "bastard street," because it was named for an illegitimate offspring of France's Louis XIV. It is, however, a very legitimate part of French Quarter life.

In the 700 block of this street look for the **Court of the Two Lions,** at no. 710, which also has an entrance at 537 Royal Street. Built in 1792 the house features a courtyard whose entrance is guarded by two lion statues. It is much photographed and has been used by at least one writer in works of fiction (it is the home of *The Crossing's* heroine, whose author is a popular American writer of the early 1900s named Winston Churchill—*not* "Sir Winnie").

In the same block, you'll find the **Casa Hinard** at 723 Toulouse Street, said to be one of the oldest in the Mississippi Valley. An old French map shows that it was here in the 1720s, although older records were destroyed in the 1788 fire and only those dating after 1797 remain. Since 1983 the ground floor has been occupied by Oaks Gallery, which features original designs in arts and crafts by local and national artists. The Casa Hinard Museum, filled with period antiques, is open for tours during June, July, and August.

The charming little **Hôtel Maison de Ville** at 727 Toulouse Street dates back to at least 1742 (its earlier records were also lost). It is expensive, but it won't cost a cent to walk back into its beautiful courtyard and take a peek at the slave quarters that are now guest accommodations.

ST. PETER STREET

St. Peter Street is one of Jackson Square's boundaries, and you'll find its 500 block described in that section of this chapter.

That rather grim building at 615 St. Peter Street was the 1839 site of the Spanish government's prison (or *calabozo*). The present building went up in 1803 as an arsenal, and it also became headquarters for a military organization known as the Louisiana Legion, an elite group of Louisiana "first family" sons of both American and Creole descent. The insignia of crossed cannons above a mound of cannon balls and the *LL* monogram of the legion are worked into the balcony railing (on the right-hand side) facing Pirates Alley. To see it, turn left off St. Peter and walk through the little alley (known as Cabildo Alley) to Pirates Alley and the rear of the arsenal. Union forces under the notorious General Butler moved in from 1862 to 1871. Since 1915 this building, known as the **Spanish Arsenal,** has been a part of the Louisiana State Museum, although it is not open to the public at present.

The Spanish-style building at 616 St. Peter Street houses **Le Petit Théâtre,** the oldest nonprofessional theater in the country. Construction of the house was begun in 1789, and it was severely damaged in the 1794 fire but was restored shortly afterward. Since then it has had such widely diverse tenants as cafés; bars; the first bishop of New Orleans; and, since 1922, the Le Petit Théâtre group. Incidentally the balconies were done by the same artisan who did the Cabildo ironwork, and they are survivors of the original building.

It was in a small apartment at 632 St. Peter Street that Tennessee Williams wrote his great play *A Streetcar Named Desire,* as that vehicle rumbled down nearby Royal Street. Later he did much of the play's rewrite in the courtyard of the Maison de Ville, over on Toulouse Street.

The **Le Monnier House,** 714 St. Peter Street, built in 1829 for a prominent physician by that name, was the home for several years during the 1860s of Antoine Alciatoire, who ran a boarding house here. His cooking became so popular with locals that he later gave up catering to "live-in" guests and moved into larger quarters on St. Louis Street to open the famous Antoine's Restaurant, which is run even today by his descendants.

You will know 718 St. Peter Street as **Pat O'Brien's,** a swinging, fun-filled nightspot (see Chapter XI), but it was known as the Maison de Flechier when it was first built in 1790 for a wealthy planter. Later Louis Tabary put on popular plays here, and it is said that the first grand opera in America was performed within its walls. Sight-seeing in New Orleans just wouldn't be complete without a look at the gorgeous courtyard, even if you pass on modern-day entertainment and liquid refreshment.

I highly recommend that you make your inspection of **Preservation Hall,** 726 St. Peter Street, after 8pm, when its walls ring with some of the best jazz in the country (see Chapter XI). But a daytime stop will give you an intriguing glimpse through the big, ornate iron gate of a lush tropical courtyard in back.

ORLEANS STREET

Orleans Street begins at **St. Anthony's Garden,** in back of the cathedral. Not only was this charming little garden a favorite dueling spot, but also it is the site of a marble monument put there by the French government in memory of 30 French marines who died doing volunteer nursing duty during a yellow fever epidemic.

Where the **Bourbon Orleans Hotel** now stands at 717 Orleans Street there once was a fine ballroom known as the Salle d'Orléans. Built in 1816 it hosted some of the grandest balls ever seen in New Orleans, including one in 1825 in honor of Lafayette. It also hosted balls whose "grandness" depends on your point of view. At the so-called quadroon balls, ambitious mothers would trot out their most beautiful mulatto daughters to be surveyed by the white gentry as possible mistresses (many of those duels in St. Anthony's Garden had their origins here as youngbloods quarreled over the lovelies). Once chosen, the lucky (?) girl could look forward to being set up for life in one of the small cottages on or near Rampart Street, and any offspring would almost certainly be given a good education, which usually included some time at European schools. If you have any difficulty understanding or accepting this practice, keep in mind that along with the title "mistress" went that longed-for label "free."

Once in its history the Orleans Ballroom was leased to the state legislature, when its own building had been destroyed by fire and it needed a temporary meeting place. Then in 1881 the quadroon balls were perhaps avenged when Thomy Lafon, a "free man of color," bought the place and gave it to the black Sisters of the Holy Family as a convent. The ballroom became their chapel, and the sisters set up an orphanage on the premises. Over the ballroom door they placed a sign that read "I have chosen rather to be an object in the house of the Lord than to dwell in the temple with sinners." Nowadays you'll see the ballroom restored in the modern hotel.

ST. ANN STREET

The mid-19th-century town house at 826 St. Ann Street is owned by the **New Orleans Spring Fiesta Association.** Furnished with lovely antiques of the Victorian era and many outstanding objets d'art from New Orleans's golden age of the 1800s, the house is open to the public for guided tours from 1 to 4pm Monday through Friday for a $3 donation. It's a lovely peek backward in time. For Spring Fiesta information, contact the association at 826 St. Ann Street, New Orleans, LA 70116 (tel. 504/581-1367).

All those stories you will have heard about Marie Laveau, New Orleans's voodoo queen, happened at her home, which stood at **1022 St. Ann Street.** The house was torn down in 1903, but that act did little to erase Marie's memory or influence on "black magic" believers. When she lived there, her powers were much sought-after, even by respectable Catholic families in the city. All and sundry looked for her to turn errant lovers and husbands into ardent, attentive slaves of those who purchased Marie's love potions and charms. And woe betide the object of her gris-gris ("gree-gree") if an enemy enlisted her help to cause sickness or death. A mixture of religion, Caribbean superstition, and African rituals, collectively known as voodoo, brought Marie a more-than-comfortable living and even a sort of "respectability." Still today her grave is sought out (although there are two burial places that purport to be her final resting place) as a place to leave gifts of food and money (in 2¢ and 11¢ combinations) to elicit good luck to the donor and bad luck to his or her enemies. I don't know if it works, but it might be worth a try—old Marie was credited with some mighty powerful stuff in her day.

DUMAINE STREET

Louis XIV's bastard son, the duke of Maine, gave his name to this street, another example of New Orleans's nonconcern with the matter of legitimacy.

There are those who say that the house at 632 Dumaine Street, known as **Madame John's Legacy,** is the oldest building on the Mississippi River. Others dispute that claim, saying that only a few parts of the original building survived the 1788 fire and were used in its reconstruction. Be that as it may, the house was erected in 1726, just eight years after the founding of New Orleans, and the reconstruction follows its design meticulously. Its original owner was a ship captain who died in the 1729 Natchez Massacre, after which the house passed to the captain of a smuggling ship. It has had no fewer than 21 owners since. The present structure went up in 1789, right after that disastrous fire, and it's a fine example of a French "raised cottage." The above-ground basement is built of brick (to protect against floodwaters), and the upper story is of brick-between-posts construction, covered with boards laid horizontally. The hipped, dormered roof extends out over the veranda. Its name, incidentally, comes from a fictional quadroon who was bequeathed the house in "Tite Poulette," a Creole short story written by George Cable. It is now a part of the Louisiana State Museum complex and is open to the public on an irregular basis.

There's another interesting little cottage at **707 Dumaine Street**—interesting because of its roof. After the 1794 fire all houses in the French Quarter were required by law to have flat tile roofs, and although most have since covered them with conventional roofs, this one is still in compliance with that long-ago ruling.

If tales Marie Laveau have captured your imagination, you'll definitely want to stop by the **New Orleans Historic Voodoo Museum,** 724 Dumaine Street (tel. 523-7685). The dark, musty interior seems exactly the right setting for artifacts of the occult from all over the globe and a fitting place in which to learn more of that curious mixture of African and Catholic religions and rituals brought to New Orleans in the late 1700s by former slaves in Santo Domingo. The museum is open from 10am to dusk daily, including holidays, with an admission charge of $3 for adults and $2 for students and senior citizens. There's also a 2½-hour guided tour (for $15 per person) that leaves the museum at 1pm daily to visit Congo Square (now Beauregard Square), Marie Laveau's reputed grave, and a pharmacy displaying voodoo potions. The museum can arrange psychic readings and visits to voodoo rituals if you want to delve deeper into this subject, which has bedeviled New Orleans for centuries.

ST. PHILIP STREET

Although there's little of sight-seeing interest today on this street, it was once peopled by those fleeing from the French Revolution or the slave uprisings in the Caribbean. Back then there were cafés, bars, and even a theater (all long gone) in which they gathered to socialize and forget for a time the upheavals they had left behind.

URSULINES STREET

Named for the long-suffering nuns whose property it bounded, this street is supposedly the hatching ground for Texas independence. It is said that Stephen Austin met with a group of Freemasons in 1835 at 829–833 Ursulines Street to plan their strategy for the Texas War for Independence. I can't vouch for that personally (and I haven't turned up any definitive research), but with New Orleans's record of encouraging military leaders and its history as a breeding ground for all sorts of plots, if they *did* meet here, they couldn't have picked a better place.

GOVERNOR NICHOLLS STREET

This was originally called Hospital Street, and it is probably where those Ursuline nuns did a good bit of nursing in the early days. It was renamed for a state governor of the Civil War era.

Henry Clay's brother, John, built **618–630 Governor Nicholls Street** for his wife in 1828, and in 1871 the two-story building was added at the rear of its garden. It was in this later building that Frances Xavier Cabrini (later sainted by the Catholic church) conducted a school.

The **Thierry House,** 721 Governor Nicholls Street, was built in 1814 and started an architectural trend that spread throughout the entire state. Designed by architect Henry Latrobe when he was just 19 years old, the house is in the Greek Revival style and features a classic portico.

BARRACKS STREET

This street, as you might guess, was named for the military barracks that once stood here between Chartres and Royal streets. The

French garrison put them up in 1757, they were used by Spanish troops in 1769, and they perished in the 1788 fire.

It is said (and again I can neither confirm nor deny) that in the 1820s John James Audubon had a studio at 706 Barracks Street while he worked on his *Birds of America* series.

Just behind the French Market fruit stands, but on Barracks Street, there's an **open-air flea market** every Saturday and Sunday from 9am to sundown in fair weather. It's absolutely free and a "don't miss." More than 100 artisans turn out to show their art, jewelry, and other handcrafts; vendors offer books, clothes, and plants (actually, I couldn't begin to list all the things on sale), along with good New Orleans food specialties such as red beans and rice, sausages, chicken, and gumbo. One native says that "It's the best street theater in town."

At the other end of the street, between Burgundy and Rampart streets, there's an interesting building known locally as the **Morro Castle,** 1001–1005 Barracks Street. It's the first all-granite house in the city (the granite was shipped from Massachusetts), and was begun in 1832 by a Paul Pandelly, who promptly went broke and had to sell it before it was even finished.

ESPLANADE AVENUE

This French Quarter boundary street (pronounced "Es-pla-*nade*") served as the parade ground for the troops quartered on Barracks Street. It is a lovely, wide avenue lined by some of the grandest town houses built in the late 1800s. It is sad to say that many of these proud homes no longer house just one family but have become boarding houses, apartments, bars, cafés, and restaurants.

The entire 400 block of Esplanade is occupied by the old **U.S. Mint.** This was once the site of Fort St. Charles, one of the forts built to protect New Orleans in 1792. (Its troops also used Esplanade as a parade ground.) It was here that Andrew Jackson reviewed the assortment of "troops" (comprised of pirates, volunteers, and a nucleus of trained soldiers) he would lead in the Battle of New Orleans. The mint was built in 1835, with three-foot-thick walls made of brick stuccoed over and a granite trim. The minting of coins commenced in 1838 (coin collectors greatly value those that show the *O* mintmark) and continued until 1862. In 1850 the mint was the scene of a glamorous ball given by its director for his daughter. When federal troops took over the city (and the mint) in the Civil War, one William Mumford staged his own rebellion by tearing down the American flag raised over the mint. He paid dearly for that act, when General Butler had him hanged from the middle of the mint's front porch as a public example. It was 1879 before coins again flowed from the mint, this time until 1910, and at its peak some $5 million poured forth each month. For a time after 1910 it was used by the Veterans Administration, then as a federal prison. More recently it has been acquired by the Louisiana State Museum, and it's currently being renovated.

At present there are two permanent exhibits, the **Jazz Museum** and the **Carnival Museum.** You'll find a complete and vivid record of the evolution of music first given life in New Orleans. There are pictures, musical instruments, and other artifacts connected with jazz greats (Louis Armstrong's first trumpet is here). Across the hall there's a stunning array of Carnival mementoes—from ornate Mardi Gras costumes to a street scene complete with maskers and a parade float.

Entrances to the Mint are on both Esplanade Avenue and Barracks Street, the hours are 10am to 5pm, and there's an admission fee to the museums of $3 for adults and $1.50 for senior citizens and students. Those under 12 are free.

And if you've wondered what has become of that well-known "Streetcar Named Desire," it's parked behind the mint—it, too, has been put in "mint condition" and is opened for public visits.

---

2. Museums

Most of the following have been included in some detail in my street-by-street examination of the French Quarter. However, as a matter of convenience, I'm listing French Quarter museums here as well, with a brief description of each.

The **Cabildo,** 709 Chartres Street on Jackson Square, is the site of the Louisiana Purchase signing. Exhibits include a Mississippi River collection of steamboat-era artifacts and paintings, Napoleon's death mask, and early Louisiana settlement items. It is currently closed for renovation following a disastrous fire; it is expected to reopen sometime in 1992.

The **Historic New Orleans Collection,** 533 Royal Street (tel. 523-4662), museum, gift shop, and research center for state and local history, is housed within a complex of 18th- and 19th-century French Quarter buildings. Guided tours are available of the founders' residence and of the Louisiana history galleries. The tour of the Williams residence, a 19th-century town house restored for 20th-century living, exhibits the elegant life-style of the collection's founders. A tour of the history galleries is a must for all visitors who would like to learn more about Louisiana's colorful and exciting past through original maps, documents, pictures, and rare books. The changing exhibition gallery at the main entrance is free of charge. The collection is open Tuesday through Saturday from 10am to 4:45pm. Tours are $2 each and are scheduled at 10am, 11am, 2pm, and 3pm. There's a touch tour for the blind, and wheelchair accommodation is available.

Musée Conti Wax Museum, 917 Conti Street, offers New Orleans history depicted by life-size wax figures with authentic costumes and settings of Louisiana legends (Andrew Jackson, Jean Lafitte, and the like), plus an added "Haunted Dungeon" illustrating well-known horror tales. It is open from 10am to 5pm daily (except Christmas and Mardi Gras Day). Admission is $5 for adults, $4.50 for those over age 62, $3 for ages 4 to 17; Children under 4 are free with parents. They also provide a self-guided Louisiana

Legends Walking Tour for $1.50 with your admission to the museum.

Pontalba Apartments, 1850 House, at 523 St. Ann Street, in the Lower Pontalba Buildings, are in a restored house of the period, authentically furnished from parlor to kitchen to servants' quarters. The apartments are open Wednesday to Sunday from 10am to 5pm. The admission is $3 for adults, and $1.50 for seniors and students. Children under 12 are free.

The **Presbytère,** 751 Chartres Street on Jackson Square, was planned as housing for the clergy but never used for that purpose. It holds exhibits of Newcomb pottery, Louisiana portraits, and changing exhibits on local history and culture. It is open Wednesday to Sunday from 10am to 5pm. The admission is $3 for adults and $1.50 for seniors and students. Children under 12 are free.

The **Jazz Museum** and the **Carnival Museum** are in the Old Mint, 400 Esplanade Avenue. These museums contain a comprehensive collection of pictures, musical instruments, and other artifacts connected with jazz greats, a videocassette theater, and a large array of Carnival mementoes. Entrances to the Mint are on both Esplanade Avenue and Barracks Streets. The hours are 10am to 5pm. The admission fee to the museums is $3 for adults and $1.50 for seniors and students. Children under 12 are free.

---

3. Tours

As I've said earlier in this book, the very best way to see the French Quarter is on foot. There's an excellent walking tour offered by the nonprofit volunteer group **Friends of the Cabildo** (tel. 523-3939). This tour furnishes guides for a two-hour, on-foot exploration that will provide a good overview of the area. Leaving from in front of the Presbytère, 751 Chartres Street, your guide will "show and tell" you about most of the Quarter's historic buildings' exteriors and the interiors of two of the Louisiana State Museum properties. You're asked to pay a donation of $7 per adult, $3.50 for seniors over age 65 and children from 13 to 20 (those 12 and under are free). Tours leave at 9:30am and 1:30pm Tuesday through Saturday and at 1:30pm on Sunday, except holidays. No reservations are necessary—just show up, donations in hand.

Cynthia Ratcliffe, a charming and knowledgeable former English teacher, conducts three two-hour walking tours of the French Quarter. The Literary Tour centers around those sites involved in the lives or works of New Orleans writers; the Tennessee Williams Tour points out nearly 50 spots linked with the writer in his beloved Quarter; the History and Architectural Tour traces the Quarter's history as portrayed in its architecture. Each tour ends with a complimentary drink in an appropriate setting. There's a $20 fee for each tour. Contact her at **Royal Walks,** 616 Royal Street, New Orleans, LA 70130 (tel. 504/566-7592).

Tours by Isabelle, P.O. Box 740972, New Orleans, LA 70174 (tel. 504/367-3963), conducts small groups on a 3-hour city tour in a comfortable, air-conditioned minibus. The tour covers the French Quarter, the cemeteries, Bayou St. John, City Park and the Lakefront, the universities, St. Charles Avenue, the Garden District, and the Superdome. The fare is $20, and departure times are 9am and 1pm.

Stop by the **Jean Lafitte National Park Service French Quarter Folklife and Visitor Center** at 419 Decatur Street (tel. 589-2636) for details of the excellent free walking tours on a variety of topics conducted by National Park Service rangers. The History of New Orleans Tour covers about a mile in the French Quarter and brings to life the historical events and ethnic groups that have contributed to the city's unique cultural mix. No reservations are required for this tour of for the Tour du Jour (also in The Quarter), which is a "ranger's choice" and varies from day to day. You must book, however, for the two tours outside the Quarter. The City of the Dead Tour visits St. Louis Cemetery No. 1, and the Faubourg Promenade Tour takes you on the St. Charles Avenue streetcar and a walk through the Garden District. Both tours are very popular, so book as much as two or three days ahead.

If you don't think your feet are up to all that walking, just head for Decatur Street at Jackson Square and hop aboard one of the **horse carriages** at the stand there. For about $8 ($5 for children under 12), you will not only view the Quarter in comfort but also be treated to what is sure to be a highly individualistic narrative on its history from your guide. I've always thought this kind of tour should come under the heading of entertainment in New Orleans because each driver has a personal collection of stories about the landmarks, and if you took several different carriages, you'd get several different versions of New Orleans history.

Gray Line, 1300 World Trade Center (tel. 587-0861 or 800/535-7786), has tours of the entire city, including the French Quarter, in comfortable motorcoaches. But take my word for it: The Quarter will demand a more in-depth examination than a view from a bus window. Take one of these excellent (and very informative) tours only after you've explored the Quarter in detail or as a prelude to doing so.

Gray Line's complete city tour begins in the French Quarter, with an informative narration on historic buildings, as well as the Creole cottages and elegant mansions along Esplanade Avenue. From Esplanade, you go to City Park, then on to Lake Pontchartrain, the cemeteries, and back to the Garden District for a look at those antebellum mansions. Before delivering you back to your hotel, they'll show you the Superdome, the New Orleans River Bridge, and the old Custom House. It's a 2-hour trip (departures at 9 and 11:45am and 2:30pm), with a $15 fare for adults and a $8 fare for children. Book ahead.

For $24 per adult and $12 per child (and five hours of your time), Gray Line will throw in a 2-hour cruise on the paddle wheeler *Natchez.* You'll have lunch on board (cost *not* included in the tour price) as you take in the sights and sounds of the harbor. This tour has 9am and 11:45am departure times and you must make an advance reservation.

A special Do The Zoo tour is a great combination of the city tour, a visit to nationally acclaimed Audubon Zoo, and a river cruise. The fare is $22.50 for adults and $14 for children. The departure time is 9am.

All tours depart from the ticket office at the corner of Jackson Brewery and Toulouse Street, just one block from Jackson Square.

IX

SIGHT-SEEING OUTSIDE THE QUARTER

1. **BASIN STREET**
2. **NEW ORLEANS BURIAL GROUNDS**
3. **CANAL STREET AND THE CENTRAL BUSINESS DISTRICT**
4. **UPTOWN AND THE GARDEN DISTRICT**
5. **THE IRISH CHANNEL**
6. **CAMP STREET**
7. **THE WAREHOUSE DISTRICT**
8. **DRYADES STREET**
9. **THE BAYOU, CITY PARK, AND THE LAKE**
10. **OTHER POINTS OF INTEREST**
11. **MUSEUMS**
12. **TOURS**

Outside the borders of the French Quarter lies "American" New Orleans. It came into being because of Creole snobbery. You see, those semi-aristocratic French Quarter natives had no use for the crass Americans who came flooding into the city in 1803 and the years that followed, so they presented a united and closed front to keep "their" New Orleans exclusive. Not to be outdone, the new-comers simply bought up land in what had been the old Gravier plantation upriver from Canal Street and set about building *their* New Orleans. With that celebrated Yankee enterprise, they very soon dominated the business scene, centered on Canal Street itself, and constructed mansions different from the traditional Quarter residences but surrounded by beautiful gardens. In 1833 what we know now as the Garden District was incorporated as Lafayette City, and—thanks in large part to the New Orleans–Carrollton Railroad, which covered the route of today's St. Charles Avenue trolley—the Americans kept right on expanding until they reached the tiny resort town of Carrollton. It wasn't until 1852 that the various sections came together officially to become a united New Orleans.

Your sight-seeing beyond the French Quarter will, because of all this, take on quite a different flavor—indeed, a mixture of flavors. You'll feel the pulse of the city's commerce, take a look at river activities that keep that pulse beating, stroll through parks more spacious than any that could be accommodated in the Quarter, drive or walk by those impressive "new" homes, get a firsthand view of the bayou/lake connection that explains why New Orleans was settled here in the first place, and run across a few places closely connected to French Quarter history.

1. Basin Street

You remember Basin Street, of course—the birthplace of jazz. But then there are those who will tell you that Storyville (the red-light district along Basin Street) served only as a place for jazz, which had been around a long time, to come in off the streets. It did that, all right, with so many houses of ill-repute—ranging from the ornate "sporting palaces" with elaborate furnishings, musical entertainment, and a wide variety of "services," to the pitiful "cribs" of poorer women of the streets—that a directory (the famous "Blue Book") listed over 700 prostitutes in the district. And jazz flourished along with the women. "King" Oliver, "Jelly Roll" Morton, and Louis Armstrong are among the black musicians who got their start on Basin Street in the houses between Canal Street and Beauregard Square (which, ironically, is now named for "Satchmo"—but more about that later). Storyville operated with wide-open abandon from 1897, when Alderman Sidney Story proposed a plan for the concentration of illegal activities in this area, until the United States Navy (the secretary of the navy, that is, not the enlisted men) had it closed down in 1917.

What you'll find there today is a far cry from what was there in those rowdy days. A public housing project for low-income families now sprawls over the site, and by virtue of a series of statues depicting Latin American heroes, it is New Orleans's equivalent of the Avenue of the Americas in New York. Simón Bolívar presides over the Canal and Basin streets intersection; Mexico's Benito Juárez comes next, with the inscription "Peace is based on the respect of the rights of others"; and Gen. Francisco Morazón, a hero of Central America whose likeness was given to the city by Honduras and San Salvador, is last in line at Basin and St. Louis streets.

The first of New Orleans's "Cities of the Dead," St. Louis Cemetery No. 1, is in the 400 block of Basin Street. This is one of the places that may or may not hold the grave of voodoo queen Marie Laveau, and if you feel the need for a little help from her powerful magic, you can hunt for her tomb (she's purported to be in the one marked "Famille VVe Paris Née Laveau Ci-Gît, Marie Philomé Glapion, décédée le 11 Juin 1897") or take the guided tour for a small charge and ask the caretaker to point it out. Some say that even now a gris-gris (which might be anything from a string around a bone to a doll stuck with a pin) left overnight there and then placed on the doorstep of the person you want to influence will absorb some of that magic. For more about this cemetery and others, see the section on New Orleans burial grounds.

Between Basin Street and North Rampart Street (in the 700 block) is an area alive with history. It began as a Native American camp, but as the old walled village of New Orleans acquired more and more black slaves (who held on to their secret voodoo ceremonies and wild native music in spite of everything their white masters could do to squelch them), the area across from Rampart Street was designated as Congo Square, to be used as a gathering spot for blacks on Sunday afternoons. It was hoped that this once-a-week opportunity to sing, dance, and generally let off steam would eliminate the voodoo rites at other times and locations. Unfortunately not only did those secret rituals continue (and even attract prominent French residents as spectators), but also Congo Square became the scene of wild, sensual dancing accompanied by beating drums; frequent fights precipitated by heightened emotions; and a source of fascination for as many as 2,000 spectators who would congregate to watch the dancing until a 9pm cannon boomed curfew for all slaves. After the Civil War it was named for the locally loved Gen. P.G.T. Beauregard (he actually *started* that war by ordering the first shot on Fort Sumter), and in April 1980 it was officially renamed **Louis Armstrong Park** in honor of the black man with a horn who carried the name of New Orleans with him all over the world.

Just behind the square you'll see the **Municipal Auditorium** and the **Theatre of the Performing Arts.** There once was a canal (about where the auditorium is now) that linked New Orleans with Lake Pontchartrain back in 1796. A prison and an early charity hospital also have stood on these grounds.

2. New Orleans Burial Grounds

In the beginning burials were made along the banks of the Mississippi, but when the little settlement of New Orleans began to grow, more cemetery space was a necessity. But there was a problem —and a big one. The soggy ground was so damp that graves would fill with water even before the coffins could be lowered. To solve that problem, above-ground tombs were constructed. The coffin would be put in place on the ground, walls of brick would be built around it, then the walls would be plastered and whitewashed. The entrances to the tombs were closed by marble tablets, and many were enclosed with iron fences. Some are even finished off with rounded roofs or topped with eaves—like tiny, windowless houses. It is easy to see why the cemeteries came to be called "Cities of the Dead" because they are arranged along narrow paths, many of which have "street" names. And these miniature cities have their "skyscrapers," since upper floors would be added as members of the same family passed away and were entombed right on top of the existing vault. Along the outer walls of the cemeteries, you'll see rows of wall vaults, or "ovens," which hold the remains of the city's poor. Incidentally you may be perplexed by the long list of names listed for just one tomb—that's because, in a miracle of space engineering, New Orleanians use the same tomb over and over, simply removing the old remains after two years have passed and interring a fresh body in the vacated space.

St. Louis Cemetery No. 1, in the 400 block of Basin Street (see above), was the first, established in the 1740s; **St. Louis Cemetery No. 2** is a few blocks away down Conti Street on Claiborne Avenue (from Iberville to St. Louis streets), and if you see one of the unmarked "ovens" with red crosses on its concrete slab, that's the other place Marie Laveau may or may not be resting from her voodoo activities. It seems that no matter how many times the slab is painted over, the faithful keep coming back to mark it and ask Marie's favors. **Lafayette No. 1 Cemetery** is in the Garden District bounded by Washington, Prytania, and Coliseum streets. Perhaps the most beautiful of all is **Metairie Cemetery,** at the intersection of Pontchartrain Boulevard and Metairie Road—and it wouldn't be here at all except for one New Orleanian's pique at being denied admission to the exclusive Metairie Jockey Club at the racetrack that once operated on these grounds. He was an American who, to strike back at those uppity Creoles who wouldn't let him in, bought up the land, turned it into a burial ground, and swore that from then on only the dead would gain admittance.

Before leaving this subject, there is one word of warning that I must add—a sad commentary on these modern days. Because there have been several muggings in St. Louis Cemeteries No. 1 and No. 2 (the oldest), it is best not to walk in them alone. Either go with a party or tour or join the excellent free "City of the Dead" walking tour guided by park rangers of the Jean Lafitte National Park and Preserve. Call 589-2636 for the schedules.

3. Canal Street and the Central Business District

There's no street more central to the life of New Orleans than Canal—the location of *everything* is described in reference to its re-

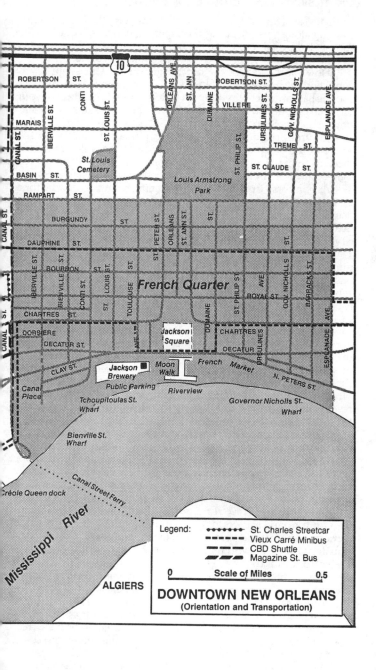

DOWNTOWN NEW ORLEANS
(Orientation and Transportation)

lation to Canal Street. It took its name from a very shallow ditch that was dug along this border of the French Quarter in its early days. Although the ditch was given the rather grand name of *canal,* it was never large enough to be used for navigational purposes.

Down at the foot of the street, right on the Mississippi River, you'll find the free **ferry to Algiers.** It's a lovely way to view the city and the harbor, whether you're on foot or behind the wheel of your car. It takes about 25 minutes each way, so be sure to allow sufficient time. Also, the **Riverfront streetcar line's** "Ladies in Red" trolley cars run from the downriver side of Esplanade to the Riverwalk. These are great stepsavers, and with ten station stops along the way, they are an excellent way to move from one point to another for sight-seeing both in the French Quarter and across Canal Street.

As you pass Canal Street's street lights, be sure to dawdle for a close look. The lights on the tall posts are arranged in the French fleur-de-lis pattern, and each post has four bronze plaques imbedded in its base, one for each government that hoisted its flag over the city: French Domination, 1718–69; Spanish Domination, 1769–1803; Confederate Domination, 1861–65; American Domination, 1803–61 and 1865 to date. Looking at the broad, neon-blighted street these days, you'd never guess it was once residential. It is here, in what is now called the Central Business District (roughly bounded by Canal toward the lake to Loyola Avenue and upriver to the elevated Pontchartrain Expressway—Bus. I-90—and the Mississippi River to the west), that you'll find several of the newest hotels; downtown department stores; all manner of clothing stores, drugstores, dime stores, movie houses, and restaurants; and all the other bits and pieces that make up a major city's leading commercial thoroughfare. Only at Mardi Gras does Canal put aside business for pleasure, and then it becomes a veritable sea of humanity intent on revelry, its tide ebbing and flowing to follow floats that drift down the street as each krewe parades.

Down at the river, the **World Trade Center of New Orleans,** 2 Canal Street, is the center of New Orleans's maritime industry as well as the home of most international consulates. On the 31st floor there's an observation deck that looks out over the city and a harbor scene that might include naval vessels (from submarines to aircraft carriers), cruise ships (those that simply ply excursions in local waters and those that leave for far-away ports), and freighters flying flags from around the world. For a stunning ride up, use the outside elevator—more timid souls can opt for the one inside. The observation deck, called Viewpoint, is open every day except Christmas and Easter from 9am to 5pm. This is truly an incomparable view. Also included in the admission price are two exciting slide shows about the city, a colorful international flag and map display, and individual recorded cassette tours of the observation deck. There are high-power telescopes to zoom in on your favorite site for only 25¢. Adults pay $2; children 6 to 12 pay $1; and children under 6 are free. For more relaxed viewing, go on up to the 33rd-floor revolving cocktail lounge (see Chapter XI).

A stone's throw away is the **Rivergate Exhibition Center,** at 4

Canal Street, a $13½-million building constructed to encourage and aid New Orleans's booming convention activity. Its huge main hall (132,500 square feet) is seldom without a trade show of one sort or another, and the kitchen can serve as many as 10,000 hungry conventioneers at one sitting. Come Mardi Gras time, however, it—like the rest of the city—puts business aside. That massive floor space is used by a Carnival krewe for its ball, and the krewe even parades its giant floats right through the Rivergate.

The **Louisiana Children's Museum,** 428 Julia Street (tel. 523-1357), is a marvelous "hands-on" wonderland for the young. They'll delight in fantasies of being a medieval knight or lady-in-waiting, a tugboat captain, or a newscaster. Special projects scheduled on Saturday include puppet workshops, storytelling, and cooking programs. The hours are 9:30am to 4:30pm Tuesday through Sunday, and there's an admission fee of $3 per person. The museum is accessible to the handicapped.

Big as it is, the Rivergate looks almost puny when compared to the colossal **Louisiana Superdome,** located in the 1500 block of Poydras Street. Tall as a 27-story building, with a seating capacity of 76,000, the windowless structure has a computerized climate-control system that uses over 9,000 *tons* of equipment. It is the largest building in the world in diameter (680 feet), and its grounds cover some 13 acres. Inside, no posts obstruct the view for spectator sports such as football, baseball, and basketball, and movable partitions and seats give it the flexibility to form the best configuration for almost any event. Most people think of the Superdome as a sports center only, but this big flying saucer of a building plays host to conventions, trade shows, and large theatrical and musical productions as well. Entertainment and instant replays are provided via two Diamond Vision screens. Guided tours are run daily at regular intervals from 9am to 4pm. For tour information and prices, call 587-3810.

That complex of five modern buildings you see surrounding the plaza on Loyola Avenue between Poydras Street and Tulane Avenue is the **Civic Center.** The 11-story City Hall is the most imposing—the others are the State Supreme Court, Civil Courts Building, State Office Building, and the Main Public Library (which many natives consider a modern monstrosity because of its cubistic architecture).

The huge granite building that fills the block of Canal Street bounded by Decatur and North Peters is the historic **Customs House.** Its construction, begun in 1847, was interrupted by the Civil War, among other things, and it wasn't actually completed until the 1880s. Its gigantic Marble Hall, 128 by 84 feet, rises to a height of 58 feet and has life-size bas-reliefs of two city heroes, Bienville and Andrew Jackson. The ceiling, a great white-and-gold iron frame holding large ground-glass plates, is supported by 14 white marble columns—it's absolutely breathtaking to walk into the sunlit hall from the dusky corridors. One part of the unfinished building was used to hold Confederate prisoners during the reign of Union General Butler.

4. Uptown and the Garden District

If you don't have time for an in-depth exploration of uptown—and, indeed, even if you do—one thing you shouldn't miss during any visit to New Orleans is the 1½-hour **trolley ride** out of St. Charles Avenue and back. The streetcars were "modernized" in the 1920s, and as late as 1948 you could take the trip "around the belt" for only 7¢. These days, you'll pay 60¢ each way—one of the best buys in town. The streetcar passes through or on the edges of the most interesting parts of New Orleans's "American" section, and for the most complete sight-seeing, climb aboard at Canal and Carondelet streets. This is a fine way to reach the Garden District, Loyola and Tulane universities, Audubon Park, or the Riverbend shopping area without the hassle of driving, and you can spend a lovely, meandering day riding the streetcar in spurts from one to another. Don't worry about lunch—there are loads of good restaurants (see Chapter VII), and an even better idea is to pick up a box lunch at your hotel or favorite restaurant and picnic in the park. Make your day as long as you please because the streetcars run around the clock. There's a description of what you'll see along the way in the "Getting Around" section of Chapter II, but you might like a general guide for the architecture you'll be viewing: If it has cupolas, gingerbread trim, and turrets, it's Victorian; those above-ground basements, covered porches, and iron-railed galleries are of the Louisiana "raised cottage" genre.

To walk around the Garden District, get off the streetcar at Jackson Street (be sure to wear comfortable shoes so weary feet won't cut short your tour). The lavish formal gardens surrounding the lovely "town" mansions (the pride of wealthy planters who many times spent part of every year on their plantations) along St. Charles Avenue and the numbered streets that cross it gave this district its name. If you could peep inside these large homes of colonnaded galleries and ironwork balconies (and you can at certain times of the year—see Chapter III), you'd see a décor of ornate moldings, mahogany bannisters, mantels of rosewood or Italian marble, winding staircases, crystal chandeliers, and priceless antiques.

The "uptown" Americans were determined to equal, if not outdo, those snooty Creoles in the French Quarter, and they certainly came close. Many of their descendants still live in these houses, although some have been sold to wealthy new owners who maintain them with loving care. Alas, some have yielded to "progress" in the form of apartments or commercial ventures. Space limitations will not, of course, permit a description of every home worthy of note, but I'll do my best to point out those of special interest. As I did with those in the Quarter, I'll simply arrange them by streets and leave you to determine your own route through this beautiful section, or you can follow the excellent walking tour provided by **The Tourist Board**, 529 St. Ann Street (tel. 504/566-5031). I'll start with St. Charles Avenue and its parallel streets, then list the streets that cross it, beginning with Jackson Avenue. Remember that you'll have to admire everything from the sidewalk—the interior details are visible to the public only during Spring Fiesta (see Chapter III).

ST. CHARLES AVENUE

The famed James Gallier, Jr., was one of the architects of 2265 St. Charles. The house was built in 1856, and the side wing was added later.

When the cottage at 2336 St. Charles was built in the 1840s, the avenue was a dirt road known as Nayades, nothing like the broad street you see today.

At 2919 St. Charles, the **Christ Church Cathedral** is one of the oldest Protestant churches in the Mississippi Valley. This is the fourth building on the site, and it suffered the loss of its steeple in a 1915 hurricane.

The house at 2926 St. Charles was built in 1882, with a gallery for every room and an early air-conditioning system—a 12-inch space between inner and outer walls. Don't be confused by the number 710 above its front door—it's left over from an outdated numbering system.

PRYTANIA STREET

There's a central hall measuring 67 by 12 feet in the house at 2127 Prytania. Dating from 1857, it has been fully restored.

The Victorian villa-style home at 2221 Prytania was built in 1850, and you'll notice that the architect, Henry Howard, added Greek Revival touches—another example of New Orleans's tolerance for mixing whatever styles appealed to the fancy of the builder.

The unpretentious "raised cottage" at 2340 Prytania is probably the oldest residence in the Garden District. It was built in 1820 by Thomas Toby, a wealthy merchant who came to New Orleans from Philadelphia and brought many of the materials for this house from there. He had the house built for his overseer but decided to live there himself. The unlucky Mr. Toby lost most of his fortune later, when he helped finance the Texas War for Independence. The structure saw some changes in an 1855 remodeling.

Wealthy sugar planter Bradish Johnson built the elegant town house at 2343 Prytania, and it cost him $100,000 even back in 1870. It was probably designed by the Paris-trained architect James Freret, and before a deadly hurricane in 1815 the magnolias out front were said to be the largest in the country.

The house at 2507 Prytania is built on a truly grand scale—every room is 22 feet square, except for the hall (which measures 11 by 44 feet) and the ballroom (which measures 22 by 44 feet). It was erected in 1850, and in 1870 the ballroom was paneled and a motif of Louisiana birds was added to its décor.

The 1857 mansion with a lovely marble entryway at 2521 Prytania houses Our Mother of Perpetual Help Chapel.

At 2605 Prytania there's a Gothic "cottage" dating back to 1850.

COLISEUM STREET

There's something reminiscent of a Swiss chalet in the 1870 house at 2627 Coliseum. Maybe that's because of its rather unique use of wooden gingerbread and cast ironwork.

A New Orleans "developer," architect William Freret (brother of James), built the houses from 2700 to 2726 Coliseum in 1861. They were identical in design, and he meant them to turn a tidy profit. But the Civil War came along and his money-making scheme was gone with the wind, leaving these houses with a local nickname of "Freret's Folly."

CHESTNUT STREET

Notice the "raised cottage" at 2838 Chestnut—it was built sometime between 1840 and 1850, and during the Civil War an "enemy" (Union) general lived here.

MAGAZINE STREET

Most of Magazine Street is now commercial, and it can furnish a fascinating day's ramble all by itself, with antiques and "classy junque" on display in many of the stores. However, in this look at the Garden District, go by 2319 Magazine to see the home architect John Turpin built for himself. He was a Londoner who went into partnership with New Orleanian James Gallier, and the house was built in 1853.

JACKSON AVENUE

At 1329 Jackson, the Trinity Episcopal Church dates back to 1851, and its architecture might be described as "Victorian Gothic."

Notice the Ionic columns, cast-iron railings, and gardens of the mid-1800s house at 1410 Jackson.

PHILIP STREET

The all-wood residence at 1220 Philip was built in the 1850s. A subsequent owner was the wealthy sugarcane and molasses dealer whose nephew, Isaac Delgado, donated his art collection to start the Museum of Art—Isaac spent most of his growing-up years in this house.

The beautiful gardens at 1238 Philip brought citywide fame to its owner, John Rodenberg. It was constructed in 1853 and has the two-story columned gallery typical of houses in this district.

Don't call the elegant home at 1433 Philip a "mansion"—in New Orleans, it's a "raised cottage" even though it has those stately columns and the fancy ironwork. It dates to the late 1850s.

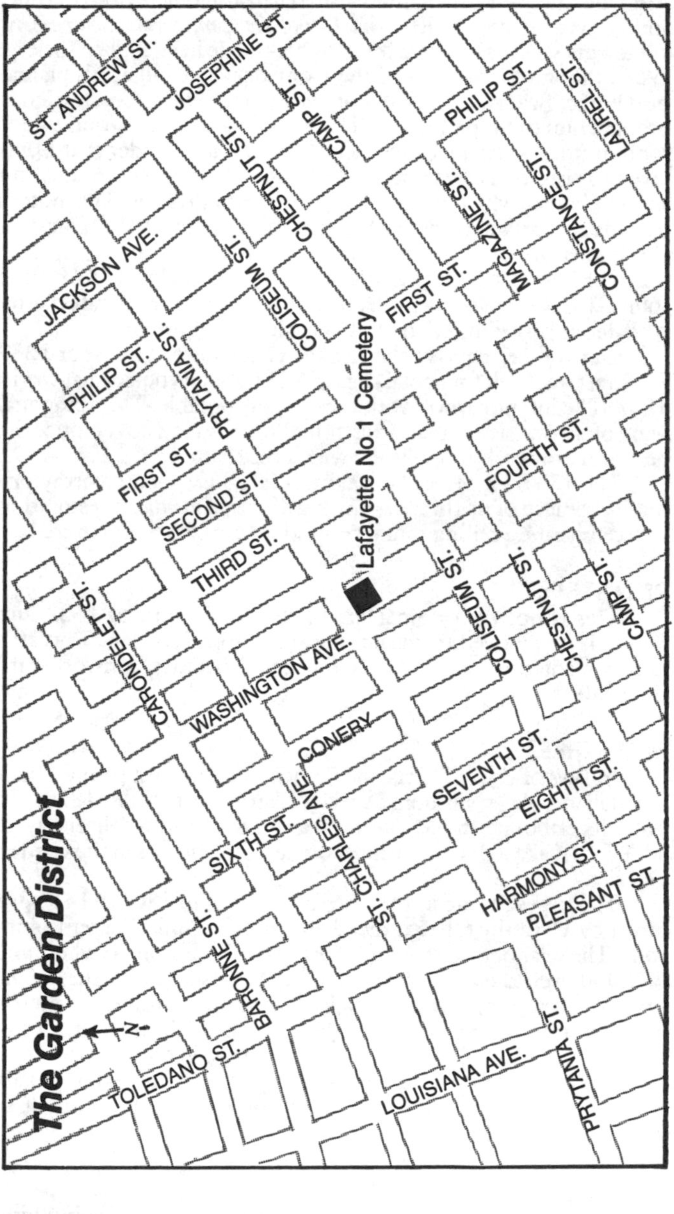
The Garden District
ST. ANDREW ST.
JOSEPHINE ST.
JACKSON AVE.
PHILIP ST.
FIRST ST.
SECOND ST.
THIRD ST.
WASHINGTON AVE.
CONERY
SIXTH ST.
SEVENTH ST.
EIGHTH ST.
HARMONY ST.
PLEASANT ST.
TOLEDANO ST.
LOUISIANA AVE.
FOURTH ST.
CARONDELET ST.
BARONNE ST.
PRYTANIA ST.
COLISEUM ST.
CHESTNUT ST.
CAMP ST.
ST. CHARLES AVE.
MAGAZINE ST.
CONSTANCE ST.
LAUREL ST.
Lafayette No.1 Cemetery
N

1ST STREET

A close friend of Confederate president Jefferson Davis, Judge Charles Erasmus Fenner used slave labor to build 1134 1st Street.

After the Civil War, Davis often visited here for long periods of time, and he even wrote *The Rise and Fall of the Confederate Government* while a guest. This is where his daughter made her debut to society. When the aging president of the Confederacy fell ill at his plantation home, Beauvoir, in Biloxi on Mississippi's Gulf Coast, friends brought him to Judge Fenner's home, and he died in a ground-floor room in this house in December 1889. It's no wonder that Davis loved to visit the 1850s house—just take a look at the gardens and summerhouse, which make a beautiful, restful retreat. The judge's descendants retained ownership of the house until 1935, and its new owners have continued its upkeep in the old style.

The house at 1236 1st Street was constructed in 1847 by one John Gayle for his young bride. Its interior features elaborate plaster medallions on ceilings and black marble mantelpieces.

Can you believe that the elegant Greek Revival house at 1239 1st Street was built for a total cost of $13,000? Of course, that was in 1857. The interior woodwork is especially notable. The hexagonal wing off to one side was an afterthought, added in 1869. Notice the beautiful ironwork embellished with a rose pattern.

The 1331 1st Street house, built in 1869, is noteworthy primarily because of its three cast-iron galleries. During its restoration in recent years, a ceiling mural painted on canvas was uncovered.

2ND STREET

This is not the original site of the 1845 house at 1427 2nd Street. It was moved to the city location from Mrs. Jane Fawcett's nearby plantation, and it didn't gain the decorative ironwork until the 1930s.

3RD STREET

In-laws of Edgar Degas, the French impressionist painter, built the Italian villa–style home at 1331 3rd Street in the 1850s. In 1884 its elaborate stables out back and the cast-iron galleries were added, to make it one of the most outstanding houses in the Garden District.

The largest home in the district was built in 1865 at 1415 3rd Street by a wealthy tobacco merchant from Virginia, Walter Robinson. The elaborate structure cost Mr. Robinson a whopping $80,000 even then (can you imagine its present-day value?). The luxurious interior boasts a marvelous winding staircase, and there's an interesting carved wooden eagle, fished from the river after a violent storm, adorning the dining room chimneypiece.

The little carriage house at 1417 3rd Street belonged originally to the large house around the corner on Prytania. It was built in 1853, with walls 13 inches thick.

4TH STREET

Louis Herman, a New Orleans cotton broker, started building from the back at 1241 4th Street. The kitchen and slave quarters went up in 1844, then when the "big house" was added up front at a later date, the two were connected.

If your French Quarter sight-seeing included the Cornstalk House on Royal Street, you'll see a twin to that fence at 1448 4th Street. This house was built in 1859 for a Col. Robert Short of Kentucky. Its double parlors measure a spacious 43 by 26 feet, and the cast-iron fence with the motif of cornstalks entwined with morning glories was cast in Philadelphia.

WASHINGTON AVENUE

There once was a gymnasium at the corner of Washington and Prytania, and that's where "Gentleman" Jim Corbett trained for his match with John L. Sullivan. The gym also held the first Turkish bath in the city.

From Prytania to Coliseum, on Washington, you'll find one of the interesting "Cities of the Dead," Lafayette No. 1 Cemetery (see "New Orleans Burial Grounds," above). This one was laid out in 1833, and yellow fever victims had it almost completely filled by 1852. The little wooden mortuary first served as a Catholic church at another location—it dates from 1844.

6TH STREET

When Newcomb College was in this district, the building at 1240 6th Street was its Music School. The other buildings were torn down when the school moved out.

7TH STREET

The two houses at 1221 and 1215 7th Street were twins when they were built as wedding gifts for two sisters. As you can see they've taken on individual personalities as modifications were made over the years.

The house at 1506 7th Street still has the original cornices and chandeliers. It dates from the 1850s.

8TH STREET

Writer George Washington Cable lived in the 1874 house at 1313 8th Street. Mark Twain and Joel Chandler Harris (author of the Uncle Remus stories) were entertained in the house, which was built off the ground to prevent flood damage and (it was hoped) yellow fever. The poet Joaquin Miller was a resident during the 1884–85 Cotton Exposition.

HARMONY STREET

The "raised cottage" at 1328 Harmony, with its wide central hall and galleries at both front and back, is typical of the 1860s, when it was built.

LOUISIANA AVENUE

There's another "raised cottage" of the 1860s at 1424 Louisiana. This one has double chimneys and brick gable ends.

ST. CHARLES AVENUE

When moving out of the Garden District along St. Charles Avenue, take note of the lovely home at **5005 St. Charles Avenue.**

The exclusive Orleans Club (a private social and cultural women's club) now occupies the premises, but it was built in 1868 by a Colonel Lewis as a wedding gift for his daughter. It is sometimes used for debut teas and wedding receptions (but no rice-throwing allowed—it might damage those beautiful floors).

The 1907 mansion at 5100 St. Charles Avenue was at one time the home of silent-screen star Marguerite Clark. In later years the house was given to the New Orleans Public Library by a prominent family as a memorial to the son they lost in World War II, and its official name now is the **Milton H. Latter Memorial Library.** It's worth a stop just to see the painted ceiling and the paneling.

Loyola University occupies the 6300 block of St. Charles Avenue on the site of a preparatory school, Loyola Academy, that stood there from 1904 to 1911, when the university was established. The campus covers some 14 acres, and its brick-front main buildings form three sides of a square facing the avenue. Behind these buildings, the modern Dana Center student union is a popular gathering spot, and its cafeteria and snack bar are open to visitors. Loyola, incidentally, is the largest Catholic university in the South.

Right next door, in the 6400 block of St. Charles, is the older **Tulane University.** It dates back as far as 1834, when the Medical College of Louisiana was founded. The University of Louisiana, begun in 1847, was merged with the Medical School, and when Paul Tulane left a bequest of $1 million to the combined schools, the name was changed in gratitude to the benefactor. That generous gift financed what is now one of this country's leading medical and law schools. (The medical school has since moved to a downtown campus on Tulane Avenue.) An interesting facet of the legal education offered here is its emphasis on the Code Napoléon, a rather peculiar system of law practiced in this country only in Louisiana. Other specialties—such as engineering, architecture, art, social sciences, and the oldest college of commerce in the country—add to the university's prestige. It is on the 93-acre campus that the Sugar Bowl used to be played every New Year's Day, but that was before the Superdome came along. Also on the campus is the Harriet Sophie Newcomb Memorial College for Women, which was founded in 1886 and was located in the Garden District until it moved here in 1918. Nowadays it's an undergraduate college of Tulane. The university's Howard Tilton Memorial Library has an unusually fine collection of rare books, documents, and early New Orleans data.

You're welcome to stop in at the University Center for a snack during your tour of the campus. And in case you're wondering about that shady oval with a gatehouse guarding its entrance, that's **Audubon Place,** one of the last privately owned streets in the city (it's been called "millionaire's row," and when you look in at the mansions that line the little street, you'll know why). The gatehouse, which is occupied around the clock, is older than any of the homes it guards. The white house out front is where Tulane's president lives.

Across the street from both Loyola and Tulane, **Audubon Park** sprawls over 340 acres, reaching from St. Charles Avenue all the way to the Mississippi River. This tract of land once belonged to Bienville, the founder of New Orleans, and later was part of the Étienne de Bore plantation, where sugar was granulated for the first time in 1794. The city purchased it in 1871, and on that section that is now a golf course the World's Industrial and Cotton Centennial Exposition was held in 1884–85. In spite of having what was then the largest building in the world (33 acres under one roof) as its main exhibition hall, the exposition was such a financial disaster that everything except a Horticultural Hall had to be sold off. (The Horticultural Hall fell victim to a hurricane a little later). After that, serious work was begun to make this into a park.

The huge trees with black bark you see here are live oaks, and some go back to the days when this was a plantation. They're evergreens and shed only once a year, in early spring. Their spreading limbs turn walkways into covered alleys, and there are winding lagoons, fountains, and statuary, as well as a very nice zoo. Look for the bronze statue of John James Audubon, for whom the park was named—it's in a grove of trees (as is altogether fitting), and the naturalist is shown with notebook and pencil in hand, as he no doubt was most of the time during his sojourn in Louisiana (perhaps on this very land). Scattered about are gazebos, shelters, and playground areas—and that funny-looking mound over near the river is called "Monkey Hill," constructed so that the children of the city could see what a hill looked like in this flat land. Especially nice is the pavilion on the riverbank that is one of the most pleasant places from which to view the Mighty Mississippi.

As far as I'm concerned, the trees and wandering paths and general atmosphere of peace and quiet are quite enough for any park. But if you're looking for recreation facilities, you'll find those here, too. There's a golf course (18 holes) in the front half, picnic facilities, tennis courts, a swimming pool, a 1.8-mile jogging track, 18 exercise stations, horseback riding, and bike rentals. The zoo, sea lion pool, and a small amusement park are toward the back of the park.

The **Audubon Zoo,** 6500 Magazine Street (tel. 861-5101), is one of the top-five zoos in the country. Here, in a setting of subtropical plantings, waterfalls, and lagoons, some 1,500 animals live in natural habitats. Don't plan to spend less than two or three hours—more if you have time to spare—in this delightful oasis of animal culture. A terrific way to visit is to arrive or depart on the sternwheeler *Cotton Blossom* (see "Tours" at the end of this chapter) and arrive or depart via the St. Charles streetcar, which is reached by way of a lovely stroll through Audubon Park itself. The zoo is open daily from 9am to 4:30pm (to 5:30pm on summer weekends) but closed for major holidays. Admission is $6 for adults and $3 for children 2 to 12.

When you reach the end of St. Charles Avenue (it's where the streetcar turns onto Carrollton Avenue), the green hill over by the river is the levee—if the water happens to be high enough, you'll see the tops of ships as they pass by.

Right here, too, is where you'll find the **Riverbend** area, and even if you don't spend a cent, you might want to wander about a bit. The place is literally crowded with shops, but they're located in charming old houses, and they hold everything from arts and crafts to elegant clothing to paintings and sculptures to fine jewelry to antiques to eating places. To reach it, turn at Burthe, then turn left on Dublin Street.

Back at St. Charles Avenue's end is what was once an independent town, **Carrollton.** When Gen. William Carrollton's troops camped here in 1812, a tiny settlement sprang up. When a railroad came along to connect it to New Orleans (along the same route covered by today's streetcars), a depot was built, and New Orleanians began flocking out of the city on weekends to this "country" town. Before long a resort hotel went up, beautiful gardens were laid out, and there was even horse racing for the town sports. Gradually the wilderness between New Orleans and Carrollton gave way to those Garden District mansions and other developments. In 1874 the resort town was annexed to the city. The depot and hotel went down when the river changed its course, and the levee was built.

At 719 S. Carrollton Avenue, that antebellum building is now the Benjamin Franklin public high school, but it was originally built as Carrollton's courthouse.

Along this section of Carrollton Avenue, you'll see yet another architectural style much used in New Orleans, the "shotgun house." Only one room wide, the little houses would permit a bullet fired through the front door to go right out the back, passing through every room in the house.

5. The Irish Channel

The area between the Garden District (Magazine Street) and the river is known locally as the Irish Channel. No one really knows why—it's true that a good many Irish immigrants settled here, but so did Germans, and for some reason it was never known as the German Channel. Whatever the reason for its name, it is an interesting, although somewhat seedy, section of town these days. It houses many of New Orleans's poor, just as it did in the early days when Irish men and women lived a day-to-day existence along these streets. An illuminating sidelight to the city's history is the fact that between 1820 and 1860 the more than 100,000 Irish newcomers were considered more "expendable" than costly slaves and were killed off by the dozens in dangerous construction work and any other manual labor that might endanger health and well-being. In spite of that, however, there was a toughness and lively spirit that gave the Irish Channel a distinctive neighborhood flavor, and although it is mostly populated by blacks and Hispanic-Americans nowadays, there is still a sort of "street camaraderie" character alive here.

At the corner of Camp and Prytania streets, you'll see a statue of one Irish immigrant, Margaret Haughery, who toiled in a bakery and dairy and devoted every spare free minute to the care of orphans. When she died she left all her hard-won earnings to charity. The Carrara marble statue, whose inscription is simply "Margaret," was unveiled in 1884; it was one of the first statues dedicated to a woman anywhere in the country. Appropriately there's a day nursery that dates back to 1850 on the edge of the small park that holds Margaret's monument.

Remember Sir Henry Morton Stanley, of "Dr. Livingstone, I presume" fame? Well, long before he set out for darkest Africa in 1871 on his rescue mission, he came to New Orleans from Wales and was taken under the wing of an American merchant named Stanley, whose name the young John Rowlands took as his own. He grew up in the house at 904 Orange Street, and his signature can still be seen cut into a windowpane of the little room that was his, just off the kitchen.

The Irish built **St. Alphonsus Church** at 2029 Constance Street in 1855, and the gallery and columns will remind you rather vaguely of the St. Louis Cathedral in the French Quarter. A beloved Redemptorist priest, Fr. Francis Xavier Seeles, is buried in the church. He is credited with the working of many miracles, and if you visit the church, you're likely to see letters of petition on his tomb.

At the foot of Jackson Avenue, the second of New Orleans's free ferries will take you across the Mississippi—this one lands at the little town of Gretna.

---

6. Camp Street

There are two sight-seeing attractions on Camp Street, which got its name when there was a slave camp here. **St. Patrick's Church,** at 724 Camp Street, was founded in a tiny wooden building to serve Irish Catholics in the parish. When the present building was begun in 1838, the new edifice was constructed around the old one, which was then dismantled inside the new building. The distinguished architect, James Gallier, Sr., designed much of the interior, including the altar. It opened in 1840, proudly proclaimed as the "American" Catholics' answer to the St. Louis Cathedral in the French Quarter (where, according to the Americans, God spoke only in French).

At 929 Camp Street, the **Confederate Museum** was established in 1889, close enough to the end of the Civil War for many donations to be in better condition than is sometimes true of museum items. There are battle flags, weapons, personal effects of Confederate president Jefferson Davis (including his evening clothes), part of Robert E. Lee's silver camp service, and many portraits of Confederate military and civilian personalities. A series of detailed pictures traces Louisiana's history from secession through Reconstruction. There's a $3 charge for adults, a $2 charge for seniors and students, and a $1 charge for children under 12. The hours are 10am to 4pm Monday through Saturday.

7. The Warehouse District

With the revitalization of an area once devoted almost entirely to abandoned warehouses into an upmarket residential neighborhood, the area between Julia and St. Joseph streets has become a mecca for artists. **The Contemporary Arts Center,** 900 Camp Street (tel. 523-1216), just beyond St. Joseph toward Howard Avenue, has facilities for presenting not only art exhibitions but also theatrical programs. For the "Arts in the Warehouse District" brochure—a complete listing of art galleries—write to the Warehouse District Arts Association, P.O. Box 80949, New Orleans, LA 70190.

8. Dryades Street

Because you wouldn't be human if you didn't wonder about that gilded dome so prominent against the skyline (especially as you drive on the elevated expressway), I'm including the **Church of St. John the Baptist,** at 1139 Dryades Street. It was built by the Irish in 1871, but its most noteworthy features (except for the exceptional brickwork of the exterior) are the Stations of the Cross and Sacristy murals that were painted during and after World War II by a Belgian artist, Dom Gregory Dewit, as well as the beautiful stained-glass windows crafted by artists in Munich.

9. The Bayou, City Park, and the Lake

BAYOU ST. JOHN

Bayou St. John was one of the most important reasons New Orleans is where it is today. When Sieur de Bienville was commissioned to establish a settlement that would protect the mouth of the Mississippi River for the French Crown against British expansion, he recognized the strategic importance of the "back-door" access to the Gulf of Mexico provided by the bayou's linkage to Lake Pontchartrain. Boats could enter the lake from the gulf, then follow the bayou to within easy portage distance of the Mississippi mouth. The Native American tribes hereabouts had used this route for years, and Bienville was quick to see its advantages.

The path from city to bayou back in those early days is today's Bayou Road, an extension of Governor Nicholls Street in the French Quarter. The modern-day Gentilly Boulevard, which crosses the bayou, was another Native American trail—it led around the lake and on to settlements in Florida after a relatively short boat trip.

As the new town grew and prospered, planters moved out along the shores of the bayou, and in the early 1800s a canal was dug to connect the waterway with the city. It reached a basin at the edge of Congo Square. The lake itself became a popular recreation area, with fine restaurants and dance halls (as well as meeting places for voodoo practitioners, who held secret ceremonies along its shores). Gradually the city reached out beyond the French Quarter and enveloped it all—farmlands, plantation homes, and resorts. So on your exploration of this part of New Orleans, you'll see traces of that development. The canal is gone, filled in long ago, and the bayou itself is no longer navigable (even if it were, bridges were built too low to permit the passage of boats of any size), but residents still prize their waterfront sites, and rowboats and sailboats make use of its surface.

The simplest way to reach the Bayou St. John from the French Quarter is to drive straight out Esplanade Avenue about 20 blocks. Just before you reach the bayou, you'll pass St. Louis Cemetery No. 3 (it's just past Leda Street), in which rest many prominent New Orleanians—among them are Thomy Lafon, the black philanthropist who bought the old Orleans Ballroom as an orphanage for black children and thus put an end to its infamous "quadroon balls," and Fr. Adrien Rouquette, who lived and worked among the Choctaw. Just past the cemetery, Esplanade reaches Moss Street, and a left turn will put you on that street, which runs along the banks of Bayou St. John.

MOSS STREET

The **Pitot House** at 1440 Moss Street is perhaps the most notable of several built along this side of the bayou in the 1780s and early 1800s. It dates from 1799, when it was built for an aristocratic family named Ducayet, and it originally stood where the nearby modern Catholic school is now. In 1810 it became the home of James Pitot, New Orleans's second mayor, and it is now known by his name. A typical West Indies–style plantation house, it has wide galleries on three sides and large columns supporting the second floor. There's a beautiful collection of Federal period antiques inside, and you can tour the interior Wednesday through Saturday from 10am to 3pm for a $3 fee for adults and $1.50 for children. Call 482-0312 for tour information.

The Greek Revival plantation house at **1342 Moss Street** was built about 1834 and now serves as a school.

At **1300 Moss Street,** you'll see an old plantation home built about 1784 in the West Indies style, with above-ground living quarters, sloping roof, and wide gallery. The land grant for a farm here dates from 1708, and because legend says that goods traveling on the bayou were sometimes checked here, the house has come to be known as the Old Spanish Custom House.

CITY PARK

Right at the entrance is yet another statue of Gen. P.G.T. Beauregard, who ordered the first shot fired on Fort Sumter to open the Civil War and whom New Orleanians fondly call the "Great Creole." The park was once part of the Louis Allard plantation; its extensive, beautifully landscaped grounds hold four golf courses, picnic areas, a restaurant, lagoons for boating and fishing, tennis courts, horses for hire for the lovely trails, a bandstand, a miniature train, and an amusement area with carnival rides for children. **Children's Storyland** is open Wednesday through Sunday from 10am to 5pm ($1.50 admission for everyone over the age of 2; all under that age don't pay) and an enchanted place for youngsters, where larger-than-life, papier-mâché figures of such Mother Goose characters as Jack and the Beanstalk and Humpty Dumpty will delight even their parents. It's right across from the tennis courts on Victory Avenue.

The huge old oaks in City Park looked down on a favorite pastime in New Orleans during the 1700s—dueling. To the proud Creoles, nothing—not even death—was to be feared so much as the loss of honor, and when a dispute ended with a heated "under the oaks at sunrise," it was here, under what came to be called the **Dueling Oaks,** that the rendezvous was kept. The practice persisted into the early 1800s (there were, in fact, ten duels fought on just one Sunday morning in 1837), but duels changed very much in character after "Americans" arrived on the scene. You see, Creoles observed a very formal and strict dueling etiquette, using the meetings to demonstrate their expertise with rapiers, broadswords, or pistols (fists were never used among gentlemen), and only seldom was either party actually killed. With the Americans, however, came a whole new concept—duels became a fight to the death, with such "rude" weapons as rifles, shotguns, clubs, and even axes. After the Civil War, when Reconstruction made life almost unbearable for Creole and American New Orleanians alike, the two factions united in overcoming their common problems, so dueling died out. It had always been forbidden by both church and law (a fact heretofore completely ignored), and after the war there was a stricter enforcement of the laws—perhaps because there was less to enforce. One of the mighty oaks became known about then as the "Suicide Oak" because of its popularity as the setting for that action. Another, McDonogh Oak, is believed to be over 600 years old, and its 142-foot branch spread served as a shady canopy as recently as 1958, when the City Park superintendent held a breakfast for 526 visitors under the tree.

You'll find the **New Orleans Museum of Art** on LeLong Avenue in City Park in a building that is itself a work of art. The neoclassical, columned main building is a beauty inside and out. Its Delgado Great Hall on the first floor leads to a branched staircase at the back that rises to a mezzanine overlooking the hall. Beautiful! Notice, too, the bronze statue of Hercules as an archer just outside the entrance. The original building, which is about 80 years old, has been expanded by the addition of three wings, and the art inside does justice to its housing. There's a lovely portrait of Estelle Musson, a relative of the French impressionist painter Edgar Degas, who painted this likeness on one of his visits to the city. The 22 sections of the Kress Renaissance collection, pre-Columbian art, and bronzes by Rodin live happily with contemporary, 20th-century art, and galleries are arranged to show the logical progression of the history of art. The museum is open from 10am to 5pm Tuesday through Sunday; it is closed Monday. There's a $4 admission fee for adults and $2 for children and senior citizens. In 1991 the museum will begin a massive renovation and expansion programs, so be sure to check the hours before you go, as there may well be some dates when parts are closed.

LAKE PONTCHARTRAIN

As you drive along Wisner, along this bank of Bayou St. John, you'll pass some of New Orleans's grandest modern homes, which provide a sharp contrast to those over on Moss Street. Stay on Wisner Boulevard to Robert E. Lee Boulevard, turn right and drive to Elysian Fields Avenue, and then turn left. That's **Louisiana State University's New Orleans campus** on your left (its main campus is in Baton Rouge).

Turn left onto the broad concrete highway that is Lakeshore Drive. It runs for 5½ miles along the lake, and in summer the parkway alongside its seawall is usually swarming with swimmers and picnickers. On the other side are more luxurious, ultramodern residences.

Lake Pontchartrain itself is some 40 miles long and 25 miles wide. Native Americans once lived along its shores on both sides, and it was a major waterway long before white people were seen in this hemisphere. You can drive across it over the **Greater New Orleans Causeway,** the 23¾-mile-long bridge, the longest in the world.

When you cross the mouth of Bayou St. John, you'll be where the old Spanish Fort was built in 1770. Its remains now nestle among those elegant modern homes. In the early 1800s there was a lighthouse here, and in the 1820s a railroad brought New Orleanians out to a hotel, casino, bandstand, bathing houses, and restaurants that made this a popular resort area.

Look for the Mardi Gras fountain on your left. Bronze plaques around its base are inscribed with the names of Mardi Gras krewes, and if you time your visit out to the lake so that you'll be there at sundown, you'll see the fountain beautifully lit in Mardi Gras colors of purple (for justice), green (for faith), and gold (for power).

Down at the end of Lakeshore Drive, you'll come to the old white Coast Guard lighthouse, and you'll know you've reached **West End.** This is an interesting little park that's home for several yacht clubs, a marina, and restaurants, many of which have been here for years and look just like lakeside restaurants should (not too fancy—more interested in the view out over the water and good eating than in "decorator-style" interiors). This old fishing community has, over the years, become the main pleasure-boating center of New Orleans, and the Southern Yacht Club here was established in 1840, the second oldest in the country. After the railroad began bringing pleasure-seekers here from the city in the 1870s, showboats and floating circuses would often pull up and dock for waterside performances. West End is an excellent place to stop for a bite to eat, if indeed it isn't your destination when you set out for the lakeside with a fresh seafood dinner in mind.

To reach **Buckstown,** which lines the banks of a narrow canal behind the restaurants on the western side of West End park, turn to the left on Lakeshore Drive at the Coast Guard station, then turn right on Lake Avenue (it's the first street you come to). Buckstown is another small fishing community which still retains its oldtime atmosphere. There are also many good seafood restaurants here.

10. Other Points of Interest

LONGUE VUE

Just off of Metairie Road, at 7 Bamboo Road, you'll find the lovely, eight-acre Longue Vue estate, one of the most beautiful garden settings in this area. The mansion is built in the classical tradition. As with the great country houses of England, here there is a close rapport between indoors and outdoors, with vistas of formal terraces and pastoral woods. Some parts of the enchanting gardens were inspired by those of the Generalife in Granada, Spain; besides the colorful flowering plants, there are formal boxwood arrangements, fountains, and a colonnaded loggia. Highlights are the Canal Garden, Walled Garden, Wild Garden (which features native iris), and Spanish Court with pebbled walkways, changing horticultural displays, and statuary. Longue Vue is open daily; call 488-5488 for the hours and admission fees.

JACKSON BARRACKS

At 6400 St. Claude Avenue (that's an extension of Rampart Street downriver from the French Quarter), there's a series of fine old brick buildings with white columns. They were built in 1834–35 for troops who were stationed at the river forts. Some say Andrew Jackson, who never quite trusted New Orleans Creoles, planned the barracks to be as secure against attack from the city as from outside forces. The Barracks now serve as headquarters for the Louisiana National Guard, and there's a marvelous military museum in the old powder magazine. It's open from 7:30am to 3:30pm Monday through Friday but closed Saturday and Sunday. There's no admission charge, but it's best to call 271-6262, ext. 242, or 278-6242 before you go, to confirm that the Barracks and museum are open.

About a mile away, you'll come to another site connected with Andrew Jackson.

CHALMETTE NATIONAL HISTORICAL PARK

To reach the park, continue on St. Claude Avenue until it becomes St. Bernard Highway. The park will be on your right. On these grounds a horrendous battle was waged on January 14, 1815. Ironically the battle should never have been fought at all, since the War of 1812 had by then been concluded by a treaty signed two weeks before in Ghent, Belgium. The treaty was not, however, in effect, and word had simply never reached Congress, the commander of the British forces, or Andrew Jackson, who stood with

American forces to defend New Orleans and the mouth of the Mississippi River.

The British, having defeated Napoleon in Europe earlier in 1814, had turned their full military might against the United States. Campaigns on Lake Champlain and the Chesapeake Bay had failed, however (in spite of their attack on Washington and the burning of the White House), and control of the Mississippi River became vitally important. In December 1814, under General Packenham, brother-in-law of the duke of Wellington (Napoleon's nemesis at Waterloo), the British had massed a huge invasion force just off the waters of Ship Island in the Gulf of Mexico, with its chief aim the capture of New Orleans.

Gen. Andrew Jackson, then in command of American forces in Louisiana (which meant mostly militiamen from the hills of Tennessee and Kentucky), hurried to the city to set up some sort of defense. With few trained troops of his own, he set about gathering volunteers, and the crew he assembled was, if not motley, certainly diverse. There were Creoles, Irish and German immigrants, "uptown" Americans, slaves, a few "free men of color," and even Native Americans. So compelling was Jackson's appeal to New Orleanians that even the privateer Jean Lafitte joined in the defense effort, not only supplying troops from his pirate band but also furnishing great quantities of weaponry and ammunition. (This is when Lafitte and Jackson held all those meetings in all those cafés and bars in New Orleans.)

The British managed to come up the river by way of Bayou Bienvenu to within 9 miles of the city. Jackson, with the help of his colorful collection of recruits, built earthworks along the river on the grounds of the Chalmette plantation and kept the British forces stalled for several days. General Packenham, faced with a serious morale deterioration among his men, ordered a head-on land attack, much to the dismay of his junior officers. Jackson's men, behind their rampart, let loose with rifles, cannons, and muskets, effectively mowing down the redcoats as they approached in tight, orderly lines of march. It was over in little or no time, with more than 2,000 British casualties littering the battleground, including Packenham, who lost his life in the fight. The British flotilla continued to fire on forts downriver, and General Packenham's men were encamped close by for another ten days before the general's successor, General Lambert, ordered them back aboard their ships, and they sailed for home. The bloody battle, so costly to the British, left only 13 American dead—as I said, however, the whole thing would never have happened had word of the Peace Treaty of Ghent reached this side of the Atlantic in time. The battle did, however, succeed in bringing New Orleanians together more than they had ever been, and in making Andrew Jackson a hero forever in this city.

You can visit the battleground and see markers that will let you follow the course of the battle in detail. In the Beauregard plantation house on the grounds, you will find interesting exhibits, and the Visitor Center presents a film and other exhibits on the battle. There is also a National Cemetery here, which was established in 1864 and holds only two American veterans of the Battle of New

Orleans, but some 14,000 Union soldiers who fell in the Civil War. For a really terrific view of the Mississippi River, climb the levee in back of the Beauregard House. There's no charge to visit the park, which is open from 8:30am to 5pm daily.

11. Museums

Here's a quick-reference list of the museums outside the French Quarter that I already discussed in detail:

The **Pitot House,** 1440 Moss Street, is a typical West Indies–style plantation home built in 1799, restored and furnished in Federal period antiques. It is open Wednesday through Saturday from 10am to 3pm. Admission is $3 for adults and $1.50 for children.

The **New Orleans Museum of Art,** LeLong Avenue (Tel. 488-2631) in City Park, is in a neoclassical building housing pre-Columbian, Renaissance, and contemporary art exhibited to show the history of art development. It is open from 10am to 5pm Tuesday through Sunday but closed Monday. Admission is $4 for adults and $2 for children. It is free to all ages on Thursday.

Jackson Barracks, 6400 St. Claude Avenue, is a plantation-style, columned military barracks built in the 1830s. The powder magazine has an extensive collection of military items that span the American wars. It is open Monday through Friday from 7:30am to 3:30pm (but call 271-6262, ext. 242, or 278-6242 to verify before coming to visit). There is no admission charge.

Chalmette National Historical Park, St. Bernard Highway, is the battlefield where the Battle of New Orleans was fought in 1815. Beauregard plantation house has several exhibits, and the Visitors Center offers both exhibits and a film. There's also a National Cemetery dating from 1864. The park is open from 8:30am to 5pm daily. There is no admission charge.

12. Tours

Once you leave the confines of the French Quarter, sight-seeing tours can save a lot of time, to say nothing of wear and tear on the nerves, especially if you're the one behind the wheel. Buses will pick you up at your hotel and deliver you back there, and guides can be depended on for complete, accurate information (as well as occasional entertainment by way of amusing anecdotes and legends about the city). Another marvelous way to view the city is from the riverboats that cruise the harbor and a little stretch of the Mississippi River. Docks are at the foot of Toulouse and Canal streets, and there's ample parking space for the car while you sit back and relax on the water. Reservations are required for all these tours, and I would remind you once more that the prices quoted here are those in effect at press time and are subject to change.

BUS TOURS

The **Gray Line,** 1300 World Trade Center of New Orleans (tel. 587-0865, or toll free 800/535-7786), has a complete city tour that begins in the French Quarter, with an informative narration on many historic buildings in the Quarter, as well as the Creole cottages and elegant mansions along Esplanade Avenue. From Esplanade, the tour travels to City Park, then on to Lake Pontchartrain and the old cemeteries, then back to the Garden District for a look at those antebellum mansions. Before delivering you back to your hotel, the tour will show you the Louisiana Superdome, the New Orleans River Bridge, and the old Custom House. It's a 2-hour trip, with departures at 9am, 11:45am, and 2:30pm. The fare is $15 per adult and $8 per child.

For $24 per adult and $12 per child (and five hours of your time), Gray Line will include a 2-hour cruise on the paddle wheeler *Natchez.* You'll have lunch on board (cost *not* included in the tour price) as you take in the sights and sounds of the harbor. Call for departure times.

An excellent Family Tour combines the City Tour with visits to the zoo and a riverboat cruise for a $22.50 fare for adults and $14 for children, with a 9am departure.

They will pick you up at your hotel, and reservations are necessary for all tours.

Tours by Isabelle, P.O. Box 740972, New Orleans, LA 70174 (tel. 504/367-3963), specializes in small groups traveling in a comfortable, air-conditioned minibus. Her City Tour is a 25-mile, 3-hour drive through the French Quarter, the city cemeteries, the Garden District, the Lakefront, and finally the Superdome. The fare is $20, and you should call as far in advance as possible to book. For $30 you can join her afternoon Combo Tour, which adds Longue Vue Gardens to all of the above.

The park rangers of the Jean Lafitte National Historic Park guide free walking tours of both the St. Louis Cemetery No. 1 and the Garden District. Call 589-2636 for schedules.

RIVERBOAT CRUISES

The steamboat **Natchez,** 1340 World Trade Center of New Orleans (tel. 586-8777, or toll free 800/233-BOAT), a marvelous three-deck stern-wheeler docked at the wharf behind the Jackson Brewery, offers three 2-hour harbor cruises daily. The narration is by professional guides, and there are an optional Creole buffet, cocktail bars, and a gift shop aboard. The fares are $12 for adults and $6 for children. Those under 3 ride free. Call for sailing schedule. Also, there are jazz dinner cruises. Call for the schedules and prices.

The stern-wheeler **Cotton Blossom,** 1340 World Trade Center of New Orleans (tel. 586-8777), offers a real departure in the cruise world—the exciting Zoo Cruise. Passengers travel the Mississippi by stern-wheeler, tour the busy port, and dock to visit the Audubon Zoological Gardens, one of the finest zoos in the world. There are three round trips daily from the Canal Street dock at Riverwalk, beginning at 9am. The fares are $14.50 round trip and $11.50 one way—including zoo admission. Call for exact sailing schedule and to make reservations.

The paddle wheeler **Creole Queen** (tel. 524-0814) departs from the Poydras Street Wharf adjacent to Riverwalk at 10am and 2pm for 3-hour narrated excursions of the port and points downriver. There is also an 8pm jazz dinner cruise. The ship has a covered promenade deck, and its inner lounges are air-conditioned and heated. Buffet and cocktail services are available on all cruises. The fares are $14 for the daytime cruises and $34 for the nighttime jazz cruise. Call to confirm sailing schedules and current fares.

X

NEW ORLEANS SHOPPING

1. THE SHOPPING SCENE
2. SHOPPING A TO Z

Like everything else in New Orleans, shopping is fun. I say that as a dedicated nonshopper, one who keeps the mail-order houses in business. Still, the shops are so different, so intriguing, that I'm in and out of them all along the streets. There's *everything* in New Orleans, and if you can't find something, you can find someone to make it for you! The place is loaded with craftspeople and artisans who use every material conceivable: cast iron, wood, leather, fabric, brass, plastic, and precious metals. You can even have one of those marvelous old-time overhead fans shipped back home.

Antique shops are really special here, many with patios and gardens that actually seem to enhance their goods. Some are located in old French Quarter homes, giving another dimension to browsing. And the emphasis that was always placed on fine home furnishings in New Orleans has left a residue of some of the loveliest antiques I've ever viewed. Many came from Europe in the early days; others were crafted right in the city by cabinetmakers internationally known for their exquisite pieces. And for the nautically minded, there are shops that specialize in marine antiques, wonderful mementoes of long-ago voyages and the ships that made them.

Because its port is the landing place for goods from all over the world, New Orleans fills its shops with a rich variety of imported items, from home furnishings to kitchen utensils to pottery to designer clothes to whatever else you can name. Art galleries, too, display the works of leading world artists as well as those closer to home. The creation of fine jewelry is a much-practiced art, and a visit to some of the jewelers is akin to an art gallery visit.

You'll notice, of course, the abundance of gift shops—postcards, sunglasses, and T-shirts displayed outside won't let you miss them. Well, don't dismiss them all as cheap souvenir places. Some of my most blissful browsing has come as a surprise when I entered such a place to buy postcards and found an interior stocked with imaginative imported gift items. (This is not true of all of these little shops, but it pays to look.)

The following listing is far from complete, but if you don't see a particular category that is of special interest to you, be assured that you'll more than likely find it when you arrive in New Orleans. For convenience, I'll show the major shopping centers first, followed by shops grouped by category.

The hours for most shops are 10am to 5pm every day except Sunday. Many, however, are open later on Saturday night and on Sunday afternoon, especially in the French Quarter, where souvenir shops are likely to remain open until 11pm every day of the week.

1. The Shopping Scene

CANAL PLACE (365 CANAL STREET)

At the foot of Canal Street, where it reaches the Mississippi River, this stunning shopping center holds over 50 shops, many of which are branches of some of this country's most elegant. The three-tiered mall has polished marble floors, a landscaped atrium, fountains, and pools. Stores in this sophisticated setting include Brooks Brothers, Polo/Ralph Lauren, Godiva Chocolatier, Saks Fifth Avenue, Laura Ashley, and Tabbi.

THE FRENCH MARKET (1008 NORTH PETERS STREET)

Shops within the Market begin on Decatur Street across from Jackson Square, and include candy, cookware, fashions, crafts, toys, New Orleans memorabilia, and candles.

JACKSON BREWERY (600–620 DECATUR STREET)

Just across from Jackson Square, the old brewery building has been transformed into a joyful jumble of shops, cafés, delicatessens, restaurants, and entertainment. The 125 shops and eateries within its walls include fashions, gourmet and Cajun–Créole foodstuffs, toys, hats, crafts, pipes, posters, and souvenirs. The Brewery is open from 10am to 10pm Friday and Saturday but to 9pm other days, although many shops close at 5:30 or 6pm.

MAGAZINE STREET

This major uptown street runs from Canal Street to Audubon Park, with some 6 miles of more than 140 shops, some in 19th-century brick storefronts, others in quaint, cottagelike buildings. Among the offerings are antiques, art galleries, boutiques, crafts, and dolls.

RIVERBEND

The Riverbend district is in the Carrollton area. To reach it, ride the St. Charles Avenue streetcar to stop 44, then walk down Maple Street one block to Dublin Park, the site of an old public market once lined with open stalls. Nowadays, renovated shops inhabit the old general store, a produce warehouse made of bargeboard, and the town surveyor's raised-cottage home. Among the outstanding shops are Yvonne LaFleur, whose romantic fashions have appeared on television and movie screens; and the Cache Pot, a concentration of unusual quality gifts.

RIVERWALK

This popular shopping development is an exciting covered mall that runs right along the river from Poydras Street to the Convention Center. Among the many specialty shops at this location, you'll find Sharper Image, Abercrombie & Fitch, and Banana Republic, plus several eateries and periodic free entertainment.

UPTOWN SQUARE

At 200 Broadway, this unique shopping center consists of a maze of one- and two-story buildings interspersed with pleasant plazas and fountains. It's a central place to find fine fashions (Holmes Department Store has a large branch here), family clothing, housewares, distinctive gifts, toys, plants, books, and wines. There's also an upstairs, cafeteria-style restaurant with balcony seating if you wish.

---

2. Shopping A to Z

ANTIQUES

Boyer Antiques—Dolls & Buttons is at 241 and 328 Chartres Street (tel. 522-4513). In addition to the usual assortment of antiques, you'll find an enchanting collection of old dolls and doll furniture. The hours are 9:30am to 5pm daily.

Magazine Arcade Antiques is at 3017 Magazine Street (tel. 895-5451). This part of Magazine Street (30 blocks from Canal Street) is right on the edge of the Garden District. This large and fascinating shop holds an exceptional collection from around the world, and on display are antique furniture, music boxes, Victrolas, and stained glass. Try to plan plenty of time to browse through it all. A 2½-mile ride from Canal Street on the Magazine Street bus, it is open from 10am to 5pm Monday through Saturday.

St. Charles Antiques Ltd., 2125 St. Charles Avenue (tel. 524-0243), is set in a turn-of-the-century mansion and filled with marvelous antiques, with heavy emphasis on the English and Asian. It also has lamps and decorative accessories and offers interior design services. The hours are 10am to 6pm Monday through Saturday.

ART GALLERIES

The Davis Galleries, 3964 Magazine Street (tel. 897-0780), features West and Central African tribal art. Give it a call to check on current showings. The hours are 10am to 5pm Monday through Saturday.

Dixon & Dixon Art Gallery, 237 Royal Street, (tel. 524-0282), features 18th- and 19th-century oil paintings, as well as decorator-quality Oriental rugs. Come by from 9am to 6pm daily.

Nahan Galleries, 540 Royal Street (tel. 524-8696), specializes in works of major artists and original graphics. It is also the publisher for Theo Tobiasse, Max Papart, and others. It is open from 9:30am to 6pm seven days a week.

Hanson Galleries, 229 Royal Street (tel. 566-0816), has a special showing of new originals and graphics by Peter Max, and also works by LeRoy Neiman, Kostobi, Tova, Joanna Zjawinska, and Frederick Hart. The hours are 10am to 7pm Monday through Saturday and 11am to 5pm on Sunday.

Bergen Galleries, Inc., 730 Royal Street (tel. 523-7882, or toll free 800/621-6179), is the place for the largest selection of posters and limited-edition graphics—including New Orleans works; Mardi Gras; jazz; and artists such as Erté, Nagel, Hoppe, and Taylor Kent. The service from Margarita and her staff is friendly and is extremely personable. The hours are 9am to 7pm daily.

Old Quarter Gallery is at 621 Chartres Street (tel. 523-6871). This is an unusual gallery owned and operated by local artists and the prices are low because the middleman is eliminated; there's a wide variety of styles and mediums: oil, acrylic, watercolor, batik, etchings, woodcuts, silkscreen, and photography. Limited-edition prints and paintings may be purchased either framed or unframed.

BOOKS

Bookstar, 414 N. Peters Street (tel. 523-6411), is a large, attractive bookshop in the Jackson Brewery complex. Without doubt, it stocks one of the largest selections of books and magazines in the city, and its enthusiastic and knowledgeable staff can help you find the printed word on virtually any subject you can name.

Beckham's Bookshop, 228 Decatur Street (tel. 522-9875), has two entire floors of old editions and some rare, secondhand books that will tie up your whole afternoon or morning if you don't tear yourself away. The owners also operate **Librairie Bookshop,** at 823 Chartres Street, and **Old Books,** at 811 Royal (both of which you'll surely have found if you're a book lover). The hours are 10am to 6pm every day of the week.

For literary enthusiasts there's the **Maple Street Bookstore,** 7523 Maple St. (tel. 866-4916), which has five locations throughout the city; as well as **De Ville Books and Prints,** 1 Shell Square (tel. 525-1846); **Beaucoup Books,** 45 Magazine St. (tel. 895-2663); and **Book Stop,** 5082 Pontchartrain Blvd. (tel. 488-5540), which has its own café. **Little Professor Book Center of New Orleans,** 1000 S. Carrollton Ave. (tel. 866-5628), stocks one of the best general collections.

In addition to the independent bookstores, above, the nationwide chain stores are well-represented: **B. Dalton,** 714 Canal Street (tel. 529-2705), open Monday through Saturday from 10am to 7p.m.; and **Waldenbooks,** 739 Canal Street (tel. 529-8418), open Monday through Saturday from 9:30 to 7p.m.

CAMERAS AND FILM

One of the city's most complete camera shops is the **K&B Camera Center,** 227 Dauphine Street (tel. 524-2266), with a wide selection of cameras and other electronics, as well as film and camera and darkroom supplies. Fast film developing is also featured. The hours are 8am to 6pm Monday through Friday, until 2pm on Saturday.

CANDIES AND PRALINES

At **Aunt Sally's Praline Shops, Inc.,** 810–827 Decatur Street in the French Market (tel. 524-5107), you can watch skilled workers cook the original Creole pecan pralines here right before your eyes in a 150-year-old process. You'll know they're fresh. The large store also has a broad selection of regional cookbooks, books on the history of New Orleans and its environs, Creole and Cajun foods, folk and souvenir dolls, and local memorabilia. They'll ship any of your purchases, which can lighten the load going home considerably. The hours are 8am to 6pm every day.

Godiva Chocolatier, 301 Canal Street in Canal Place, offers a complete assortment of these deluxe chocolates. It is open from 10am to 6pm Monday through Saturday.

Laura's Original Praline and Fudge Shoppe, 115 Royal Street (tel. 525-3880) and 600 Conti Street (tel. 525-3886), is New Orleans's oldest candy store, established in 1913. There are seven varieties of pralines on sale here, plus hand-dipped chocolates, rum-flavored pecans, Vieux Carré Foods, and their great praline sauce. Take home a feast, or have it shipped. And drop in almost anytime —they're open from 8am to 10pm every day of the week.

CANDLES

At the **French Market Candle Shop,** 824 Decatur Street (tel. 522-6004), there's a delightful collection of handcrafted beeswax candles in beautiful artistic shapes and sizes. Brass candlesticks and other candle-related items, as well as a large array of gift items and collectibles (clowns, masks, music boxes, and so on) make this much more than just a candle shop. The hours are 9am to 7pm daily.

CLOTHING

Perhaps as a leftover from their elegant past, New Orleanians love fashion, and shops around the city accommodate them by providing everything from high-fashion designer clothes to the latest "funky" styles. Men and women will find stylish garb to suit almost any taste readily available.

Meyer the Hatter is at 120 St. Charles Avenue (tel. 525-1048; or toll free 800/882-4287). Men will find distinguished headwear —one of the largest selections of fine hats and caps in the South— with labels such as Stetson, Dobbs, and Borsalino in this fine shop, which opened in 1894 and is now run by third-generation members of the same family. It is open Monday through Saturday from 9:30am to 5:30pm.

Saks Fifth Avenue is at 301 Canal Street in Canal Place (tel. 524-2200). In addition to the high-quality fashion (for men, women, and children) for which they are nationally known, Saks also offers a personalized shopping service, the Fifth Avenue Club. It is open from 10am to 6pm Monday through Saturday (until 8pm on Thursday).

Town and Country is at 1432 St. Charles Avenue (tel. 525-9572). Opened almost a half century ago, this shop has a warm, friendly atmosphere that encourages leisurely examination of the fine fashions. There are designer collections, distinctive dresses and jewelry, and some truly smashing accessories. The hours are 9:30am to 5:30pm Monday through Friday, until 5pm on Saturday.

Yvonne LeFleur/New Orleans is at 8131 Hampson Street (tel. 866-9666), in the Riverbend shopping district. Yvonne Le-Fleur, a confessed incurable romantic, is the creator of original designs so beautifully feminine that they'll invite fantasies of past golden ages. Her custom millinery, silk dresses, evening gowns, lingerie, and sportswear are surprisingly affordable, and all are enhanced by her own perfume. The hours are 9:45am to 6pm Monday through Saturday (until 8pm on Wednesday and Thursday).

COSTUMES

The following is just one of the shops specializing in Mardi Gras finery. One tip to remember is that New Orleanians often sell their costumes after Ash Wednesday and you can sometimes pick up a one-time-worn outfit at a small fraction of its cost new.

Mardi Gras Center, 831 Chartres Street (tel. 524-4384), carries sizes 2 to 50 and has a wide selection of new, ready-made costumes as well as used outfits. It also does custom costumes and carries all accessories such as wigs, masks, hats, makeup, and jewelry. The hours are 10am to 5pm Monday through Saturday.

FLOWERS AND PLANTS

For that special "thank-you" gift to your New Orleans host or hostess, go by **H & J Plants,** 1209 Decatur Street (tel. 561-5849), where Harold Cinquigranno and Jesse St. Croix, the knowledgable owners, will give you expert guidance in making your selection.

FOODS

If you want to try your hand at making those scrumptious beignets, you can buy the mix at the **Café du Monde Coffee Shop,** 800 Decatur Street in the French Market. To make it complete, pick up a tin of their famous coffee. It is open around the clock, seven days a week. The shop also has a very good mail-order service.

GIFT SHOPS

There are literally hundreds of gift shops in New Orleans, with merchandise ranging from very expensive to junky. The following are the ones I found most attractive.

Little Mex, is at 1017–1021 Decatur Street (tel. 529-3397). I don't really know how to tell you about this amazing store. From a rather unimposing entrance, you walk into an interior that just goes on and on. And it's filled with just about everything under the sun. There are imports from all over the world—a huge selection from

Mexico—leather goods; straw, wheat, and bamboo products; baskets (I bought a great one to carry an accumulation of purchases already made); metal sculpture; dolls; brass and copper items; and . . . well, all I can say is to be sure to allow some extra time for some of the best browsing in the French Quarter. It is open from 9am to 5pm every day.

Pontalba Historical Puppetorium is at 514 St. Peter Street on Jackson Square (tel. 522-0344 or 944-8144). There's an excellent puppet presentation of New Orleans history here (see Chapter VIII) but you can also purchase puppets. In fact, the puppetorium has the largest collection in the United States. It is open every day from 10am to 6pm.

Santa's Quarters is at 1025 Decatur Street (tel. 581-5820). If you're walking down Decatur Street in July and suddenly hear "Jingle Bells," you'll know you've found this year-round Christmas store. It's an enchanting place, with ornaments from around the world, all kinds of decorations, and so many Christmas ideas that you may finish up all your holiday shopping months in advance. It is open from 10am to 5pm daily.

JEWELRY

At **New Orleans Silversmiths,** 600 Chartres Street (tel. 522-8333), you'll find jewelry, both old and new, in gold and silver, as well as a variety of reproductions of antiques. The hours are 9:30am to 5pm Monday through Saturday.

Mignon Faget Ltd. is at Level One, Canal Place, 365 Canal Street (tel. 524-2973). The striking originals of New Orleans's own Mignon Faget have won national fame, and a visit to her studio display room is a real treat. Handcrafted designs in gold, silver, and bronze d'oré include pendants, bracelets, rings, earrings, shirt studs, and cufflinks. The hours are 10am to 6pm Monday through Saturday.

LEATHER GOODS

Rapp's Luggage and Leather, 604 Canal Street (tel. 568-1953), carries an extensive selection of leather goods, from the most expensive designer luggage to duffle bags, wallets to attaché cases, and many unique gifts that you'd never expect to find in a leather goods store. Gift wrapping and monogramming are free. The quality is high, and the prices are reasonable. This store can also repair luggage. The hours are 10am to 5:30pm, and there are branches at Uptown Square, 200 Broadway (tel. 861-1453); Esplanade Mall, Kenner (tel. 467-8283); 3250 Severn at 17th Street, Metairie (tel. 885-6536); New Orleans Centre (tel. 566-0700); and Oakwood Shopping Center, Gretna (tel. 362-5408).

PIPES AND TOBACCO

Ye Olde Pipe Shoppe is at 306 Chartres Street (tel. 522-1484). Mr. Edwin Jansen's shop won my heart in about two seconds flat (or maybe it was Mr. Jansen himself). His grandfather, August, founded the place way back in 1868, and at one time repaired Jefferson Davis's pipes. Nowadays, *my* Mr. Jansen hand-makes beautiful briar pipes, repairs broken pipes, and sells pipe accessories and enough tobacco blends to keep you puffing all year long. This is not a fancy shop but a warm, comfortable stopping-off place for pipe lovers. While you're there, take a look at the marvelous collection of antique pipes put together by his father and grandfather. In keeping with the character of this special place, the pipes aren't shown off in a velvet-lined display, but are just heaped in a glass case, making it sort of an adventure to run your eyes over one after the other, trying to imagine each in the fond hand of its original owner. Over the years Mr. Jansen has developed a firm philosophy about pipes and their smokers and has written an excellent book about them. If pipes are your thing, don't fail to search this place out and spend some time with a kindred spirit. It is open from 10am to 5pm Monday through Saturday.

TOYS

The dolls in **The Little Toy Shoppe,** 900 Decatur Street in the French Market (tel. 522-6588), are some of the most beautiful I've ever seen, especially the Madame Alexander and Effanbee ones—and the New Orleans–made bisque and rag dolls. In addition to "heros" wood toys from Germany and "All God's Children" collectibles, there are cuddly stuffed animals, dollhouses and furniture, toy soldiers, and miniature cars and trucks. Stop by from 9:30am to 5:30pm Monday to Thursday, to 9pm on Friday and Saturday, and 10am to 9pm on Sunday.

UMBRELLAS

They call her "the Umbrella Lady," but her real name is Anne B. Lane. You'll find her in her upstairs studio at **1107 Decatur Street** (tel. 523-7791). She's a Quarter fixture and the creator of wonderful Secondline umbrellas as well as fanciful "southern belle" parasols.

XI

NEW ORLEANS NIGHTS

1. THE CLUB AND MUSIC SCENE
2. THE PERFORMING ARTS

We'll be talking about entertainment in this chapter, and in New Orleans entertainment starts with jazz. It's everywhere—on the streets of the French Quarter, in jazz clubs all over the city, and in the heart and soul of everyone who lives here. Its counterpart, the blues, moans through the city in the soft, throaty notes of the clarinet. But there's more to New Orleans than just its heady nightlife. Its rich French heritage, strongly spiced by the Italians who've become such a part of its life, has left a real love of classical music and opera. Theater, too, plays a part in New Orleans entertainment. As for sports—well, just say "Superdome" and eyes light up. We'll take a look at all of these and tell you where to find them.

1. The Club and Music Scene

When the sun goes down, New Orleans lights up. In the French Quarter, Bourbon Street turns into a ten-block-long street party, posh downtown hotel supper clubs start to swing, and uptown hideaways come to life with music. Jazz, that uniquely American contribution to the world's music, was born here. It grew out of the anger, fear, love, joy, pride, and back-breaking toil that made up the emotional lives of blacks in New Orleans from the days of slavery right up to the advent of "Storyville." Slaves, remembering the rhythms and chants of West Africa or the Caribbean, danced in Congo Square to the accompaniment of homemade instruments (a skin stretched across a piece of bamboo, reed flutes, banjos made of gourds, and clicking bones) as their white masters looked on, convinced that the Sunday-night revelry would be sufficient outlet for week-long frustrations and would squelch black magic voodoo rites. Creole gentlemen fathered a large group of "free men of color" by their quadroon mistresses and sent them off to Europe to be educated, and these free men brought back a knowledge of classical music and instruments that they promptly integrated with the black music of their native city. No longer confined to once-a-week happenings at Congo Square, the joyous, soul-lifting sounds moved out into the streets of the city to capture the attention of a white population who was already music oriented. "Spasm bands," made up of blacks using whatever instruments were available, played at street corners to audiences of foot-tapping whites.

When the restricted area around Basin Street opened up a world of highly competitive bordellos, saloons, and nightclubs, black musicians moved their vibrant, expressive music inside to provide entertainment for paying customers. It wasn't long before it began showing up in the white man's world of college campuses, riverboats, and "respectable" nightclubs and restaurants. New Orleans–born masters of the art such as Louis Armstrong and "Jelly Roll" Morton, left New Orleans and moved upriver to St. Louis and Memphis, eventually carrying their music to Chicago, New York, and the West Coast. Others—"Papa" Celestin, Bunk Johnson, and Sweet Emma Barrett, to name just a few—stayed at home, keeping the free-spirited music alive at the scene of its birth. Today jazz permeates the city, as black and white, newcomers and old-timers, join together to fill the air with its strains at all hours in the French Quarter and after dark outside the Quarter. And you'll still find uninhibited dancers performing in the streets outside jazz spots (sometimes passing the hat to lookers-on), jazz funerals for departed musicians (the trip to that final resting place accompanied by sorrowful dirges and "second liners" who shuffle and clap hands to a mournful beat; the return, a joyful, swinging celebration of the deceased's "liberation"), and occasionally a street parade (even when it isn't Carnival), complete with brass band.

IN THE FRENCH QUARTER

Dear to the hearts of all jazz devotees (and I count myself among them) is **Preservation Hall,** 726 St. Peter Street, where jazz is found in its purest form, uncluttered by such refinements as air conditioning, drinks, or even (unless you arrive very early) a place to sit down. The shabby old building offers only hot, foot-tapping, body-swaying music, played by a solid core of old-time greats who never left New Orleans. Nobody seems to mind the lack of those other refinements—indeed, not only is the place always packed, but also its windows are filled with faces of those who stand on the sidewalk for hours just to listen.

Admission is an unbelievably low $2, and if you want to sit on one of the much-sought-after pillows right up front or the couple of rows of benches just behind them, be sure to get there a good 45 minutes before the doors open at 8pm. Otherwise, you must stand. The music goes on until 12:30am, with long sets interrupted by 10-minute breaks and the crowd continually changing as parents take children home at bedtime (the kids *love* the hall) and sidewalk listeners move in to take vacant places. There's a marvelous collection of jazz records on sale, some of them hard-to-find oldies.

Pat O'Brien's, at 718 St. Peter Street (tel. 525-4823), has been famous for as long as I can remember for its gigantic, rum-based

Hurricane drink, served in 29-ounce hurricane-lamp-style glasses. But more than the drinks, the let-your-hair-down conviviality has earned it a special place among so many residents that it sometimes has a neighborhood air usually associated with much smaller places. There are three bars here—the main bar at the entrance and one of the loveliest patio bars in existence have no entertainment—but it's the large lounge just off the entrance that is the center of a Pat O'Brien's fun night. The fun comes from several teams of pianists alternating at twin pianos and an emcee who tells jokes. The entertainers seem to know every song ever written, and when they ask a patron "Where're you from?" quick as a wink they'll break into a number associated with the visitor's home state. Requests are quickly honored, and sing-alongs develop all night long, sometimes led by a patron who's been invited up to the bandstand. There's no minimum and no cover (in fact, I once went in when things were so lively that I never *did* get a drink but just had a terrific time enjoying the show and left unalcoholic but happy). The main bar is open from 10am to 4am, the patio is open from 10am to 4am, and the lounge is open from 2pm to 4am (to 5am on Friday and Saturday).

Don't confuse the **Old Absinthe House Bar** at 400 Bourbon Street (tel. 525-8108) with the Old Absinthe House at 240 Bourbon. That's right, they both have the same name, and what's more, they're both entitled to it. The one on the corner of Bourbon and Bienville streets (that's no. 240) can claim the original *site,* while all the original fixtures are now to be found at no. 400, on the corner of Bourbon and Conti. That situation came about when federal agents padlocked the original (it was operating as a speakeasy) during the 1920s, and some enterprising soul broke in, removed the bar, the register, 19th-century prints, ceiling fans, an antique French clock, and a handsome set of marble-based fountains once used to drip water into absinthe (which has been banned in the United States since 1918 because it's a narcotic). They all turned up soon afterward in the establishment on the next corner a block away, and New Orleans was blessed with two "original" Old Absinthe Houses. Anyway, it's the one at 400 Bourbon where you'll find rhythm and blues and progressive jazz—and you'll find drinks only at the other. Beginning at 9pm nightly, the music is continuous, sometimes with as many as three groups alternating, until all hours—there's no legal shutdown time in New Orleans, and it isn't unusual to find things still going strong here as dawn breaks. On weekends there's also daytime music. Blues dominate on the bandstand. There's a cover charge on Friday and Saturday night (drinks are $2 and up).

I once heard a horse-and-carriage driver state unequivocally that the corner of St. Peter and Bourbon streets was "the world's heaviest jazz corner." He may well be right, for jazz pours out of just about every door (and most are wide open) in this area. Not just any jazz, mind you, but *great* jazz, and it begins early in the day and doesn't stop until there's no one left to tap a toe. Almost anyplace along here will be a good spot to spend an evening, but if you're like most, you'll pop into several. The only charge is a one-drink minimum (and of course, you aren't encouraged to spend the night at one place nursing that one drink). You might start at **Maison Bour-**

bon, 641 Bourbon Street (tel. 522-8818), which keeps its doors open to the sidewalk and employs three bands every day to play from 11am to 2am (or later). **& Mo' Jazz,** 614 Bourbon Street (tel. 522-7261), has Dixieland on tap from 8:30pm, as well as ballads, pop standards, and Big Band–era songs. At 339 Bourbon Street, **The Famous Door** (tel. 522-7626) holds forth with Dixieland jazz from 7pm to 3am and beyond, and the **Famous Door Patio,** at 327 Bourbon Street (tel. 581-4784), is an outdoor Dixieland spot.

Lulu White's Mahogany Hall, 309 Bourbon Street (tel. 525-5595), occupies what was once the much-loved Paddock Lounge. The 200-year-old building has been restored to a replica of the original Lulu White's, a thriving bordello from 1897 to 1917. There's a huge mahogany bar, mahogany floors, brick walls, and pressed-tin ceilings. Even more important, this is now the home of the world-famous Dukes of Dixieland. The bar opens at noon, and show times are 9:15, 10:35, and 11:55pm—with a two-drink minimum during shows. From 3:30 to 7:30pm, you'll hear the Mahogany Hall Stompers. You should reserve at this popular spot.

The **New Storyville Jazz Hall,** 1104 Decatur Street (tel. 525-8199), is open from 8pm to midnight Sunday through Thursday, until 3am on Friday and Saturday, with a one-drink-per-set minimum and a cover charge determined by who's playing at the moment. Traditional Dixieland played by top bands gets things started, and on some nights the beat takes on a contemporary note as the evening progresses. Children are welcomed here with their parents, and there's limited food service.

One of the most stylish jazz haunts in the Quarter is the **Palm Court Café,** 1204 Decatur Street (tel. 525-0200). Nina and George Buck have created an oasis of civilized dining (linen on the table, lace curtains at the street windows, and international cuisine—see Chapter VI) in which to present top-notch jazz groups Wednesday through Saturday and on Sunday for a jazz brunch. One very special feature is the collection of jazz records for sale in a back alcove, many of them real finds for the collector. The café is open Wednesday through Sunday from noon to 11pm.

You might walk right past the small **Fritzel's European Bar and Cuisine,** 733 Bourbon Street (tel. 561-0432), but that would be a big mistake, for since 1974 this 1836 building has attracted some of the city's best musicians, who perform on the tiny stage in back. There are frequent jam sessions here in the wee hours when musicians end their stints elsewhere and gather to play just for themselves. Richard Payne, bassist with the late Lou Sino's jazz band, put me on to it—such is its fame among musicians that he had learned about it from a friend in the Vienna Symphony. The bar stocks a variety of German liqueurs, as well as imported beers, and there's a menu of German sandwiches (knockwurst, bratwurst, and so on, on Black Forest bread), hamburgers, po-boys, and red beans and rice—all at budget prices. But go along late at night if you want to catch "musicians' music."

It's not jazz that will set your feet tapping at **Ryan's Irish Pub,** 441 Bourbon Street (tel. 566-1507), but the lively tones of Irish jigs, reels, and ballads. Michael Ryan, who came to New Orleans to run a pub at the 1984 World's Fair, stayed on to open one of Bourbon Street's better establishments. The interior is a nice mix of signposts and other memorabilia from Ireland and ceiling fans with fluted light globes that are pure New Orleans. The Innisfree lads sing traditional Irish songs and play the rousing tunes (sometimes affectionately called "rowdy dow" tunes) that quite often bring patrons to their feet for a bit of a dance. Noel Nash, as fine an Irish balladeer as you'd ever want to hear, alternates with the group. Guinness stout is on tap and comes in the "proper" Irish pint glass; there's Harp lager from Ireland; and there's a terrific Irish coffee as well as Bass Ale, domestic beers, 14 imported beer brands, and the usual array of cocktails.

A smaller bar in the rear is called the Irish Harp and opens to St. Louis Street. Dart teams compete on Tuesday nights, and there's always a game to be had along with a "proper pint." An upstairs bar sports a balcony and also has a view of the stage.

If rock 'n' roll is more your thing—or if you just feel like a break from all that jazz—you can find it at the **Original Melius Bar,** 622 Conti Street (tel. 581-2723), after 9pm.

If you like your entertainment on the sexy side but aren't quite game for Bourbon Street's strippers, the place to go is the **Chris Owens Club,** on the corner of Bourbon and St. Louis streets (tel. 523-6400). This talented and very beautiful woman puts on a solo show of fun-filled jazz, popular, country-and-western, and blues music while (according to one devoted fan) revealing enough of her physical endowments to make strong men bay at the moon. Between shows, there's dancing on the elevated dance floor. The $10.50 door charge covers the show and one drink. Call for show times and to make reservations.

Incidentally those *other* sexy shows, where they often exhibit more skin than talent, can be found in the 300 and 400 blocks of Bourbon—and if you walk by slowly, you can take in more than just a peek, since doors are opened to the sidewalk frequently to lure in the paying public.

It's old-time gospel music with a bit of rhythm and blues thrown in for good measure at the **Bourbon Street Gospel and Blues Club,** 227 Bourbon Street (tel. 523-3800). To catch the gospel music, go by from 8 to 10pm; the blues take over from 10pm to 1am. There's a cover charge of $3, and it's $25 for the Gospel Brunch from 11am and 1pm on Saturday and Sunday.

For a nightcap to the strains of top-notch piano music in one of the city's loveliest settings, stop by the **Esplanade Lounge** in the Royal Orleans, 621 St. Louis Street (tel. 529-5333).

Before leaving nightlife in the Quarter, there are two just-plain-bars I'd like to tell you about. Both are a bit out of the center of things and have a special appeal in this city full of good drinking spots. **Lafitte's Blacksmith Shop,** at 941 Bourbon Street, dates back to 1772. Legend has it that the privateer brothers Pierre and Jean Lafitte used the smithy as a "blind" for their lucrative trade in contraband (and, some say, slaves they'd captured on the high seas). It had pretty much deteriorated by 1944, when a honeymooning visitor fell in love with it and devoted most of the rest of his life to making it a social center for artists, writers, entertainers, and journalists. He did this all without changing one iota of the musty old interior—even today you can see the original construction and "feel" what it must have been like when it was a privateers' hangout. Unfortunately Tom Caplinger's penchant for treating good friends such as Tennessee Williams, and Lucius Beebe, to refreshments "on the house" was stronger than his business acumen, and he eventually lost the building. Friends say that it broke his heart, but he rallied and a little later opened a new place down the block toward Canal Street called the **Café Lafitte in Exile** (the exile is his own, from that beloved blacksmith shop), which flourishes (even after his death) as an elite gay bar. All this is, of course, history, but I think it helps explain the comfortable, neighborhood air that still pervades Lafitte's Blacksmith Shop. The interior is all exposed brick, wooden tables, and an air of authenticity. It's a good drop-in spot any time of day, but I especially enjoy relaxing in the dim, candlelit bar at the end of a festive night when "Miss Lily" Hood holds forth at the piano.

The younger set will find a friendly home at the **Cosimos Bar,** on the corner of Burgundy and Governor Nicholls streets. There are nothing fancy and no special history here; it is just a favorite gathering place for a lively neighborhood crowd who welcome strangers and make them feel right at home. If fact, it's that sociability that sets the Cosimos apart.

On the fringes of the French Quarter (one street beyond Esplanade), **Snug Harbor,** 626 Frenchmen Street (tel. 949-0696), has earned top popularity from residents and locals alike for its nightly presentation of contemporary jazz and blues. Seating is on two levels to provide good viewing of the bandstand, and there's full dinner service (local Cajun and Creole specialties and steak) as well as a light menu of sandwiches. The cover charge varies from $5 to $10, depending on the performers. Two acts are booked nightly, and they change every night. It is open seven nights a week from 6pm to midnight Sunday through Thursday and until 2am on Friday and Saturday.

OUTSIDE THE QUARTER

Pete Fountain is one of those royal native sons who has never been able to sever hometown ties. For more than 20 years he held forth in his own Bourbon Street club, but these days you'll find him at the **New Orleans Hilton** at 2 Poydras Street and the Mississippi River in a re-creation of his former Quarter premises, which seats more than twice the number that could be accommodated in the old club. The plush interior—gold chairs and banquettes, red velvet bar chairs, white iron-lace-railinged gallery—sets the mood for the popular nightspot. Pete is featured in one show a night, Tuesday through Saturday at 10pm. The club, on the hotel's third floor, is named simply **Pete Fountain's** (tel. 523-4374 or 561-0500) and is closed Sunday and Monday. You'll need reservations. Call for rates and to confirm show times.

The view is breathtaking any time of day, but especially so after dark, from the **Top of the Mart,** World Trade Center of New Orleans, 2 Canal Street at the river (tel. 522-9795), and it keeps changing as the large lounge makes a complete circle every 90 minutes. From up there you'll see the bend in the Mississippi that gives New Orleans its "Crescent City" title, and the reflected lights of ships in the harbor remind you that this is not only a fun town, but also a very busy and important port. As you revolve, the layout of the city unfolds all the way to Lake Pontchartrain. There are no admission charge and no cover. Since no meals are served (only drinks), children aren't permitted. One tip to women: Don't lay your purse on the windowsill when you're seated—*it* doesn't revolve, and you'll wind up either chasing it around the room or waiting in the hope that it'll come back around to you. Top of the Mart is open from 10am to midnight weekdays, 11am to 2am on Saturday, and 4pm to midnight on Sunday.

Another up-high spot with a glorious view (but one that stays still) is the **Rainforest,** atop the New Orleans Hilton, 2 Poydras Street at the Mississippi River (tel. 561-0500), which is as popular with residents as it is with out-of-towners. In daylight hours the Rainforest is a sunny luncheon spot (see Chapter VII); at sundown it's a perfect place for cocktails; but come 9pm there's dance music and a spectacular light-and-sound show that simulates a thunderstorm (sound effects operate during the day, as well). The décor is that of a tropical paradise, with gnarled cypress trees, bamboo furnishings, and lots of greenery. There are no cover and no minimum here, just one of the most action-packed dance floors in town.

Tipitina's, 501 Napoleon Avenue (tel. 895-9144), is open from 2pm until closing, seven days, with a small cover charge depending on who's performing. Here there's jazz, rhythm and blues, and almost every other form of music—at Tip's, it all depends on the artist playing, and that covers a *lot* of territory. Past performers in this New Orleans staple have included the Neville Brothers and Bo Diddly. Back in its 1977 beginnings this was home for the revered Professor Longhair up until his death in 1980, and you'll be greeted by a bronze bust of the beloved musician as you enter. Their Creole restaurant is open from 5 to 10pm daily, and things begin to liven up musically around 9:30pm.

Local artists also perform every night at **Tyler's Beer Garden,** 5234 Magazine Street (tel. 891-4989). There's no cover and no minimum—but there are delicious raw oysters that go for 15¢ apiece. *Note:* You'll most likely find the front door locked in this informal, sometimes noisy place, so just go around to the side door and settle in.

Uptown in the Carrollton area, at the **Maple Leaf Bar,** 8316 Oak Street (tel. 866-9359), music begins at 10pm, seven days a week, with a $3 to $7 cover charge depending on the day of the week and the performer. This may be the best place outside the bayous to hear Cajun music (mostly on Thursday and weekends) played by top musicians of that genre. Other nights it might be rhythm and blues, rock 'n' roll, or reggae. Dancing is "encouraged" so you may find yourself out on the floor doe-see-doeing to that Cajun beat. There's a jukebox offering an eclectic mix of musical styles, from classical to jazz to ragtime to Cajun, and there's a strong tradition of good conversation ranging from literary subjects (poetry readings every Sunday afternoon feature local and visiting poets and writers) to music to sports to almost any topic you choose. Come 10pm, however, the jukebox gives way to live music. Thursday nights and some weekends celebrate the lively music and dancing from southwest Louisiana's Cajun country, with standouts such as the Filé Cajun Band and the black Cajun zydeco renditions of Dopsie and his Cajun Twisters.

You'll also find good Cajun music over in the Warehouse District at **Michaul's Live Cajun Music Restaurant,** 701 Magazine Street (tel. 361-4969 or 566-0515). If your feet begin tapping to the catchy rhythms but you're uncertain of the steps, Michaul's will give you free dance lessons. The cuisine is as Cajun as the music. The hours for lunch are 11am to 2pm Monday through Friday; the hours for dinner are 5 to 10pm Tuesday through Sunday. Reservations are required.

Lenfants, 5236 Canal Boulevard (tel. 486-1515), also has no cover charge, and the hours are 9pm to 2am. This art deco disco is one of the city's most "in" spots. Dinner is available from the excellent adjacent restaurant. Opening days vary, so call ahead to check.

You'll find good comedy cabaret every Saturday night at **Ernst Café,** 600 S. Peters Street (tel. 525-8544), with professional comics holding forth at 8pm, 10:30pm, and 1am. On Wednesday at 8pm drop in to see local comedians perform.

ON THE RIVER

A lovely night out in New Orleans is one on the water. The *Creole Queen* (tel. 529-4567, or toll free 800/445-4109) is a paddle wheeler built in the tradition of its forebears, which made its debut at the 1984 World's Fair and now offers superb Créole dinner and jazz cruises nightly. Departures are at 8pm (boarding at 7pm) from the Poydras Street Wharf. There's a covered promenade deck and dance floors on all decks. The fare is $34 per person (which includes a sumptuous Cajun buffet), and there's continuous bar service, as well as live jazz and dancing against a backdrop of the city's sparkling skyline. Schedules are subject to change, so call ahead to confirm days and times.

2. The Performing Arts

In spite of the fact that it's a little off the regular routes for touring Broadway shows, New Orleans attracts some very good national companies, and there's surprisingly good local theater. The city has a long-standing love affair with footlight entertainment—Le Petit Théâtre du Vieux Carré is one of the oldest playhouses in this country, light opera appeared as early as 1810, and grand opera was first sung here in 1837. Opera enjoyed its peak years during the Gay '90s and the early part of this century, and thrived until a fire destroyed the famous old French Opera House in 1919. It wasn't until 1943 that the New Orleans Opera House Association was formed to present several operas a season, with Metropolitan Opera stars in lead roles supported by talented local voices. Occasionally the Met's touring company will also book performances here. If you're an opera buff and in town during one of the local offerings, don't pass it up—there's nothing amateurish about these productions. You'll likely find them (as well as concerts by top performers, symphony orchestras, ballets, and recitals by local and imported talent) in one of two buildings: the New Orleans Theatre for the Performing Arts or the New Orleans Municipal Auditorium (which also accommodates such general-audience shows as circuses, prize fights, ice shows, and the popular summer pops symphony concerts). The New Orleans Philharmonic Symphony Orchestra plays a subscription series of concerts during the fall-to-spring season, and the pops concerts on June and July weekends. Live theater got a big boost in early 1980 when the grand old Saenger Theatre was reopened after being rescued from demolition by a determined group of New Orleanians. There's also a good dinner theater going strong and sometimes good cabaret in bar or lounge settings. In short, you're unlikely to hit town when there *isn't* something worthwhile going on in the performing arts.

Since the **Saenger Theatre,** 143 N. Rampart Street (tel. 525-1052), is *the* theater news in New Orleans, let's start with it. First opened in 1927, it was regarded as one of the finest in the world, and it has now been completely restored in all its finery. The décor is Renaissance Florence, with Greek and Roman sculpture, fine marble statues, and glittering cut-glass chandeliers. The ceiling is alive with twinkling stars, with realistic (although manmade) clouds drifting by. It's a setting the likes of which are fast disappearing from the American theater scene, and New Orleans is to be congratulated on preserving such opulence. First-rate Broadway productions such as *Cats, Les Miserables, Fiddler on The Roof,* and Chita Rivera in *Can Can* play here regularly. Check to see what's on when you're in town.

Le Petit Théâtre du Vieux Carré, 616 St. Peter Street (tel. 522-2081), is right in the heart of the French Quarter, and if you hear people talking about "The Little Theater," this is it. It's one of the oldest nonprofessional theater troupes in the country and periodically puts on plays that rival the professionals in excellence. Check when you're in New Orleans to see if the footlights are up.

The **Theatre of the Performing Arts,** 801 N. Rampart Street (tel. 522-0592), opened in early 1973 and has become the home of lavish touring musical shows, as well as concerts by cultural artists. Opera and ballet also appear here in season. It's a part of the 32-acre New Orleans Cultural Center complex in Louis Armstrong Park, adjacent to the French Quarter.

The **Municipal Auditorium,** 1201 St. Peter Street (tel. 522-0592), is just across a flowered walkway from the Theatre of the Performing Arts in the Cultural Center complex in Louis Armstrong Park and is used for just about every kind of entertainment—from the circus to touring theatrical companies to ballet and concerts. This is where most of those marvelous, elaborate Mardi Gras balls are held.

Other possibilities for theatrical performances (check when you're here, because none of these is open on a regular basis) include **N.O.R.D. Theatre** (tel. 586-5275), for productions sponsored by the New Orleans Recreation Department; **Tulane University Theatre** (tel. 865-6204), which puts on student plays of very high caliber; and the **Louisiana Superdome** (tel. 587-3810)—yes, that's right, the Superdome—which frequently hosts entertainment not even remotely connected with sports.

EASY EXCURSIONS

New Orleans can serve as the hub for four interesting side trips. The banks of the Mississippi River are lined with great plantation homes; a little over 100 miles to the west is the heart of Acadiana, where the unique, delightful culture of the Cajuns lives on; and to the east is the resort-filled Gulf of Mexico coastline. Although a day trip is possible to see some of the plantation houses that are open to the public, the other trips will probably require overnight stops, and each is likely to lure you for more than just one night. I must warn you, too, that should you become hooked on the romanticism of the plantations, it is quite possible to keep rambling north of the River Road to visit those in the St. Francisville area, an exploration that also calls for an overnight stay—and I'll tell you about old homes in which you can actually spend the night if you plan far enough ahead.

1. The Plantations

BACKGROUND

In the beginning the planters of Louisiana were little more than rugged frontierspeople as they spread out along the Mississippi from New Orleans. Swamplands had to be cleared, with a mighty expenditure of sweat and muscle. And the indigo, which was first cultivated as a cash crop, had to be transported downriver to New Orleans before there was any return on all that work, no mean feat in itself. Even today, when you ride modern highways through some of the bayous, your imagination will almost automatically present a very vivid picture of what it must have been like for those early settlers.

Fields were cleared, swamps were drained, and crops were

planted, however, in spite of all the obstacles. And rough flat boats and keel boats (with crews even rougher than their vessels) could get the produce to market in New Orleans—sometimes. Once the boats were on the river, if they weren't capsized by rapids, snags, sandbars, and floating debris, there was the danger that their cargos would be captured by murdering bands of river pirates. It was the crudeness of these men (and a few amazing women) who poled the boats to New Orleans; collected their pay for the journey; and then went on wild sprees of drinking, gambling, and brawling that first gave Creoles of the French Quarter their lasting impression of all "Americans" as barbarians, a conviction that was later to influence the growth and development of the city.

By the 1800s Louisiana planters had introduced farming on a large scale, thanks to their use of (and dependence on) slave labor—a fact that would ultimately bring about their downfall. With large numbers of blacks to do the back-breaking work in the fields, more and more acres went under cultivation, and King Cotton arrived on the scene to prove the most profitable of all crops. Sugarcane, too, brought huge monetary returns, especially after one Etienne de Bore discovered the secret of successful granulation. Rice became a secondary crop. Always there were natural dangers that could spell disaster for planters—a hurricane could wipe out a whole year's work, and the capricious river could, and did, make swift changes in its course to inundate entire plantations. Nevertheless the planters persevered, and for the most part they prospered.

The Riverboats

As for getting their crops to market, the planters could, after 1812, turn to the newfangled steamboat for speedier and safer transportation. When the first of these (built in Pittsburgh and named *New Orleans*) chugged downriver belching sooty smoke, it was called by some a "floating volcano"—it was that dirty, dangerous, and potentially explosive. It wasn't long, however, before vast improvements were made, and over a 30-year period the image of the steamboats changed to that of veritable floating pleasure palaces. Utilitarian purposes (moving goods to market and the planters and their families to town) were always primary, but the lavish staterooms and ornate "grand salons" put a whole new face on river travel and made a profound change in plantation life. A planter could now travel in comfort with his wife, children, and slaves, which induced many to spend the winters in elegant town houses in New Orleans. After months of isolation in the country, where visitors were few and far between, the sociability of the city—with its grand balls, theatrical performances, elaborate banquets, and other entertainments—was a welcome relief. It was now possible, too, to ship fine furnishings back upriver to plantation homes, and thus the planters could enjoy a more comfortable and elegant life-style along the banks of the river.

Those wonderful floating pleasure palaces did, alas, add another element of danger to the lives of some planters. For along with

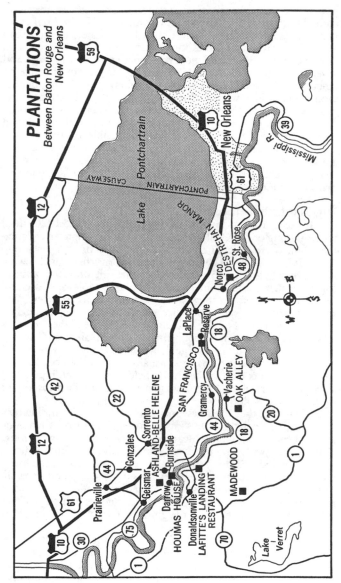

Map courtesy of the Louisana State Tourist Office

the prosperous plantation families, northern merchants, carpetbag-carrying peddlers, European visitors, and poor immigrant families who made up passenger lists, came the most colorful and dramatic passenger of all—the riverboat gambler. Perhaps because they were natural-born gamblers (didn't they gamble on Nature itself every year?), plantation owners were drawn like magnets to the sharp-witted, silver-tongued professionals. Huge fortunes were won and lost on Ole Man River, and more than once when cash, luggage, and jewelry were depleted, the deed to a plantation went on the table, to be raked in by a well-dressed, cigar-smoking pro. During one famous game, which went on for three days without interruption, it was said that over $37,000 in gold was on the table at one point. Thus a planter might leave his plantation home a wealthy man and arrive at journey's end a pauper. And if the gamblers didn't get him, the steamboat captains might. As the vessels became grander and grander and more and more efficient, the captains and pilots took to racing one another—a hazardous practice that caused the loss of many boats and even more lives and fortunes.

The Plantation Houses

It was during this period of prosperity, from the 1820s until the beginning of the Civil War, that most of the impressive plantation homes were built. They were the focal point of a self-sustaining community and almost always were near the riverfront, with a wide avenue of oaks leading to a wharf. On either side stood *garçonnières* (much smaller houses, sometimes used to give adolescent sons and their friends privacy; others were guesthouses for travelers who stopped for a night's lodging). Behind the main house, the kitchen was built separately because of the danger of fire, and the overseer's office was close enough for convenience. Some plantations had, behind these two structures, pigeon houses, or dovecotes—and all had the inevitable slave quarters, usually in twin lines bordering a lane leading to cotton or sugarcane fields. When cotton gins and sugar mills came along, they were generally across the fields, out of sight of the main house.

What were they like, these main houses? In the beginning they were much like the simple "raised cottage" known as Madame John's Legacy, on New Orleans's Dumaine Street—with long, sloping roofs, with cement-covered brick walls on the ground floor, and with wood and brick (brick between posts) used in the living quarters on the second floor. They suited the sultry Louisiana climate and swampy building sites, and they made use of native materials. There's a distinct West Indies influence in houses of this colonial period, much unlike the grander styles that were to follow in the 1800s.

In the 1820s homes were built that combined traces of the West Indian style with some Greek Revival and Georgian influences—a style that has been dubbed Louisiana Classic. Large rounded columns usually surrounded the main body of the house, wide galleries reaching from the columns to the walls encircled upper floors, and the roof was a dormered one. The upper and lower floors consisted of four large rooms centered by a wide central hall. Their construction was entirely of native materials, with a few imported interior details such as fireplace mantels. Remember that there were no stone quarries in Louisiana, and if stone was used (which wasn't very often), it had to be shipped from New England and transported up the Mississippi from New Orleans. The river, on the other hand, flowed through banks of clay, there were all those slaves, and bricks could be made right on the spot. Cypress, too, was plentiful—and more than that, the water-loving wood was perfect for the hot, humid climate, which could quickly deteriorate those woods less impervious to its destructiveness. Thus the damp-resistant wood was used for house beams, and even for railings on the galleries (unlike the fancy cast iron so much used in New Orleans). To protect the homemade bricks from dampness, they were plastered or cement covered, and sometimes the outer coating was tinted, although more often it was left to mellow into a soft, off-white color. The columns were almost always of plastered brick and very occasionally of cypress wood. Even their capitals were of these materials, except for a rare instance when cast iron was used. These houses, then, took some features from European architecture, and some from the West Indian styles that so well suited the location, and adapted them to local building materials.

By the 1850s planters were more prosperous, and their homes became more grandiose. The extravagance of Victorian architecture was embraced and given a unique Louisiana flavor, the features of northern Italian villas crept in, and some plantation homes followed Gothic lines (notably the fantastic San Francisco Plantation, sometimes called "steamboat Gothic"). As planters and their families traveled to Europe more frequently, they brought home elegant furnishings for their houses, which had begun to grow in size as well as ornateness. European masters were imported for fine woodworking, until Louisiana artisans such as Mallard and Seignouret developed skills that rivaled or surpassed those from abroad. Ceilings were adorned by elaborate "medallions" from which glittering crystal chandeliers hung, and on wooden mantels and wainscoting the art of *faux marbre* ("false marble") began to appear. In short, plantation owners seemed determined to make their country homes every bit as elegant as their New Orleans town houses. They were developing a way of life dedicated to graciousness and hospitality unlike any other in American history.

As they grew in opulence, the plantation houses expanded in size—some had as many as 30 or 40 rooms. They were so large because families were quite large in those days. But even more important, if there was to be any social life in the country, it had to come from neighbors or friends visiting for several days or weeks. After all, travel being what it was, there just was no such thing as "popping in for a call." But there were other reasons, too, and they had to do with that well-known southern pride. Madewood, for example, over on Bayou Lafourche, was built for no other reason than to outshine the builder's brother, who had a beautiful home, Woodlawn, nearby. Two suitors of one young woman put up rival, massive houses in an attempt to win her affections. It was a simple case of antebellum "keeping up with the Joneses."

But underneath the planters' enormous wealth and power lay an economy built on the backs of slaves. It was, as world history has many times shown, an unhealthy foundation, and it crumbled, as was inevitable, with the beginning of the Civil War. Farming as it was then practiced was impossible without that large, cheap labor base. And, of course, as plantation owners went away to fight, the management of the plantations deteriorated even where slaves stayed on during the war. During Reconstruction, lands were often confiscated and turned over intact to those unfit or unable financially to continue the large-scale operation or broken up into smaller, more manageable farms. With increasing international competition, the cotton and sugar markets that had built such large fortunes started to crumble. And as industrialism moved south, there was no place for life as it had been lived in the golden plantation years.

It is hard to remember when you walk through the grand old homes left in the wake of the plantation era that the culture they embody had its beginning, reached a lofty pinnacle, and then died away in the span of less than 100 years. It has left as almost its only—and certainly its most eloquent—relic, houses the like of which will undoubtedly never again be seen.

The Plantation Houses Today

What has happened to these houses since the beginning of this century? Several have been the victims of fires or floods. Some have been torn down to make way for other things, such as industrial plants. Others, too costly to be maintained in modern times, have been left to the ravages of dampness and decay. But for a few, fate has been more kind—wealthy families have bought the houses and restored them with love and affection, retaining their feeling for "the good life" and filling them with family heirlooms or treasured antiques. The encroachment of modernity is restricted primarily to the installation of plumbing and electricity. Some are used only as private residences, but you can visit others for a small admission fee (which, in some instances, supplements the owner's own resources to keep up the old house). Not one single home open to the public is owned by descendants of the original owners. Today's visitors are, then, truly indebted to those "outsiders" who have gone to such lengths to preserve one part of our heritage that might otherwise disappear completely.

PLANNING YOUR TRIP

All the plantation homes shown on the map are within easy driving distance of New Orleans. How many you take in on any one day will depend, I suspect, on your endurance behind the wheel, your walking stamina (you'll cover a lot of ground touring the houses), and how early you set out. You'll be driving through "country" Louisiana, and I might as well warn you that some of what you'll see is really quite tacky—that modern, industrial economy just isn't pretty to look at. Also, don't expect to enjoy broad river views as you drive along River Road (the name given to the roadway on *both* sides of the Mississippi)—you'll have to drive up on the levee for that. You will, however, pass through little towns that date back to plantation days, and in your own car you'll have the luxury of turning off to inspect interesting old churches or above-ground cemeteries that can be glimpsed only from a tour bus window. I think it's a good idea to make your first plantation inspection via one of the excellent tours that you'll find listed, then take the car exploring after you've gained some familiarity with the territory. Another advantage of the tours is the detailed background information furnished by the guides—your own ramblings will be the better for it.

One more word about this particular group of homes: If you should happen to be in New Orleans on Christmas Eve and drive along River Road, your way will be lit by huge bonfires on the levees —they're to light the way for the Christ Child (an old Latin custom), and residents along here spend weeks collecting wood, trash, and anything that's flammable to make the fires blaze brightly.

Because not all Louisiana plantations actually bordered the Mississippi River (many were on bayous that also provided water transportation), some of the grand old homes have survived at locations too far away from New Orleans to be visited in a single day. I'm listing those separately, with the recommendation that you try to stay overnight at one of those that offer guest accommodations. I'll also include accommodations in Baton Rouge and St. Francisville, either of which can serve as a convenient tour base.

Tours from New Orleans

As I said in the beginning, it's an excellent idea to take a plantation-house bus tour from New Orleans before setting out on your own. Most of the tours visit only one or two of the houses I have described, leaving plenty for your private exploration. My experience has been that tour guides are exceptionally well informed, and the buses are an easy, comfortable way to get around in unfamiliar territory. Almost every tour company operates a River Road plantation tour.

One tour I especially like is the **Gray Line,** 2345 World Trade Center (tel. 504/587-0861), a 7-hour River Road Plantations Tour. The two plantations visited are San Francisco and Houmas House. All admissions are included in the $31 charge. Tours depart at 9am, and they pick you up and deliver you at your hotel. The cost of lunch at a country restaurant, however, is not included and generally runs $5 to $6, sometimes more.

If you prefer a smaller tour group, **Tours by Isabelle,** P.O. Box 740972, New Orleans, LA 70174 (tel. 504/367-3963), takes no more than 14 people in a comfortable minibus on a 10am to 5pm expedition to visit Houmas House and Nottoway Plantation. The price of lunch is included in the $65 tour fare. Call for information about half-day plantation tours and the Oak Alley Tour, which includes lunch and a swamp boat ride.

WITHIN THE NEW ORLEANS AREA

I'll start with the plantations nearest New Orleans and describe them, for ready reference, in the order in which they appear on the map, although that is not necessarily the order in which you will view them.

Destrehan Manor

Twenty-three miles from New Orleans, on the River Road, is Destrehan Manor, La. 48, Destrehan, LA 70047 (tel. 504/764-9315). A free person of color named Charles built this house in 1787. The wings on either side were added in 1805, and between 1830 and 1840, it was renovated from French Colonial to Greek Revival. Some of the largest live oaks in the state are on the grounds. Its double galleries are surrounded by Doric columns that support the central structure's hipped roof. Inside you can see the original woodwork and some interesting antiques. There's also a gift shop, and you can purchase light refreshments. The American Oil Company, which had bought the property, presented the house (in a state of deterioration) to the River Road Historical Society, and during its restoration some of the earliest methods of construction were uncovered. The society has left some glimpses of the construction open for visitors to see. Destrehan is the oldest plantation home remaining intact in the Lower Mississippi Valley that is open to the public.

It is open every day from 10am to 4pm (with guided tours) at a $5 admission charge for adults, $4 for teenagers and senior citizens, $3 for ages 6 to 11. It is free to preschoolers.

Ormond

A mile and a half above Destrehan (not shown on the map because it isn't open to the public), look for Ormond plantation house, a two-story structure with columns and gallery and a wing on each end. The house has in recent years been bought and beautifully restored as a private residence, but its early history is one of tragedy. Built sometime before 1790 by one Pierre de Trepagnier on land granted him by the Spanish government, it witnessed the mysterious disappearance of Pierre, when he went off with a complete stranger and was never seen or heard from again; the wiping out of almost an entire family by yellow fever; and the murder of its owner during Reconstruction, when his body was found riddled with bullets and hanging from a live oak tree. From all appearances it has now fallen on happier days and its future looks bright.

You can't go inside, but it is certainly worth a slowdown and long look as you pass by.

San Francisco

This fantastic mansion on La. 44 two miles north of Reserve (P.O. Drawer AX, Reserve, LA 70084; tel. 504/535-2341) was built in 1856 by a man who was obsessed by the great pleasure boats on which he had traveled. He was determined to transmit their lighthearted joyousness into a house that would forever remind him and his many friends of the gaiety aboard the steamboats. So, beginning with the Gothic architecture then in vogue, he overlaid it with overtones of the river queens, and what he came up with has been called "steamboat Gothic," a term later used as the title of a book by novelist Frances Parkinson Keyes in which the house itself appears. Sadly, the owner died shortly after his dream house was completed. His health and his finances (strained by the heavy construction costs) failed and he died, wryly calling the mansion "Sans Fruscin," which can be roughly translated as "without a red cent in my pocket" (from whence comes its present name, a corruption of that term). It was left to his sons.

His legacy is a fantasy come true even after all these years. The three-story house has broad galleries that look for all the world like a ship's double decks, and twin stairs lead to a broad main portal much like one that leads to a steamboat's grand salon. Galleries are trimmed with lacy railings between the fluted columns. Inside the owner created sheer beauty in every room through the use of carved woodwork and paintings alive with flowers, birds, nymphs, and cherubs on walls and ceilings of cypress tongue-and-groove boards. The dazzling restoration includes English and French 18th-century furniture and paintings.

You can go through the house daily except major holidays (including Mardi Gras Day) from 10am to 4pm. Admission is $5.50 for adults, $3.75 for ages 12 to 17, and $2.50 for ages 6 to 11. Children under 6 are free. There's also a small gift shop.

Tezcuco

On La. 44, just upriver from the Sunshine Bridge (55 miles from New Orleans), Tezcuco (it means "Resting Place") was one of the last plantation houses built before the Civil War. Although small, the raised cottage was some five years in the building, using slave labor, wood from surrounding swamps, and bricks from kilns on the plantation. Although the house follows the traditional floor plan of a central hall flanked by two rooms on either side, an unusual feature is the staircase leading to the gallery at each end, as well as the expected central stair. The grounds, densely planted with shrubs, wisteria, honeysuckle, and other native plants, contain huge live oaks draped with great cascades of moss, giving an almost ghostly appearance even in bright sunlight. There's a pleasant gazebo on the lawn and a rather large giftshop in the basement.

Tezcuco is open from 10am to 5pm daily May to October, to 4pm in other months. Admission is $5 for adults, $3.50 for teenagers 13 to 17, and $2.50 for children 4 to 12.

Oak Alley

On La. 18 between St. James and Vacherie, Oak Alley (mailing address: Route 2, Box 10, Vacherie, LA 70090; tel. 504/265-2151), is 60 miles from downtown New Orleans and probably the most famous plantation house in Louisiana. It was built in 1839 by Jacques Telesphore Roman III and named Bon Séjour—but if you'll walk out to the levee and look back at the quarter-mile avenue of live oaks (estimated to be about 300 years old), you'll see why steamboat passengers quickly dubbed it "Oak Alley," a name that soon replaced the original. Those trees were planted, it is thought, by an early settler; Roman was so enamored of them that he planned his house to have exactly as many columns—28 in all. The fluted Doric columns completely surround the Greek Revival house and support a broad second-story gallery. Inside, the floor plan is traditional, even to the attic, with a wide central hall flanked by two large rooms. Oak Alley lay disintegrating until 1914, when Mr. and Mrs. Jefferson Hardin, of New Orleans, bought it and moved in. Then in 1925 it passed to a Mr. and Mrs. Andrew Stewart, whose loving restoration is responsible for its National Historic Landmark designation. Both the Stewarts have passed on now, but two members of their staff, who have been here for years, stay on to guide visitors through the home. It is furnished just as it was during the Stewarts' lifetime—with a comfortably elegant mix of antiques and more modern pieces.

Oak Alley is open to the public from 9am to 5:30pm daily, and the admission is $5 for adults, $2.50 for students, and $1.50 for children. Overnight accommodations are available in several cottages at rates of $65 to $85. Also, there's a restaurant open for lunch, from 11am to 3pm daily.

Houmas House

Right on La. 942 near Burnside (tel. 504/473-7841) and 58 miles from New Orleans, this lovely old house had very humble beginnings in a four-room cabin built in the 1700s on land originally owned by members of the Houmas tribe. When the massive Greek Revival main house was built out front, the original house was retained and survives today. The impressive main house is 2½ stories tall, with 14 columns on three sides supporting the wide gallery. At either side are hexagonal *garçonnières* (remember, those were for the young male family members or for travelers who were put up for the night), and a carriageway is formed where the original house is connected to the main house. The late Dr. George Crozat, of New Orleans, purchased the house some years ago and went about restoring it as a comfortable home for himself and his mother, bringing in authentic furnishings of the period in which it was built.

The live oaks, magnolias, and formal gardens that surround Houmas House are magnificent and frame this house in a way that is precisely what comes to mind when most of us think "plantation house." It so closely fits that image that it's been used in the movies —you may, in fact, already have seen its exterior if you saw *Hush, Hush, Sweet Charlotte*. There's an interesting gift shop out back.

Dr. Crozat's heirs now open Houmas House daily (except major holidays) from 10am to 5pm February through October (closes at 4pm other months), and there's an admission fee for the guided tour of $7 for adults, $4 for ages 13 to 18, and $3 for ages 6 to 12. Children under 6 are free.

Ashland–Belle Hélène

On La. 75 between Geismar and Darrow (tel. 504/473-1328), about 70 miles from New Orleans and 25 miles from Baton Rouge, this huge house, taller than any other you're likely to see (its square columns are 4 feet square and some 30 feet high), was built in 1841 as a wedding present by Duncan Kenner, Confederate minister plenipotentiary to France, for his beautiful young bride. The galleries, surrounded by a colonnade of eight columns to a side, are 20 feet wide, the ground floor level paved with brick and tile. Originally the thick walls (plastered brick marked off to resemble stone) were tinted a lemon yellow, the shutters were an aqua blue, and the pillars were white—a study in pastels. At the end of the large central hall there's a spiral staircase, and all the rooms have marble mantels. Kenner named his home Ashland, after Henry Clay's residence, and it became well known for its gracious hospitality and fine wine cellar. A lover of horses, its owner also maintained locally famous stables.

After the Civil War the house was bought by a John Reuss, who renamed it Belle Hélène, after his granddaughter, but the original name was too closely associated with it to be dropped, so it gained the double title. By the mid-1900s the house was standing vacant, prey to the destructive forces of nature. Such was its visual appeal, however, that in 1957 it was used for scenes in *Band of Angels,* and *Beguiled* was filmed there in 1970.

Partially restored and partially furnished, Ashland–Belle Hélène is now open to the public daily from 9am to 5pm; the $5 admission goes toward further restoration of the house.

Madewood

You won't want to miss this magnificent house on Bayou Lafourche, just below Napoleonville on La. 308, one of the best preserved of the plantation mansions (mailing address: 4250 Highway 308, Napoleon, LA 70390; tel. 504/369-7151). It was built by the son of a wealthy planter who had originally come from North Carolina in 1818. Madewood was the creation of the youngest of three brothers, and it was built for the sole purpose of outdoing his older brother's elegant mansion, Woodlawn. Four years were spent cutting lumber and making bricks, and another four were spent in actual construction. It was finally completed in 1848, but its owner never got to gloat over his brother, for yellow fever carried him off just before it was finished.

The large, two-story Greek Revival house of stucco-covered brick is set on a low terrace, and on either side connecting wings duplicate its design. Inside the ceilings are 25 feet high, the central hallways are huge, as are the bedrooms; and there's a carved, winding walnut staircase. Madewood has more than 20 rooms, including a tremendous ballroom. Outside there's a carriage house and the family cemetery. Truly, it's more than worth the drive.

Madewood is open daily from 10am to 5pm (except major holidays), and admission is $4 for adults, $3 for students, and $2 for children under 12.

Overnight accommodations are offered here and are really rather special. If you elect to stay in one of the main-house guest rooms, you'll have the run of the place, much more like a guest in a private home than a paying member of the public. For example, you'll be greeted with wine and cheese in the library, dine by candlelight in the dining room, and have brandy and coffee in the parlor. There's no telephone or television in your room, only antique furnishings, wonderful old canopied beds, and coffee in bed the next morning. The rate ($150 for two) covers a sumptuous multicourse dinner of regional specialties (shrimp gumbo, fresh seafood and/or poultry, bread pudding, and so forth) and a plantation breakfast, as well as the cheese, wine, and brandy. Choose one of the four suites in an 1820s raised cabin and your rooms will be a little more informal in furnishings; the management will bring you wine and cheese, then leave you alone—and charge you only $85 for two. To reserve, call 504/369-7151.

Where to Dine

Lafitte's Landing Restaurant, at the foot of Sunshine Bridge on La. 70 Access Road (tel. 504/473-1232), is a huge raised cottage, built in 1797. It was said to be one of Jean Lafitte's hangouts, and today there's a good restaurant and lounge in the building, a good stopping point for lunch. The hours are 11am to 3pm and 6 to 10pm Tuesday through Saturday, 11am to 8pm on Sunday, and 11am to 3pm on Monday. Since the hours can change, you might want to call ahead to check or make reservations.

The Cabin is another good eating place appropriate to a day of plantation viewing. Located on La. 44 at La. 22 (tel. 504/473-3007), it is a slave cabin from the Monroe plantation, built about 1830. Nowadays it holds interesting antiques and good Cajun cooking. Hours are 8am to 3pm Monday through Wednesday, to 9pm on Thursday, to 10pm on Friday and Saturday, and to 6pm on Sunday.

BEYOND THE NEW ORLEANS AREA

Most of the plantations described below are clustered in the area around St. Francisville, north of Baton Rouge. An overnight stay is a virtual necessity if you want to see any number of these houses, and you'll really get into the spirit of things if you plan your overnight at any of the accommodations described below. You may, however, wish to stay in St. Francisville itself or even in Baton Rouge. At the end of this section, I'll tell you about accommodations in both places. If you plan to make Baton Rouge your base, the St. Francisville tour will cover approximately 100 miles, and you will want to set aside at least one full day, probably two. In Baton Rouge itself, there is one plantation home, and about 30 miles northwest there is another, both of which you may want to include in your sightseeing.

The very first thing you should do is contact the **Baton Rouge Area Information Center,** 730 North Blvd., Baton Rouge, LA 70802 (tel. 504/383-1825), to ask for their useful "Baton Rouge Visitors Guide," which contains maps of attractions in the city and surrounding area.

Magnolia Mound

This old home at 2161 Nicholson Drive, Baton Rouge, LA 70802 (tel. 504/343-4955) was built in the late 1700s as a small settler's house. As prosperity came to the lower Mississippi Valley, the house was enlarged and renovated, eventually becoming the center of a 900-acre plantation. Its single story is nearly 5 feet off the ground and has a front porch 80 feet across. The hand-carved wood-work and thick plank floors inside are still in excellent condition. Magnolia Mound takes its name from the grove of trees on a bluff overlooking the Mississippi, which is its setting. It is one of the oldest wooden structures in the state and is typical French Creole in architecture and furnished in Louisiana and early Federal style. Costumed guides take you through.

Tuesday through Saturday the house is open from 10am to 4pm, on Sunday from 1 to 4pm. Adults pay $4, students pay $2, and children pay $1.

Mount Hope Plantation

Mount Hope Plantation, 8151 Highland Road, Baton Rouge, LA 70808 (tel. 504/766-8600), is one of the earliest plantations in this area, built in 1817 by a German planter. The house has been beautifully restored and is furnished with Federal, Sheraton, and Empire antiques. There's also a small Civil War museum, and if you decide to stay overnight, your moderate bed-and-breakfast rate will include wine and fresh flowers on arrival, a tour of the house, and a full plantation breakfast.

House tours are conducted from 9am to 4pm Monday through Saturday (closed holidays), and admission is $4 for adults and $2 for children 12 and under.

Rural Life Museum

Louisiana State University's Rural Life Museum, 6200 Burden Lane, Baton Rouge, LA 70808 (tel. 504/765-2437) is a marvelous open-air museum on Burden Research Plantation at Essen and I-10. Authentically restored buildings include an overseer's house, slave cabins, a one-room school, country church, and a barn that holds artifacts dealing with rural life from the 18th century to the early 20th century. The hours are 8:30am to 4pm Monday through Friday, with a $3 adminission for adults and $2 for children under 12.

Nottoway Plantation

To reach Nottoway Plantation (mailing address: Mississippi River Road, White Castle, LA 70788; tel. 504/545-2730) from Baton Rouge, take I-10 West to the Plaquemine exit, then La. 1 south for 18 miles. (From New Orleans, follow I-10 West to the La. 22 exit, then make a left on La. 70 across the Sunshine Bridge; exit onto La. 1 and drive 14 miles north through Donaldsonville).

This magnificent house has been likened to a castle, and you're likely to agree when you see its 22 enormous columns that support the original slate roof. Built in 1859, a blend of Greek Revival and Italianate, the house has 64 rooms and a total area of over 53,000 square feet. It was saved from Civil War destruction by the kindness of a northern gunboat officer who had once been a guest there, and kindness still blesses it, for the present owners have lovingly re-stored its rooms to their former glory. The white ballroom, with its hand-carved cypress Corinthian columns, archways, delicate plaster friezework, and original crystal chandeliers, is especially lovely.

Randolph Hall restaurant serves lunch from 11am to 3pm and dinner from 6 to 9pm, and you may stay overnight in one of those restored bedrooms with private bath for $120 to $250 double occupancy, which includes a wake-up tray of hot sweet-potato muffins, a full plantation breakfast served on the garden veranda, and tour of the house. Even if you're not staying, take the tour: 9am to 5pm daily (except for Christmas), for which there is an $8 fee for adults and a $3 fee for children 12 or under.

Parlange

To reach this plantation, one of the few that still functions as a working farm, drive 19 miles west on U.S. 190, then 10 miles north on La. 1 (HC62, New Roads, LA 70760; tel. 504/638-8410). Built in 1750 by the Marquis Vincent de Ternant, the house is one of the oldest in the state, and its two stories rise above a raised brick basement. Galleries encircle the house, and there are two brick *pigeonniers,* one on either side. Indigo was planted here at first, then in the 1800s sugarcane became the plantation's main crop. Today, sugarcane, corn, and soybeans are grown, and the plantation also supports its own cattle. During the Civil War this house was host to generals from both sides (Gen. Nathaniel Banks of the Union and Gen. Dick Taylor of the Confederacy)—not, of course, at the same time.

You can visit Parlange daily from 9am to 5pm. There's a $5 admission charge for adults and $2.50 charge for children 6 to 12.

Asphodel

Located on La. 68 (south of La. 10 and north of U.S. 61), Asphodel (Rt. 2, Box 89, Jackson, LA 70748; tel. 504/654-6868) is a charming example of the Greek Revival style popular in the 1800s. It was built about 1833 and consists of a raised central section with two identical wings of brick covered with a smooth plaster made with sand from a nearby creek. Doric columns line the gallery of the central section and support its gabled roof. Each of the wings has its own small porch. Asphodel has been seen in films, such as *The Long Hot Summer.* On the grounds, the old Levy house (built in the 1840s) was moved here in recent years and is now used as an inn and a very fine restaurant. In addition to the mansion itself (now the private home of its current owners), there are leafy forest trails open to visitors.

Asphodel is open Monday through Friday from 10am to 4pm and by appointment only on Saturday and Sunday for groups. Admission is $3.

Oakley

Oakley Plantation (tel. 504/635-3739) is on La. 965, three miles east of U.S. 61. This lovely old house is where John James Audubon came to study and paint the wildlife of this part of Louisiana. The house itself was built in 1799 and is a three-story frame house with the raised basement so typical of that era. The two galleries are joined by a curved stairway, and the whole house has a simplicity that bespeaks its age. When Audubon was here, he tutored a daughter of the family and painted some 32 of his *Birds of America* series. When you visit it today, you will see some original prints from Audubon's *Elephant Folio* and many fine antiques. A walk through the gardens and nature trails will explain why this location had such appeal for Audubon. Oakley is, as a matter of fact, now a part of the 100-acre Audubon State Commemorative Area, a wildlife sanctuary that would have gladdened the naturalist's heart. In the kitchen building there is now a gift shop, but you can still see the huge old kitchen fireplace where the family's meals were once cooked.

The house is open from 9am to 5pm Monday through Saturday, and from 1 to 5pm on Sunday. There is a $4 charge (for up to four people in a car, 50¢ for each additional) to visit the grounds and an additional $3 fee if you would like to tour the house. Those under 6 or over 61 are admitted free.

Rosedown Plantation and Gardens

Just east of St. Francisville on I-10 and U.S. 61, you'll find Rosedown (mailing address: Box 1816, St. Francisville, LA 70775-1816; tel. 504/635-3332). This truly magnificent home was built in 1835 by a descendant of George Washington on land that was a Spanish land grant back in 1789 to one of the founders of the Port of Bayou Sara on the Mississippi River. The two-story house, flanked by one-story wings, combines classic and indigenous Louisiana styles. There are the typical columns and wide galleries across the front, and the house is made of cement-covered brick. A wide avenue of ancient oaks, their branches meeting overhead, leads up to the house, and the formal gardens are as impressive as the house itself. As is altogether fitting in such a garden, marble statues of gods and goddesses are dotted along the winding pathways. Inside the house still holds the massive furniture of its original owner, as well as a winding stairway and many beautiful murals and paintings. Rosedown is one of the most beautiful examples of antebellum plantation homes, and whether you're into architecture, antiques, or horticulture—or simply a lover of beauty—you'll find this an interesting stop.

Rosedown is open March through October from 9am to 5pm every day, and November through February from 10am to 4pm. It is closed December 24 and 25. There's a $7 admission charge for the house and gardens, and $4 for the gardens only.

Catalpa Plantation

This lovely old plantation (P.O. Box 131, St. Francisville, LA 70775; tel. 504/635-3372) is 5 miles north of St. Francisville off U.S. 61. The great oaks that line the unusual elliptical drive leading up to the house were planted from acorns by Mamie Thompson's great-great-great-grandfather. This charming woman, Catalpa's present owner, leads guests through her home, regaling them with stories about the many family heirlooms and priceless antiques within its walls (the slightly dented silver tea service, for example, lay buried in a pond during the Civil War, and the lovely hand-painted china was done by none other than John James Audobon). Mrs. Thompson often greets guests with sherry and homemade cheese biscuits, then invites them to linger on the front porch for coffee at the tour's end.

Catalpa is open from 9am to 5pm every day, except during the months of December and January when it's closed (except by appointment). Admission is $4 for adults and $2 for ages 6 to 12. Children under 6 are free.

The Myrtles

Located on U.S. 61, a little over one mile north of La. 10 (mailing address: P.O. Box 1100, St. Francisville, LA 70775; tel. 504/635-6277), this beautiful house was built in 1795. Its gallery measures 110 feet in length and the elaborate iron grillwork is reminiscent of French Quarter houses in New Orleans. The Myrtles is in an astonishingly good state of preservation, especially inside, where the intricate plaster moldings are still intact in each room, and the silver doorknobs (glass-coated) and even colonial wallpaper in the entry hall are just as they were when the house was built. The 1½-story house is set in a grove of great old live oaks, as is only fitting for a place that is locally believed to have at least one ghost. When this old home was restored in recent years, much attention was given to filling it with furnishings authentic to the period in which it was built. You can visit the Myrtles from 9am to 5pm daily except Christmas. Adults pay $4.50 admission; children pay $2.50. Overnight accommodations are available with private or shared baths at rates of $65 to $120 double, which includes plantation breakfast and tour. There are also "Mystery Weekends" that are great fun—call for details and prices.

Afton Villa Gardens

There's no longer a great plantation home on this site (a little over 3 miles north of St. Francisville on U.S. 61), but Afton Villa (mailing address: Box 993, Highway 61 N, St. Francisville, LA 70775; tel. 504/635-6773) was one of the finest until it burned in 1963. Its alley of great oak trees (one of the longest known) is still there, as are the beautiful formal gardens with their boxwood maze and statuary. The Gothic gatehouse also remains. The gardens are a real delight, with something flowering almost every season. It is perhaps at its best, however, in March and April, when you can visit from 9am to 4:30pm Wednesday through Sunday; it is closed July through September and December through February. Admission is $2 for adults. Children under 16 are free.

The Cottage

This rambling country home on U.S. 61 five miles north of St. Francisville (mailing address: Box 425, St. Francisville, LA 70775; tel. 504/635-3674) is really a series of buildings constructed between 1795 and 1859. For my money, this is *the* place to make your headquarters (see "Where to Stay," below). The low, two-story house has a long gallery out front, a perfect place to sit and relax for an evening. The first house was built entirely of virgin cypress taken from the grounds. Many of the outbuildings date from 1811, when Judge Thomas Butler (of "the Fighting Butlers," so prominent in American history) acquired the property. The judge carried on the family tradition of involvement in national affairs, as did his children after him. In fact, after his victory at the Battle of New Orleans, Gen. Andrew Jackson, along with a troop of officers (including no fewer than *eight* Butlers), stopped off here for a 3-week stay on his way from New Orleans to Natchez. Among the historic treasures on the grounds is a shiny, custom-designed carriage made for the judge in 1820.

There are several outbuildings still intact, one of them a miniature cottage that was Judge Butler's office until his death, after which it became the plantation schoolhouse. Only 2 of the original 25 slave cabins remain. The interior of the Cottage looks very much as it did when the Butlers lived here, with hand-screened wallpaper, an 1800s love seat (with space for a chaperone), and needlepoint fire screens made by the ladies of the Butler family. This is a working plantation of some 360 acres. It takes little or no imagination when staying at the Cottage to feel that you've managed to step through a time warp back to the days when plantation homes were not "open to the public" but were the center of a gracious, now-vanished way of life.

Even if you don't stay as a guest, do visit. The hours are 9am to 5pm daily; admission is $4 per person.

WHERE TO STAY

In Baton Rouge there's the **Hilton Baton Rouge,** 5500 Hilton Ave., Baton Rouge, LA 70808 (tel. 504/924-5000). Rooms are all Hilton quality, there's a pool room and health spa, a lounge with entertainment and dancing, and a very good dining room. Doubles range from $69 to $90, and family rates are available.

If a motel suits you better, try the **Best Western Baton Rouge,** 10920 Mead Rd. (at the Sherwood Forest Boulevard exit off I-12), Baton Rouge, LA 70816 (tel. 504/293-9370, or toll free 800/528-1234). The nicely furnished rooms have some oversize beds, and there's a pool, dining room, and a lounge with entertainment and dancing Tuesday through Saturday. Double rates start at $38.

In St. Francisville your best bet is the **St. Francis Hotel on the Lake,** P.O. Box 440, St. Francisville, LA 70775 (tel. 504/635-3821, or toll free 800/826-9931 in La., 800/523-6118 in all other states). It's on Highway 61 Bypass, with 101 attractive guest rooms with cable TV (some with handicapped facilities), a restaurant, a coffee shop, a lounge, an outdoor pool, and dog kennels. The rates are in the $41 to $53 range.

To really get into the spirit of a plantation homes tour, you can't do better than **The Cottage,** on U.S. 61 five miles north of La. 10 (mailing address: Box 425, St. Francisville, LA 70775; tel. 504/635-3674). A full description of the house has already been given above, but I probably should add that the owners have, rather whimsically, planted a few rows of cotton between the camellias and azaleas in the garden, so if you've never seen King Cotton in its native habitat, this is your chance. On steamy hot days you can cool off in the swimming pool. There are two rooms in the main house and three in the wing added in 1850, all furnished with lovely antiques (even some canopied four-poster beds). A highlight of any stay here is the early-morning (8am) serving of steaming chicory coffee, with fresh cream and sugar, on a silver tray with bone china cups—and it comes, in old plantation style, right to your bedroom door. Half an hour later you sit down to a full plantation breakfast in the formal dining room. It's a splendid repast of hickory-smoked bacon, eggs, grits (naturally), coffee, and homemade biscuits—an absolutely perfect way to begin the day. There's also Mattie's House Restaurant on the grounds for dinner. Best of all, there's no extra charge—it comes with your room. A tour of the house and grounds is also included in room rates, which are $75 for doubles and $65 for singles. This place is popular with weekenders from New Orleans and other neighboring towns, as well as with tourists, which makes it essential to book as far ahead as you possibly can.

See also the accommodations at Mount Hope Plantation, Madewood, Nottoway Plantation, and the Myrtles (above). All should be booked well in advance.

For bed-and-breakfast, the **Barrow House,** 524 Royal St. (P.O. Box 1461), St. Francisville, LA 70775 (tel. 504/635-4791), is right in the heart of St. Francisville's historic district in a quiet neighborhood of antebellum homes. The original 1809 two-story saltbox structure had four rooms connected by an outside staircase, architecture typical of the times. Later a cottage with a Greek Revival–style façade was added. Owned now by an enterprising couple who moved here from Houston, the house has been lovingly restored and furnished in period pieces circa the 1860s. All guest rooms have French doors opening to balconies or porches overlooking Royal Street. Shirley and Lyle, the personable owners/innkeepers, serve morning coffee and evening drinks on the large screened porch. With advance notice, they'll also dish up dinner. Two of the five guest rooms have shared baths, three have private facilities, and you can opt for a full or continental breakfast. Rates are $50 single and $75 for a two-room suite.

For help in finding other bed-and-breakfast facilities throughout Louisiana, contact the **Southern Comfort Bed & Breakfast Reservation Service,** 2856 Hundred Oaks, Baton Rouge, LA 70808 (tel. 504/346-1928 or 928-9815, or toll free 800/749-1928).

WHERE TO DINE

Steak lovers who became addicted to **Ruth's Chris Steak House** in New Orleans will be happy to know there's a branch at 4836 Constitution, Baton Rouge (tel. 504/925-0163), with the same high-quality meats and the same moderate price range ($10 to $15 at lunch, $10 to $25 at dinner). The hours are 11:30am to 11:30pm Monday through Friday and 4pm to midnight on Saturday. It is closed Sundays.

There's also a branch of the famous **Mulate's Cajun Restaurant** (from Breaux Bridge) in Baton Rouge at 8322 Bluebonnet (near I-10; tel. 767-4794), with the same Cajun friendliness, great food, and live Cajun music every night of the week.

Mike Anderson's Seafood, 1031 W. Lee Dr., (tel. 766-7823), is one of Baton Rouge's better seafood eateries, yet it's surprisingly inexpensive. The menu holds a multitude of finny and shelly choices, prepared in every manner you can imagine. Freshness is everything here; the portions are quite large, and the prices are low (under $15 for a full dinner). The hours are 11:30am to 10pm Monday through Thursday, 11:30am to 11pm Friday and Saturday, and 11:30am to 9pm Sunday.

---

2. Cajun Country

Just what *is* Cajun Country? Its official name is Acadiana, and it consists of a rough triangle of Louisiana made up of 22 parishes (counties), from St. Landry Parish at the top of the triangle to the Gulf of Mexico at its base. Lafayette is its "capital," and it's dotted with towns and names such as St. Martinville and New Iberia and Abbeville and Jeanerette. Oh, you won't find its boundaries marked on any map with the name "Acadiana" stamped across it. And yet, there lives within those 22 parishes a people whose history and culture and way of life is so distinctive that crossing into this area is not much different from stepping over the portals of another country. Even their language differs from that found anywhere else in the world.

BACKGROUND

The People

And just *who* are these Acadians, or "Cajuns"? If you've gone through the standard American schooling, you probably already know something about them. Think of Henry Wadsworth Longfellow's epic poem *Evangeline*—the story of two lovers who spent their lives wandering the face of this land searching for each other after being wrenched from their own homeland. Evangeline and her Gabriel were Acadians, part of a tragic band of French Canadians who became the forefathers of today's Cajuns.

Their story began in the early 1600s, when colonists from France immigrated to the southeastern coast of Canada. There, in a region they named Acadia, they developed a peaceful, agricultural culture based on the simple values of a strong religious faith (Catholic), a deep love of family, and an abiding respect for their relatively small land holdings. Isolated from the mainstream of European culture for nearly a century and a half, their way of life was one of hard work lightened by pleasant gatherings of families and friends when work was over and punctuated by their unwavering devotion to their church. It was a satisfying, pastoral existence until 1713, when Acadia became the property of the British under the

Treaty of Utrecht. Even then, the Acadians were determined to maintain their peaceful existence under the new rulers, but that was to prove impossible. For more than 40 years they were continually harassed by representatives of the British king in an attempt to force them to pledge allegiance to that monarch, and in so doing to renounce Catholicism and embrace the king's Protestant religion. That course was so abhorrent to Acadians, and they were so steadfast in their refusals, that in 1755 the British governor of the region sent troops to seize their farms and ships to deport them. Villages were burned; husbands and wives and children were separated as ships were loaded; and a 10-year odyssey began for these sturdy, gentle people.

Some were returned to France, some went to England, many were put ashore in the English colonies along America's east coast, and some wound up in the West Indies. The deportation voyages, made on poorly equipped, overcrowded ships—none had enough food, clothing, or other provisions for their large human cargos—took a huge toll, and hundreds of lives were lost in the process. As for the survivors, so strongly ingrained was their Acadian culture that many who were sent to France and England returned to America as much as 20 years later. Those who went ashore in Massachusetts, Connecticut, New York, and Pennsylvania went varied ways—some went into indentured service for a few years to labor-hungry colonial merchants and farmers, some immediately took to the long overland walk back to Canadian territory, but *all* held foremost in their aims a reunion with families from whom they'd been so rudely torn. Those taken to Maryland were met with a somewhat warmer welcome by colonists there and were given greater latitude in work and living quarters until they, too, could take up the search for loved ones.

Louisiana, with its strong French background, was a natural destination for Acadians hoping to re-establish a permanent home, and it was probably those who were transported to the West Indies who first headed in that direction. By 1763 there was a fairly large contingent in the New Orleans area. The territory was under Spanish domination at the time, but the shared Catholic religion and the natural industriousness of the newcomers made them welcome by the governing bodies, and many Acadians were given land grants in outlying areas. In 1765 one Bernard Andry brought a band of 231 men, women, and children to the region now known as Acadiana. Joseph Broussard, one of the Acadian leaders, was instrumental in making an agreement with one of the largest landowners to give each immigrant family the use of one bull and five cows with calves for six consecutive years. They agreed, at the end of that time, to return the same amount of livestock, plus one-half the increase or the money realized from the sale of one-half the increase.

The land on which they settled differed greatly from that they had left in Nova Scotia. The swampy land was low-lying and boggy, interlaced with bayous and lakes. No one has ever come up with an exact description of the bayous (called "bayuk" by the Choctaw). Longfellow's poem comes close when he relates about the arriving Acadians:

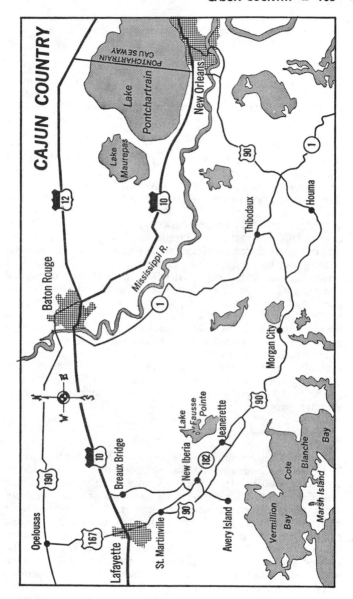

Soon were lost in a maze of sluggish and devious waters,
Which, like a network of steel, extended in every direction.
Over their heads, the towering and tenebrous boughs of
    the cypress

Met in a dusky arch, and trailing mosses in mid-air,
Waved like banners that hang on the walls of ancient
cathedrals.

Suffice it to say that a bayou is something less than a river but more than a creek; and it is sluggish, with little or no current. But the swamps were forested with live oak, willow, ash, and gum, and they were teeming with wildlife. Granted land that mostly bounded the bayous, the Acadians went to work with a will, building small levees, or dikes, along the banks, draining fields for small farms and pastures, and taking to the swamps to hunt and trap the plentiful game for food and furs. The isolation of their new home did not bother them a bit—it was perhaps the only thing this location had in common with the homeland they had left.

Always attuned to family closeness, sons would build homes close to fathers, and thus small settlements developed. The homes they constructed were marvelously adapted to the locale. From the swamps they took cypress for their houses. To provide insulation between inner and outer walls, they again turned to natural materials, filling spaces with a mixture of mud and Spanish moss (*bousillage*). They pitched roofs high so that the frequent rains would drain off, and they utilized the attic space thus created as sleeping quarters for the family's young men (this was called a *garçonnière*). And in order to get maximum use from every inch of interior space on the ground floor, stairways up to the *garçonnières* were placed outside on the front porch. The stairs did double duty as seating space when families gathered at one house (for that matter, so did the porch itself, which was many times used for extra sleeping space).

Cuisine

From their surroundings, too, came much of what has come to be known as Cajun cooking. Taking foods that could be locally grown, the Acadians based the preparation of these foods on their own French culinary heritage, threw in some of the Spanish treatment, added a bit of Native American methods (they'd always gotten on well with local Native Americans, both in Nova Scotia and in Louisiana), picked up African secrets from blacks, and came up with a unique cuisine that is now justly famous. The dishes that evolved are based on a roux, made by combining oil and flour, which is slowly browned in a heavy pot. Into the roux go seasonings and native meat or seafood (sometimes both), and the mixture is left to simmer until (as one Cajun told me) it is "good." As a variation, okra is sometimes used to make gumbo instead of the roux. In that case, one final step is omitted—filé (ground sassafras leaves), which is added to all roux-based gumbo when it is served into the bowl (*never* during cooking), does not appear in the okra-based dishes. Served over rice, either version is delicious. Combining various meats and seafoods with rice and seasonings, the Acadians created jambalaya. And from the plentiful crayfish, they came up with crayfish étouffée, a rich blending of the small, fresh-water cousin of the lobster with those delectable seasonings, again serving the result on a bed of rice. What all this adds up to is some of the best, and most unique, eating in the world—the food alone is sufficient justification for an expedition into Cajun Country. One final word about this wonderful feast: The Cajuns will invariably doctor any or all of these specialties with a dash of hot sauce (usually that produced on the large hot-pepper plantation near New Iberia, known to us all as "Tabasco"). If you follow their lead, do so with caution—when they say "hot," they mean *hot!*

Music

Cooking is an important ingredient of any large family gathering whatever the occasion, whether it be to help one another with harvests or slaughtering, celebrate the end of such tasks, or just to enjoy a sociable hour or two together. Another ingredient, equally important, is the music, which any Cajun will tell you makes the food taste better. Its roots are probably those of medieval France, and it is almost wholly an orally transmitted art form (few Cajun melodies have ever been committed to paper). The simple lyrics and strains are either very sad or very happy, and I defy you to listen to one of the numbers and keep your feet still. From the time when they used only a fiddle and triangle, Cajun musicians have expanded and now play guitars, harmonicas, accordions, and drums, but always with the distinctive sound of their special music. The best possible place to hear the music is at a *fais-dodo* (a term once used to tell the babies to "go to sleep" when they were stashed in a room apart from the one in which there would be dancing in someone's home). Nowadays a *fais-dodo* usually takes place in a dance hall, in a village square, or even in the streets, and if you're lucky enough to run across one, stop the car and join in—the Cajuns *love* company, and in no time at all you'll be dancing with the best of them. And if you don't just happen on a dance, feel free to drop in at any dance hall you pass, no matter its outer appearance. (If you can hear live music, don't hesitate to go in, for you won't be a stranger long.)

Special note: If you become completely beguiled by this special music and the special people who play it—and if you're hardy enough for an early Saturday-morning drive—there's a unique happening you won't want to miss in the little town of Mamou, some 53 miles northwest of Lafayette. (To get there, take I-10 West to the Crowley/Eunice exit, turn right on La. 13, and Mamou is about 32 miles north of Crowley, 11 miles north of Eunice.) Every Saturday, at about 8am, Cajuns from miles around congregate in **Fred's Lounge,** 420 6th Street (tel. 318/468-5411), for a live broadcast of music, local news, and commercials the likes of which you won't hear anywhere else. Broadcast times are 9:15 to 11am (on station KVPI, 1050 AM on the dial), but the music swings right on to 1pm. Never mind the early hour, the ambience is that of a nighttime get-together, with conviviality running high and the bar doing a brisk business. This is no slick broadcast—the "studio" is a roped-off section of the dance floor, the men behind the mikes and instruments are rugged Cajuns who work hard in the outdoors all week, and the audience crowds the floor dancing with friends and neighbors. It's a memorable experience! Incidentally if you should meet Fred, his last name is Tate.

PLANNING YOUR TRIP

Well, that's Cajun Country and the people who inhabit it, albeit in very abbreviated form. Just one thing remains to be straightened out, and it has to do with Mr. Longfellow and his poem. The real Evangeline was Emmeline Labiche, and her sweetheart was named Louis Pierre Arceneaux. And their story has a different ending from the one the poet assigned to his two lovers. Emmeline found her Louis Pierre, after many years of searching, right in Cajun Country in the town of St. Martinville. The real-life tragedy was that by then Louis had given up hope of ever finding her and was pledged to another. She died of a broken heart in Louisiana, *not* in Philadelphia as in the poem. With that set right, let's talk about the best way to explore Acadiana as a visitor and what you can expect to find there.

The Cajun Country map shows a circular drive that could allow you to take in one or two of the plantation homes en route to Baton Rouge (if you take River Road instead of I-10 as shown here) before turning west on I-10 to reach Lafayette. The Interstate highway runs along the edge of Acadiana, but the little town of Breaux Bridge, just off it on La. 31, is real Cajun Country, and of course Lafayette is its heart. A return to New Orleans via U.S. 90 will take you right through the history, legend, and romance of this region. It's too long a drive for one day, and you'll want to book accommodations in Lafayette for at least a one-night stay. If you take I-10, the distance from New Orleans to Lafayette is 134 miles; from Lafayette to New Orleans via U.S. 90 is 167 miles. You should know in advance, however, that this is true "wandering country," which explains why I wouldn't *dare* set out a step-by-step itinerary. I'll list some of the things to be sure not to miss, confident that you will find scores of other Cajun Country attractions on your own. Along the way I'll mention some of the outstanding Cajun restaurants (but rest assured, it's almost impossible to get bad food out here), and tell you about places to stay overnight.

The best tip I can give you, however, is that you write or call ahead to the **Lafayette Parish Convention and Visitors Commission Center,** P.O. Box 52066, Lafayette, LA 70505 (tel. 318/232-3808, or toll free 800/346-1958 in the U.S. outside Louisiana, 800/543-5340 in Montreal and Quebec)—it'll send you tons of detailed information to make your trip even more fun. The center is open from 9am to 5pm seven days a week, if you want to stop in while you're there (the driving directions are in the section on Lafayette, below).

If there is just no way you can find time to get out to Cajun Country for an extended visit, I suggest that you take one of the excellent day tours listed at the end of this section. It's a good introduction to the area, and maybe on your next New Orleans visit (and rest assured, there will be another) you will be able to drive out for an in-depth exploration of this fascinating region.

If, on the other hand, you can get here during festival time (see Chapter III), you'll have a terrific time, right along with native Cajuns, who enjoy their festivals with real gusto.

BREAUX BRIDGE

Just off I-10 on La. 31, this little town, founded in 1859, prides itself on being the "Crayfish Capital of the World." Its famous Crayfish Festival and Fair has drawn as many as 100,000 to the town of 4,500 permanent residents, and it's the most Cajun affair you can imagine, with music, a unique "bayou" parade, crayfish races, crayfish-eating contests, and lots more. It's such a splendiferous party, in fact, that it takes a full year to recover. It's always held the first week in May. Lucky you, if that's when you plan to come. Otherwise, you'll have to be content with stopping by for some of the best Cajun eating to be found (see the "Where to Dine" section that follows, for one very special recommendation).

LAFAYETTE

If you haven't written to it in advance, make your first stop at the office of the **Lafayette Parish Convention and Visitors Commission Center,** where the helpful staff will tell you everything you could possibly want to know about their region and send you out loaded with material to enlighten your stay. You'll find the center by turning off I-10 onto U.S. 167 South (it's the first exit), and the office is in the center of the median at 1400 NW Evangeline Thruway (tel. 318/232-3808, or toll free 800/346-1958 in the U.S. outside Louisiana, 800/543-5340 in Montreal and Quebec). Located near the intersection of Willow Street and the Thruway, the attractive offices are housed in Cajun-style homes set in landscaped grounds that include a pond and benches. It is a restful spot to sit and plan your Cajun Country excursion. The center is open from 9am to 5pm daily.

Acadian Village

Just south of La. 342, on Mouton Road, you'll find a reconstructed (actually, a reassembled) Cajun bayou community at Acadian Village (tel. 318/981-2364). Houses have been moved from original locations to this site beside a sleepy bayou and a footpath on its banks takes you past these historic structures. The buildings hold a representative collection of Cajun furnishings. There's a gift shop, too, where you can buy Cajun handcrafts and an interesting selection of books on this unique culture. The village is open daily (except holidays) from 10am through 5pm, with a small admission fee.

Vermilionville

A recent addition to the Lafayette scene is the marvelous reconstruction of a Cajun/Creole bayou village from the 1765 to 1890 era. Vermilionville, 1600 Surry Street, Beaver Park (tel. 318/233-4077, or toll free 800/99-BAYOU), sits on the banks of the brooding Bayou Vermilion, directly adjacent to the airport on U.S. 90. Hundreds of skilled artisans labored to restore original Cajun homes and to reconstruct others that were typical of such a village but unavailable. Homes of every level in society are represented, from the most humble to one of a well-to-do farmer. The costumed staff in each give a vivid demonstration of daily life back then; craftspeople ply their crafts in traditional ways; and, in the performance center, authentic music, plays, dancing, and storytelling hold sway. There's a restaurant serving Cajun/Creole cuisine and a gift shop. It's a great introduction to the Cajun way of life and a pleasant way to spend an afternoon. Vermilionville is open 9am to 9pm from Memorial Day to Labor Day; 10am to 6pm weekdays, 9am to 9pm weekends other months. Adults pay $8, senior citizens pay $6.50, and students pay $5. It is free for those under 6.

The Lafayette Museum

Louisiana's first Democratic governor, Alexandre Mouton, once lived in the antebellum town house (built in the early 1800s) with square columns and two galleries that now houses the Lafayette Museum at 1122 Lafayette Street (tel. 318/234-2208). Its cupola, attic, and entire second floor, incidentally, were added in 1849. Inside, in addition to the antiques, paintings, and historic documents you might expect to find, there's a colorful collection of Mardi Gras costumes that were worn by Lafayette's krewe kings and queens. Admission is $3 for adults, $2 for senior citizens, and $1 for students (of any age). The hours are 9am to 5pm Tuesday through Saturday and 3 to 5pm on Sunday (except for major holidays, when it's closed).

Cypress Lake

In the very heart of Lafayette, on the University of Southwestern Louisiana grounds, there's a lovely **natural swamp** environment. Although small, it gives the effect of being in the wild, and during warm months you'll actually see alligators. Water birds of several varieties, as well as turtles, are almost always on hand, and during the month of April the swamp is abloom with Louisiana irises. If you want to know more about the lake and how it is used as a teaching tool, contact the University News Service, University of Southwestern Louisiana, Lafayette, LA 70504 (tel. 318/231-6475). If you just want to get closer to the sort of swampland seen most often from highways, you'll find Cypress Lake next to the Student Union on the USL campus, between St. Mary Boulevard and University Avenue, Hebrard Boulevard and McKinley Street.

One of Cajun Country's most intriguing plantation mansions is only a short drive (about 15 miles) north of Lafayette. To reach **Cretien Point Plantation,** Rt. 1, Box 162, Sunset, LA 70584 (tel. 318/233-7050 or 662-5876), take I-10 west to Exit 97, then drive north about 8 miles through Ossun, Vatican, and Cankton. A little over 2 miles north of Cankton, turn left onto Parish Road 356 (toward Bristol), then turn right on Cretien Point Road, and the plantation is about a mile farther on your left.

Allow yourself at least an hour to explore this columned home that was built in 1831 on a 1776 Spanish land grant. The house itself is fascinating, but even more so are the tales of its owners in the past. Its history includes links to privateer Jean Lafitte, a flamboyant gambler, his equally flamboyant widow, a ghost or two, a buried treasure (never recovered), and a Civil War battle fought right out front. And if you remember the scene in *Gone with the Wind* in which Scarlett O'Hara shoots a marauding soldier on the staircase at Tara, you'll see the staircase that was copied for the movie. The plantation is open daily from 10am to 5pm (last tour starts at 4pm) except for major holidays. Adults pay $5 and those under 12 pay $2.50.

A Special Sports Note

If you're in Cajun Country between the first week in April and Labor Day and happen to be a devotee of the "sport of kings," you can enjoy an evening of racing at **Evangeline Downs,** 3 miles north on U.S. 167. Post time and racing days change periodically, so be sure to check. Don't bring the kids, though—no minors are allowed. For current schedules and clubhouse reservations, call 318/896-RACE.

Near Henderson

Having met the engaging Cajuns who live in this region, you really shouldn't leave without exploring the bayous and swamps that have helped shape their hardy character. Gliding through misty bayous dotted with gnarled cypress trees dripping Spanish moss, seeing native water creatures and birds in their natural habitat, and learning just how Cajuns harvest their beloved crayfish—it's an experience not to be missed. To arrange just such a voyage, contact Terry Angelle at **Angelle's Atchafalaya Basin Swamp Tours,** Whiskey River Landing, P.O. Box 111, Cecilla, LA 70521 (tel. 318/228-8567). His tour gives you nearly 2 hours in this third-largest swamp in the United States, and guides are Cajuns who have spent their lives thereabouts and who travel the mysterious waterways as easily as you and I walk city streets. There's a glass-enclosed boat for large groups and a small, open boat for up to four. The fares are $8 for adults and $4 for those under 12, with a $25 minimum per tour. Departure times are 10am and 1, 3, and 5pm (the last only during summer months).

To reach Whiskey River Landing from I-10, take Exit 115 to Henderson, go through Henderson to the levee, and turn right. The Landing is the third exit on the left.

OPELOUSAS

This historic old town to the north of Lafayette on U.S. 167 was founded in 1720 and was the longtime home of an early American hero. Jim Bowie, a hero of the Alamo and the inventor of the Bowie Knife, lived here, and you can see a fine collection of his possesions and memorabilia at the **Jim Bowie Museum,** at 220 Academy Street (tel. 318/984-6263). It's open from 8am to 4pm Monday to Friday, and the museum is free. The Acadiana Tourist Information Center is in the same building.

No matter what time of day you arrive in Opelousas, do drop in at the **Palace Café,** on the corner of Market and Landry streets (tel. 318/942-2142), for a bite to eat. This is a family-run, old-style café that's been in business for more than half a century, and the home cooking just can't be beat. Gumbo in several versions, étouffée, all kinds of seafood, frogs' legs, steaks, fried chicken—well, the list of offerings is *extensive*. My personal favorites, however, are the Greek specialties on the menu, such as the marvelous salad with feta cheese, black olives, green olives, anchovies, mixed green vegetables, and hard-boiled egg tossed with imported olive oil and vinegar (and, I'm convinced, a great deal of affection from Pete or Steve Doucas, the owners). Or the sticky-sweet, mouth-watering baklava, an unequalled pastry made with honey and pecan butter. Prices are very, very low (anywhere from $2.25 for a sandwich to $4.50 for that salad to $8 for a whopping seafood platter), service is friendly, and you'll be surrounded by locals who make this a regular eating place. They're open seven days a week from 6am to 9pm, until 10pm on Friday and Saturday. It is closed holidays.

ST. MARTINVILLE

This historic old town goes all the way back to 1765, when it was a military station known as the **Poste des Attakapas.** It is also the last home of Emmeline Labiche, Longfellow's Evangeline. There was a time, too, when it was known as "la Petite Paris," when many aristocrats fled their homeland during the French Revolution and settled here, bringing with them the tradition of fancy balls, lavish banquets, and other forms of high living.

See "Where to Stay" for a bed-and-breakfast recommendation if you decide to make this lovely little town an overnight stop. That same bed-and-breakfast serves marvelous home-cooked meals (see "Where to Dine").

St. Martin de Tours Church

This is the Mother Church of the Acadians, and the building you see on Main Street was constructed in 1834, on the site of the original. It is also the fourth-oldest Roman Catholic church in Louisiana. Fr. George Murphy, an Irish priest, was the first to associate it with its patron saint, St. Martin, back in the 1790s, and there's a noteworthy portrait of the saint behind the main altar. You'll also see the original box pews, a replica of the grotto of Lourdes, an ornate baptismal font (which some say was a gift from King Louis XVI of France), and the lovely old altar itself.

Evangeline Monument

Longfellow's heroine is commemorated by a statue to the side and slightly to the rear of St. Martin's Church. It was donated to the town in 1929 by a movie company that came here to film the epic. The star of that movie, Delores del Rio, is supposed to have posed for the statue. Legend says that the real-life Evangeline lies buried here.

Evangeline Oak

On Port Street, where it ends at Bayou Teche, this ancient old oak is where her descendants say Emmeline's boat landed at the end of her long travels from Nova Scotia. Legend has it that it was here, too, that she learned of her lover's betrothal to another.

André Olivier Museum

Not a museum in the usual sense, this is a typical country store of the old days. If you're really interested and the least bit friendly, you'll hear some colorful Cajun stories from the proprietor. Look for it on Bridge Street.

Longfellow–Evangeline Commemorative Area

Situated on the banks of Bayou Teche, just north of town on La. 31, 157 acres hold a park on land that once belonged to Louis Arceneaux, Emmeline's real-life Gabriel. The Acadian House Museum on the grounds (tel. 394-7334) dates from about 1765 and is typical of the larger Acadian homes, with bricks that were handmade and baked in the sun, cypress frame and pegs (instead of nails), and *bousillage* construction on the upper floor. You can also see the *cuisine* (outdoor kitchen) and *magazin* (storehouse) out back. Admission to the Acadian House is $1 for adults, 75¢ for seniors, and 50¢ for children.

Thibodeaux Café

I am going to recommend that you stop in at a local eatery. The menu is not extensive and the **Thibodeaux Café and Barber Shop** is definitely not for everyone—but for mingling with locals on a one-to-one basis in a "down-home" setting, it is not to be missed. It's on Main Street just across from St. Martin de Tours Church, and you'll find the tiny eating space a warm, homey, friendly place to relax from all that sight-seeing. Best of all, you'll find good, home-cooked dishes—from gumbo or soup to complete dinners of local origin—at incredibly low prices. It's open for all three meals (and I heartily recommend breakfast here) on weekdays, breakfast and lunch on weekends.

Special note: When you're in the Thibodeaux Café and Barber Shop, ask about Max Greig, and if he's available, strike a deal to have him take you on one of his very special Cajun Country tours. Max is a true Cajun raconteur who grew up in the Acadian House in Longfellow–Evangeline State Park. Although he claims to speak only "Cajun French, Creole French, Parisian French, and a little bit of English," he's actually quite fluent in English (with a beautiful French accent, of course), and he probably knows more tall tales of the Cajun variety than anyone else going. You'll find this fascinating charmer in the café nearly every afternoon—if not, the people there will know how to get in touch with him, and it's worth the effort.

JEANERETTE

This lovely little town on the banks of the Bayou Teche is filled with beautiful old antebellum homes and is worth a visit just for the scenic beauty (as well as for an excellent restaurant described in the "Where to Dine" section that follows).

NEW IBERIA

This interesting town had its beginnings in 1779 when a large group of Malagueños, 300 in all, came up Bayou Teche and settled here. It was incorporated in 1813, and its history changed drastically after the arrival of the steamboat *Plowboy* in 1836. New Iberia became the terminal for steamboats traveling up the bayou from New Orleans, and it promptly developed the rambunctious character of a frontier town. In 1839, however, yellow fever traveled up the bayou with the steamboats and laid low over a quarter of the population—many more were saved through the heroic nursing of a black woman called Tante Félicité who had come here from Santo Domingo and who went tirelessly from family to family carrying food and medicine. (She had had the fever many years before and was immune.) During the Civil War, New Iberia was a Confederate training center and was attacked again and again by Union troops. Confederate and Union soldiers alike plundered the land to such an extent it is said that local Acadians threatened to declare war on *both* sides if any more of their chickens, cattle, and farm produce were appropriated. The steamboats continued coming up the bayou until 1947 (I'll bet you didn't know the steamboat era lasted that long anywhere in the United States). New Iberia has continued its growth and is known as the "Queen City of the Teche."

Shadows-on-the-Teche Plantation

This splendid home at 317 E. Main Street (tel. 318/369-6446) was built in 1834 for David Weeks, a wealthy planter, and it is beautifully preserved. It reflects the prevailing classical taste of the times, and its columns and architectural features are of the Tuscan style. The two-story house is built of rose-colored brick and sits amid oak trees, camellias, and azaleas. This is one of the most authentically restored and furnished homes in the state, and it is now the property of the National Trust for Historic Preservation. You can visit any day of the week from 9am to 4:30pm for a $4 admission fee.

Tabasco Sauce Factory and Jungle Gardens

Avery Island, on La. 329, south of New Iberia, is underlaid by a gigantic salt dome and the oldest rock-salt mine in the Western Hemisphere. But it is the fiery-hot peppers that grow especially well here that have brought Avery Island its greatest claim to fame. Tabasco brand pepper sauce, so loved not only in Cajun country but also all over the world, is made by a closely knit family and equally close workers who cultivate and harvest the peppers, then nurse them through a fermentation process first developed by Edmund McIlhenny, founder of McIlhenny Company. You can tour the Tabasco sauce factory (at no charge) and Visitor's Center, which includes an old-fashioned Tabasco Country Store, Monday through Friday from 9am to 4pm and on Saturday from 9am to noon. You may want to take a driving or walking tour (for a fee) of the Jungle Gardens afterward. The gardens cover more than 200 acres, and there's something in bloom continously from November through June. There's a Buddha from A.D. 1000 in the Chinese Garden, sunken gardens, a bird sanctuary (with great numbers of egrets and herons), and tropical plants. The hours for the gardens are 9am to 5pm daily.

Live Oak Gardens

If time permits, plan to spend a morning or an afternoon at Live Oak Gardens, 284 Rip Van Winkle Road, in New Iberia (tel. 318/367-3485). Its location is known as Jefferson Island, although it isn't a proper island at all but a piece of land held up higher than its surroundings by one of the five massive salt domes in coastal Louisiana. Set on the shores of Lake Peigneur, it's a place of huge old oak trees, some 350 years old or more, that are draped with Spanish moss and colorful blooming plants. So beguiled by its beauty was actor Joseph Jefferson, who gained national fame for his role of Rip Van Winkle, that in 1869 he purchased land there and erected an extravagant three-story home, much of which he designed himself, with elements of French, English, Moorish, and Victorian Steamboat architecture. The result is a surprisingly gracious home with ingenious practical touches—such as the natural air conditioning afforded by a "well" in the center of the house.

Although Jefferson did more than a little landscaping and gardening on the grounds, it was the Bayless family who bought the estate from Jefferson's heirs in 1917 and are responsible for the colorful panorama you see today. The gardens were well developed when disaster struck in 1980—the lake disappeared after an oil company drilled into the salt mine, creating a gigantic whirlpool so powerful that it sucked in all the waters of the lake and huge portions of the gardens adjacent to it. Today all has been repaired, the gardens have been rebuilt, and you'll see only the glory of camellias, azaleas, crape myrtles, tulips, and even a Japanese garden. Tour the home, which is filled with antiques and landscapes painted by the talented Jefferson, then take time to stroll among the blossoms and beneath the live oaks. An old legend of buried Jean Lafitte treasure gained some credence in 1923, when three boxes of ancient gold and silver coins were unearthed beneath the trees.

Live Oak Gardens is open daily from 9am to 5pm in summer, until 4pm in winter; it is closed major holidays. Admission is $5 for adults, $3.60 for children over 6, and $2.50 for those under 6. If you opt for a boat ride on the lake as well, admission is $10, $8.50, and $5, respectively.

Houma

Take one of Annie Miller's **Terrebone Swamp and Marsh Tours** for a unique, close-up look at the bayou and its wildlife. In a comfortable boat, you'll visit a rookery of nesting egrets and herons and say hello to "Smilin' Sam," the alligator who has come to look for his daily feeding from the friendly operators of this very personal and delightful cruise. Call 504/879-3934 for current schedules and rates. *Note:* This is also worth a drive out from New Orleans. Take U.S. 90 West through Houma (about 57 miles), exit right at the Tourist Office on St. Charles Street, then turn left at the stoplight onto Southdown/Mandalay Road and proceed to Miller's Landing on Big Bayou Black.

WHERE TO STAY

The **Hotel Acadiana,** 1801 Pinhook Rd., Lafayette, LA 70508 (tel. 318/233-8120, or toll free 800/826-8386, 800/874-4664 in Louisiana), has some 300 guest rooms, most with wet bar and refrigerator. There's a plush lounge with live entertainment, the informal Café Raintree, a New Orleans–style courtyard with swimming pool, and a Crown Service floor with concierge service. Doubles run from $46 to $68.

The centrally located **Lafayette Hilton and Towers,** 1521 Pinhook Rd., Lafayette, LA 70508 (tel. 318/235-6111, or toll free 800/33-CAJUN), has over 300 nicely appointed studio rooms, guest rooms, and suites. All have cable TV, and some have private patios. There's a good restaurant overlooking the bayou, a lounge with live music and dancing every day except Sunday, and a heated pool. Studio rooms are $69; singles range from $60 to $80; doubles range from $65 to $85; and suites range from $150 to $200. Special rates are available for senior citizens, students, faculty members, and members of the military and during the weekend.

The **Holiday Inn Central—Holidome,** 2032 NE Evangeline Thruway, Lafayette, LA 70509 (tel. 318/233-6815, or toll free 800/942-4868), has more than 200 superior guest rooms, all with cable TV and some equipped for the disabled. There's a lounge, a coffee shop, a good restaurant, an indoor pool, a whirlpool, a sauna, a game room, lighted tennis courts, a jogging track, a playground, a picnic area, a gift shop, and kennels. The rates range from $46 to $120.

Guest rooms at the **Days Inn,** 1620 N. University, at I-10, Lafayette, LA 70506 (tel. 318/237-8880, or toll free 800/325-2525), are above average, which is typical for this reliable chain. There's cable TV in all rooms and facilities for the disabled in some, a coffee shop, a restaurant, and an outdoor pool. The rates are in the $30 to $40 range.

The **Southern Comfort Bed & Breakfast Reservation Service,** 2856 Hundred Oaks, Baton Rouge, LA 70808 (tel. 504/346-1928 or 928-9815, or toll free 800/749-1928), can help you locate carefully screened bed-and-breakfast accommodations throughout Louisiana.

In Lafayette, the three suites at the **Bois Des Chenes Inn,** 338 N. Sterling, Lafayette, LA 70501 (tel. 318/233-7816), are in the carriage house of an 1820s Acadian-style plantation home, the Charles Mouton House. Now listed on the National Register of Historical Houses, Bois Des Chenes was once the center of a 3,000-acre cattle and sugar plantation. Its restoration has been a labor of love that is reflected in the careful selection of antique furnishings, most of Louisiana French design. All guest accommodations are tastefully furnished with antiques of different periods, and all have cable TV, a small refrigerator, and down pillows. The rates of $55 to $75 for a single room and $65 to $95 for a double include a complimentary Louisiana-style breakfast, a bottle of wine, and a tour of the house. Smoking is not permitted. Booking as far in advance as possible is recommended.

In St. Martinville, the **Old Hotel Castillo Inn (La Place d' Evangeline),** 220 Evangeline Blvd., St. Martinville, LA 70582 (tel. 318/394-4010), also appears on the National Register of Historical Places. Set on the banks of the Bayou Teche, virtually under the branches of the Evangeline Oak, the Greek Revival building began life in the early 1800s as a residence and inn and for many years served as a high school for girls. It blossomed into its present incarnation under the loving direction of Peggy and Gerald Hulin. There are five spacious rooms, comfortably furnished with some antiques and four-poster beds that are either double- or queen-size. Daybeds can be furnished at no extra charge, and one room is so gigantic that it quite easily accommodates two queen-size beds. The rates of $50 to $75 include a complimentary breakfast.

WHERE TO DINE

As I said before, almost any place you stop will serve good food —it's one of the things that makes Cajun Country such a special place to visit. Indeed, this section would be much smaller if I could tell you where not to eat—then I could just skip the whole thing. However, the restaurants listed below are those I especially like, and like all recommendations in this book, they make up a highly subjective list. You won't see some of the towns on the Cajun Country map, but never mind, you'll find them. Also, because of space limitations, these are not full-blown reviews, just short mentions to point you in the right direction.

Mulate's Cajun Restaurant, 325 Mills Ave., Breaux Bridge (tel. 318/332-4648), is a roadside café with cypress-board walls, where Cajun owner Kerry Boutte takes great care to make every dish authentic to his heritage. Stuffed crab is a specialty. There's also an excellent Cajun breakfast Monday through Saturday. Seven nights a week and every day at noon there's live Cajun music. Mulate's is a good introduction to the Cajun world of friendliness, unique food, and music. The hours are 7am to 10:30pm Monday through Saturday and 11am to 11pm on Sunday. The prices are quite reasonable.

Chez Pastor, 1211 Pinhook Rd. (tel. 318/234-5189), differs a little from most Cajun restaurants in that its décor borders on being "fancy." But at heart it's still the easy, informal sort of place where food and friendship prevail. Their Cajun canapés are terrific bite-size bits of boudin (hot smoked sausage) cooked and served in a cast-iron skillet. A wide range of seafoods, crayfish, and beef dishes are cooked in the Cajun manner, with a touch of Creole in some. The prices are moderate. Chez Pastor is open Monday through Saturday from 11am to 2pm for lunch, 5 to 10pm for dinner. It's a favorite with locals.

Prejean's, 3480 U.S. 167 North (tel. 318/896-3247), is a place to experience as well as fill yourself with superb traditional Cajun cooking. You'll almost always find a large gathering of locals in attendance, either in the big main dining room or in the lounge with its oyster bar and marvelous stained-glass mural depicting a cypress shrimp boat on bayou waters. Other trappings in the rather plain interior consist of fish nets, crayfish traps, trawling boards, and similar items associated with the Cajuns' close affinity with fishing. In season, heaping platters of boiled crayfish come out of the kitchen in a continuous stream, along with shrimp, oysters, gumbo, alligator, steaks, and all sorts of other local dishes. Every night from 7 to 10:30pm there's live Cajun music, which transforms all those happy diners into happy party-goers at a Cajun *fais-dodo*. Lunch is served daily from 11am to 5:30pm; dinner is served on weeknights from 5:30 to 9:30pm but to 11pm on weekends. The prices are in the $5 to $16 range, and there's a children's menu with prices from $2 to $6.

Angelle's, on U.S. 167 North, across from Evangeline Downs Racetrack (tel. 318/896-8416), is in a Cajun-style building with high-pitched roof, three fireplaces, and surrounding porch. It's a relaxed, friendly establishment known for its Cajun seafood dishes and steaks. The hours are 11am to 2pm and 5 to 9pm Tuesday through Friday, 5 to 10pm on Saturday, and 11am to 9pm on Sunday; it is closed Monday.

Randol's Seafood Restaurant et Salle de Danse, 2320 Kaliste Saloom Rd. (tel. 981-7080), is a happy combination of good Cajun food and Cajun music that is sure to have you up two-stepping on the dance floor between courses. Your fellow dancers are likely to be locals enjoying their own *fais-dodo* at this popular place. In fact, so imbued are they with that lively Cajun spirit that they eagerly volunteer when owner Frank Randol is in need of dancers for his traveling Cajun food and dance show, which has been booked as far north as New England. Back home, seafood is the star of the menu, all of it fresh from bayou or gulf waters, and Randol's will serve it fried, steamed, or grilled, as you prefer. The prices are in the moderate range. The hours are Monday through Thursday and Saturday and Sunday 11am to 2pm and 5 to 10pm, Friday until 10:30pm. It is closed major holidays.

In a beautifully restored historic Acadian building of cypress and handmade brick that dates from 1799, **Café Vermilionville,** 1304 Pinhook Rd. (tel. 237-0100), seats you in a glassed-in dining room overlooking the courtyard and herb garden. The superb menu represents the best of Louisiana French and Cajun cuisines, with lots of fresh seafood featured. The prices are in the $6 to $16 range at lunch and in the $10 to $19 range at dinner. Lunch is served from 11am to 2pm Monday through Friday, and dinner is served from 5:30 to 10pm Monday through Saturday. There's a jazz brunch from 10:30am to 2pm on Sunday at $7 to $13. The café is closed major holidays.

Near Henderson

To reach **McGee's Atachafalaya Café,** McGee's Landing, Henderson (tel. 228-8519 or 228-2384), take Exit 115 off I-10 to Highway 352 and follow signs to McGee's Landing. Built right out over bayou waters, this large, bright, family-run restaurant is a delight from both a visual and a culinary point of view. Wide windows line the walls, with views of the bayou, house boats anchored in the Atachafalaya Basin, fishing boats puttering about, and the occasional tour boat heading for the inner depths of the bayou. As for the food, it is delicious. Home cooking is the style here, using the freshest of seafood and other local products and a deft touch of Cajun seasoning. I instantly fell head over heels for their shrimp étouffée, then made an absolute glutton of myself with their spicy hushpuppies. The prices are extremely moderate for the quality, with entrees in the $7 to $12 range on the à la carte menu. It is open daily from 10am to 10pm; there's music on Friday and Saturday night. They can also book you on one of those bayou tours to round out your Cajun Country experience.

At **Pat's Fisherman's Wharf Restaurant & Oyster Bar,** just across the bridge at Henderson, overlooking the bayou (tel. 228-7110), you actually have seven choices for your crayfish to be prepared, and no matter which you pick, it's bound to be among the best you've ever tasted. Shrimp, lobster, redfish, snapper, catfish, and crab are also featured on the menu. Lobster is the only entree that exceeds $13 (it's $22), and most run around $8 to $10. It is open daily from 10am to 11pm.

Near Carencro

From Lafayette, **Prudhomme's Cajun Cafe,** 4676 NE Evangeline Thruway (tel. 896-7964), is off Exit 7 of Highway 49, some 7 miles north of I-10 and 3 miles north of Evangeline Downs. Set in an Acadian country home built of cypress, the restaurant is run by Enola Prudhomme, who is easily the equal of her famous brother, Paul, in the kitchen. Assisted by her son and two sons-in-law, she dishes up wonderful dishes from a menu that changes often, according to what fresh ingredients are available at the time. Blackened redfish and eggplant pirogue (eggplant skiff filled with seafood in a luscious cream sauce) are just two of her specialties. Entrees start at $7 and run to $15. The hours are 11am to 10pm Tuesday through Saturday but to 2:30pm on Sunday. There's ramp access for the disabled.

St. Martinville

La Place d'Evangeline, 220 Evangeline Blvd. (394-4010), in the historic Old Castillo Hotel (see "Where to Stay," above), is a warm, homey room, where "friendly" certainly defines the service. All three meals are served. Breakfast features regional favorites of beignets, pain perdu, and café au lait. Seafood and steaks share the à la carte menu with soup-and-salad combinations, po-boys, and such traditional homemade desserts as peach cobbler and fudge pecan pie. The prices are in the $5 to $13 range. The hours are 8am to 9pm Sunday through Thursday but to 10pm Friday and Saturday.

TOURS

And what if you simply cannot spare the time to wander around Cajun Country? Well, you can still go home with at least a taste of this totally different region that is New Orleans's neighbor. If you have a day for out-of-town activities, one of these tours will give you a glimpse of how and where the Cajuns live.

Tours by Isabelle, P.O. Box 740972, New Orleans, LA 70174 (tel. 504/367-3963), specializes in small-group tours via a comfortable, air-conditioned minivan. You are driven across the Mississippi to visit Cajun Country and then provided with a 1½-hour narrated swamp tour. The Cajun Bayou Tour fare is $40 and leaves New Orleans at 1pm, returning around 6pm.

The *Bayou Jean Lafitte,* 1340 New Orleans World Trade Center (tel. 586-8777), a modern passenger ship, departs daily at 11am from the Toulouse Street wharf across from Jackson Square for a 5½-hour Bayou Cruise. The 45-mile route takes you back into the intrigue and charm of Bayou Barataria, where Jean Lafitte and his notorious buccaneers once thrived. A professional guide fills you in on the history of the region. There's a snackbar, a cocktail bar, and a gift shop on board. Adults pay $15 and children over 3 pay $8; children under 3 sail free.

---

3. The Mississippi Gulf Coast

East of New Orleans stretches the sunny Mississippi Gulf Coast, a resort area that not only features all the water sports, but also adds lots of golf, tennis, and after dark, enough spice to liven up the day's relaxation. Within easy and pleasant driving distance of New Orleans, the small towns along the gulf have personality, charm, and—I must add reluctantly—a touch of commercialism that comes from having so many diversions packed into such a comparatively small area. Nevertheless, because those diversions are centered in historic old towns that have never grown into cities, there's none of the frantic, "enforced joy hour" feeling that pervades so many "high-rise" resort areas. Instead, a leisurely "Old South" atmosphere prevails, and a few days spent winding down along the gulf is the perfect end to a New Orleans visit.

Closest to the city is the Mississippi coast, and the two have close historical ties. The Spanish were the first Europeans along here, when DeSoto explored the coastal territory in the early 1500s, but it remained for the French to make the first settlements. Sieur d'Iberville (brother of New Orleans's founder, Bienville) did just that in 1699 at what is now Ocean Springs, calling the little post Fort Maurepas. On the site of present-day Mobile, Alabama, Fort Condé was established in 1702. When Bienville set out for the Mississippi a few years later to plant the French flag at New Orleans, the Fort Maurepas headquarters were moved to a location near where the Biloxi Lighthouse stands. Along the Pascagoula River, some 300 German colonists moved onto land grants in 1718 and set about farming, with the village of Pascagoula as a focal point. Through the years these little settlements along the Gulf Coast changed hands time and time again—with rulers sometimes French, sometimes Spanish, sometimes English, and finally American.

From New Orleans, take I-10 to its intersection with U.S. 90 just past Slidell, then leave that highway and follow U.S. 90 for a delightful drive along beautiful bays and a long stretch of artificial beaches. Offshore, the coastal islands are administered by the National Park System and offer all sorts of recreation, with a bit of sight-seeing thrown in for good measure. The route leads through Gulfport, Biloxi, and Pascagoula, any one of which is a good base for an overnight stop or a few days' stay.

Even though there are many hotels and motels that line Mississippi's Gulf Coast, reserve ahead if you can, especially between Memorial Day and Labor Day, when it is quite possible to find virtually every room booked as residents of Mississippi and its neighboring states head for Gulf Coast holidays. Also, you should know that prices rise rather sharply during the Christmas and New Year holidays and during Mardi Gras week. Remember, too, that the prices quoted below are subject to change, so check carefully when you book.

One thing you most certainly won't want for anywhere along the Gulf Coast is good food. Our recommended restaurants are only the tip of a culinary iceberg. Fresh seafood is found all long the coast in an amazing variety, with more eateries (which range from the most elegant to some that are not far from waterfront shanties) than you'll be able to sample. And because this is a resort area, the prices are more sensitive to change than they are in other locations.

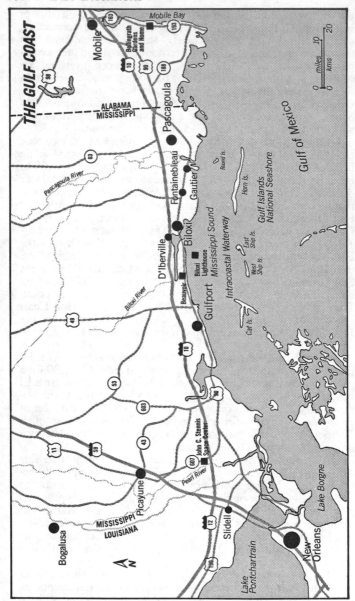

GULFPORT

Unlike most Gulf Coast towns, Gulfport from the first was laid out with broad streets along the gulf front. Planned as an important railroad center and port in the early 1900s, it has since blossomed into a first-rate resort area. With an abundance of water sports; easy access to the Gulf Islands National Seashore; and scenic lakes, rivers, and bayous only minutes from downtown, it draws hordes of sun and sea devotees. Sports enthusiasts who are up on their history will remember that Gulfport was the setting for John L. Sullivan's historic boxing victory over Paddy Ryan beneath the live oaks at the corner of U.S. 90 and Texas Street.

What to See and Do

For complete information on all that Gulfport has to offer, visit or write to the **Chamber of Commerce,** 140 20th Avenue, Drawer FF, Gulfport MS 39502 (tel. 601/863-2933).

One of the very special pleasures of a Gulfport stay is a trip to one of the four **offshore islands:** East Ship Island, from which a large British armada launched an unsuccessful attack on New Orleans in 1815 as the War of 1812 was winding down; West Ship Island, the site of Fort Massachusetts, a pre–Civil War bastion that changed hands even before its completion, occupied first by Confederates, then by Unionists (who housed prisoners of war there); and Horn Island and Petit Bois Island, both designated wilderness areas. Wilderness camping is permitted on all except West Ship Island, and all the islands are ideal for swimming, surf fishing, hiking, and picknicking, but the restrictions against bringing any motor vehicles or glass containers ashore are strictly enforced. There's daily round-trip boat service to West Ship Island in good weather from the Gulfport Small Craft Harbor, Jct. U.S. 49 and U.S. 90 (tel. 601/864-1014 or 436-6010 for schedule and rates). Do-it-yourselfers will also find charter boats available at the Small Craft Harbor.

As far back as 1836, Gulfport has drawn summer visitors, and **Grass Lawn,** 720 E. Beach (tel. 864-5019), is a gracious example of the "summer cottages" along the Gulf in that era. Its 10-foot-wide galleries are typical of much antebellum architecture. It is open Monday, Wednesday, and Friday except on legal holidays, with a small admission fee.

The scientific-minded will surely not want to miss the **John C. Stennis Space Center,** NASA's second-largest field operation and testing site, as well as a base for some 18 earth science agencies in the fields of oceanography, meteorology, and the like. It's a 38-mile drive west of Gulfport on I-10, and you can call the Visitor Center (601/688-2370) for times of the free guided tours, films, demonstrations, and other activities.

Where to Stay

Overlooking the harbor, **Best Western Beach View Inn,** 2922 W. Beach Blvd., Gulfport, MS 39501 (tel. 601/864-4650), has some 150 rooms. There's a pool, a restaurant, and a lounge with entertainment and dancing from Memorial Day through Labor Day. Guest room amenities include cable TV. The rates are seasonal, with a high of $40 to $60 for a double room and $35 to $55 for a single; children under 16 stay free with their parents. Weekend packages are available.

Most guest rooms at **Holiday Inn—Beachfront,** 1600 E. Beach, Gulfport, MS 39501 (tel. 601/864-4310), have balconies overlooking the beach. There's a pool, a wading pool, a restaurant, a lounge with entertainment and dancing every day except Sunday and Monday during the high season (Memorial Day through Labor Day), a coin laundry, and a playground for children. The high season rates range from $70 to $76 for a double room and $58 to $64 for a single; the rates drop during other months.

Where to Dine

Seafood fresh from Gulf waters are featured in the many small Gulfport eateries, as well as in the restaurants of both motels listed above. For finer dining you'll probably want to make the short drive over to Biloxi.

BILOXI

This is one of the prettiest towns along the Gulf, with Spanish moss trailing from tall trees and magnolias, camellias, roses, and crape myrtle lining its streets. On a peninsula with some 25 miles of coastline, Biloxi first became a resort about the mid-19th century, when inland cotton planters discovered the pleasures of the shore. The only industry that intrudes is the seafood industry, and hundreds of shrimp boats operate out of the town. In early June there's a Shrimp Festival that culminates in a beautiful Blessing of the Fleet ceremony.

What to See and Do

For full details of Biloxi's many visitor attractions, stop by the **Visitor Center,** Main Street and U.S. 90, or write to P.O. Box 346, Biloxi, MS 39533 (tel. 601/435-6248).

There's daily boat service from Biloxi to West Ship Island (see "Gulfport," above) in good weather from Memorial Day through Labor Day. Call 601/432-2197 for schedules and rates.

If you're a Civil War buff, you'll want to visit **Beauvoir,** Jefferson Davis's home for the last 12 years of his life. Some years after his release from a federal prison, the former Confederate president came South and, among other things, wrote *The Rise and Fall of the Confederate Government.* After his death, Beauvoir was used as a home for Confederate veterans, and in 1941 it became a Confederate shrine. On the 70-acre grounds are the home, a little white pavilion Davis used as his library and study, a guest cottage, a museum, a Confederate cemetery, and the "Tomb of the Unknown Soldier of the Confederate States of America." Beauvoir is 5 miles west of Biloxi on U.S. 90 (West Beach Boulevard). It is open daily except Christmas from 9am to 5pm; there is a small admission fee, but there are reductions for those over 65 and for military personnel.

Not far from Beauvoir is the **Biloxi Lighthouse,** built in 1848 (on West Beach Boulevard—U.S. 90—at the foot of Porter Avenue). During the Civil War, when federal forces were approaching, the intrepid woman lighthouse keeper climbed to the top, removed the lens, and buried it. Still, when Lincoln was assassinated, the citizens of the town painted the entire structure black. It's white now and automated (but for some 62 years the light was faithfully tended by a mother–daughter team). Call 432-2563 for opening hours and admission charge.

If fishing is your sport, you'll find deep-sea charter boats at the **Small Craft Harbor** at the junction of Main Street and U.S. 90. That's where you can also watch local fishing boats bring in their catch at the end of the day.

Where to Stay

The Royal d'Iberville, 1980 Beach Blvd., Biloxi, MS 39531 (tel. 601/388-6610), has large rooms, many with balconies, extra basins in separate dressing rooms, and oversize beds. There are lighted tennis courts, a swimming pool, a hot tub, and golf privileges at a nearby course. The dining room is above average, and the lounge has dancing and entertainment. Double rooms are in the $75 to $95 range.

There are kitchen suites as well as spacious guest rooms at **Days Inn,** 2046 Beach Blvd., Biloxi MS 39531 (tel. 601/385-1156). Free coffee is dispensed in the lobby, and there's a free continental breakfast. Amenities include an adjacent restaurant, a pool, lighted tennis courts, a coin laundry, and cable TV. The rates are $70 for a double room and $65 for a single; children under 18 stay free with their parents. There are some attractive golf plans.

Where to Dine

For pure atmosphere and excellent food, Biloxi's star is unquestionably **Mary Mahoney's Old French House,** 116 Rue Magnolia (tel. 374-0163). The house and slave quarters date from 1737 and have been converted into a fine restaurant that fairly oozes charm, with fireplaces, antiques, a patio for cocktails, and courtyard dining. Of course, you can't eat charm, but at this place, the food measures up to its surroundings. Try the baked shrimp Dolores or the red snapper. Semi-à la carte prices range from $5 to $12 at lunch and from $10 to $25 at dinner. The hours are Monday through Saturday from 11am to 10:30pm (closed Christmas week). It's a good idea to reserve.

There's outdoor dining and home baking at **French Connection,** 1891 Pass Christian Rd. (tel. 388-6367). Set on land that was once part of Jefferson Davis's estate, Beauvoir, the antique-filled restaurant specializes in fine continental dishes with a French accent, such as the excellent scampi belle meunière. The hours are Monday through Saturday from 11am to 2pm and 5:30 to 10pm (closed holidays). Lunch will run from $6 to $10 and dinner will run from $10 to $20.

For more casual dining at family-oriented prices, it's hard to beat **Sea 'n' Sirloin,** 1983 Beach Blvd. (tel. 388-6387). This eatery is a big place right on the water, with wide windows that let you enjoy the view as well as the food. The extensive à la carte menu features shrimp boiled in the shell, oysters on the half shell, a selection of cold seafood items, mesquite charbroiled fresh fish, fried crab claws, blackened fish, and a host of other specialties. The prices range from $5 to $10 for lunch and $9 to $24 (for the sea 'n' sirloin combination of seafood and steak) for dinner. There's also a terrific lunch buffet for just $6.75. It is open daily from 10am to 10pm.

PASCAGOULA

This ship-building center dates from 1718, and its colorful history dates from even further back. Long before the advent of white settlers in Mississippi, the peaceful Pascagoula tribe lived here; when a young warrior fell in love with a princess from the fierce Biloxi tribe and spirited her away, the Biloxis went on the warpath. Finding themselves outnumbered and outfought, the Pascagoulas (so the legend goes) walked into the river holding hands and chanting a song of death until the last voice was hushed by the dark waters. There is, to this day, an unexplained singing sound plainly heard in the late summer and autumn months in the stillness of Pascagoula evenings, and it seems to come from the river—scientists have yet to come up with a satisfactory explanation.

What to See and Do

Before setting out to explore this romantic old town, go by the **Jackson County Chamber of Commerce,** 825 Denny Ave., or write to P.O. Box P, Pascagoula, MI 39567 (tel. 601/762-3391).

Then, if you want to become a true believer in that old Native American legend, go down to the **Pascagoula River** (two blocks west of the courthouse) on a hot summer evening just about twilight. You'll hear the sound faintly at first; then you'll experience the odd sensation of hearing the humming swell in volume and seem to come closer to where you stand. The strangest thing of all is that although you know it is very near—almost underfoot—you are totally unable to pinpoint exactly where it comes from.

Five blocks north of U.S. 90 (or 8 miles south of I-10), the **Old Spanish Fort,** 4602 Fort St. (tel. 769-1505), was built in 1718 by the French and later captured by the Spanish. Said to be the oldest fortified structure in the Mississippi Valley, its walls are of massive pine timbers held together with a mixture of oyster shells, mud, and moss. Among the historic exhibits in its present-day museum are many interesting Native American relics. It is open Friday through Wednesday from 9am to 4:30pm (closed holidays.) There's a small admission fee.

Where to Stay

Just off U.S. 90 East, the **La Font Inn,** 2703 Danny Ave., Pascagoula, MS 39567 (tel. 601/762-7111, or toll free 800/821-3668 in Miss., 800/647-6077 in other states), is a large, pleasant motel. Spacious rooms—with free coffee, refrigerators, and cable TV—overlook the pool. Other amenities include a steam room, a sauna, bicycles, exercise equipment, lighted tennis courts, and a restaurant (see below). Double rooms run $45 to $75; single rooms run from $50 to $65; and kitchen units run from $50 to $65.

Where to Dine

At the **La Font Inn** (see above), Sunday dinner is an event, with a fixed-price menu that features such specialties as baked ham with wine sauce, fresh crabmeat Newburg, and roast leg of lamb. The vegetables are really fresh and nicely prepared. The lunch buffet (11am to 1:30pm) is also a standout at the modest price of $6.50, and children have a choice of several special plates. They do their own baking here (in fact, this is very much a home-cooking establishment), and almost any seafood choice will delight you. From the semi–à la carte menu, breakfast will run from $3 to $5, lunch will run from $5 to $12, and dinner will run from $6 to $20. It is open 6am to 10pm.

---

4. The Alabama Gulf Coast

Alabama's Gulf Coast beaches and holiday resorts are among the best-kept secrets in the southeastern United States. This is not surprising, because the state's actual Gulf frontage measures less than 50 miles: Florida's panhandle underpins about three-quarters of the coast's southern border and Mobile Bay cuts a wide swath more than 35 miles inland, to give Alabama its only port city, Mobile.

Along with what is left of its Gulf Coast, however, Alabama offers some of the Gulf's most beautiful white sand beaches, a vast array of holiday facilities, and a venue almost totally devoid of commercialization (which is guaranteed to stay that way, since more than 30% of the coastline has been designated public lands under federal and state management, safe from the often-destructive influence of big-time developers).

Only 214 miles from New Orleans, this is an ideal place to begin or end a visit to the Crescent City, although I must issue the warning that if you start here, you may become so beguiled that you'll save New Orleans for another visit. At any rate, it is easy to opt for a fly/drive vacation, picking up or leaving a rental car at Pensacola airport, a 40-minute drive from Gulf Shores. Delta, Northwest, and Northwest Airlink provide good daily schedules.

U.S. 90 from New Orleans joins I-10 at the Alabama state line. A short distance on is Alabama Highway 193, the detour for Bellingrath Gardens and Home (see below). You have two options: you can visit the estate, then drive the 20 miles up Mobile Bay's western shore to Mobile and continue to Gulf Shores down its eastern banks; or you can take the half-hour ferry ride ($8 for each car and its occupants) from Dauphin Island (across a causeway at the southern end of Highway 193) to the western end of 30,000-acre, 32-mile-long Pleasure Island. To reach the beaches from Mobile, take U.S. 90 or U.S. 98 to their intersections with Alabama Highway 59, also known as the Gulf Shores Parkway, and on to Alabama Highway 180, which runs the length of Pleasure Island.

BELLINGRATH GARDENS AND HOME

On more than 800 tropical acres (65 of them spectacularly landscaped), the gardens were developed on the banks of the Isle-aux-Oies River as a private estate by Walter D. Bellingrath (a Coca-Cola bottling executive) and his wife, who first opened them to the public in 1932. Supported by a nonprofit foundation, both the gardens and the home are open every day of the year from 7am to dusk. French, English, and American landscape architects worked to create this wonderland. In addition to some 70 varieties of native trees, azaleas (200 varieties), camellias, roses, water lilies, and countless other blooming plants are featured. There's an outstanding Oriental-American garden, complete with teahouses and a Moon Bridge, and hundreds of waterfowl and other birds flock to this bird sanctuary. A gardening staff of 35 to 50, depending on the season, assures masses of colorful displays at almost any time of the year.

Late winter and early spring are the times to see azaleas at the height of their beauty, as well as spring flowers and roses. In late spring and through the summer, the stars are roses, salvia, coleus, hibiscus, crotons, and copper plants. Late autumn and winter bring chrysanthemums by the millions, poinsettias during the holidays, and camellias from September to February. No matter when you visit, be sure to allow time to enjoy the lovely wooded walks through the gardens.

The two-story Bellingrath home is made of soft, handmade pink brick, with lots of antebellum iron lacework, and it clearly reflects a pleasant mingling of French, English, and Mediterranean influences. Its 15 rooms are fairly bursting with Mrs. Bellingrath's vast collections of porcelain, glassware, and antiques. Adjacent to the home is a gallery housing more than 200 pieces of Boehm porcelain, the largest public display in the world.

There's a Visitors Center, a multimedia slide show, a gift shop, and a cafeteria that serves excellent home-cooked meals featuring fresh local produce from 7:30am to 3pm. Admission to the gardens is $5, and admission to the home $6.25 (children pay half). You can write ahead for blooming dates to Bellingrath Gardens and Home, Theodore, AL 36582 (tel. 205/973-2217).

MOBILE

Mobile, Alabama's only seaport, sits near the head of Mobile Bay on the west side of the Mobile River. The docks that are the lifeblood of the busy port are stretched along the eastern side of the bay. Don't make the mistake, however, of thinking that Mobile is simply an industrial center—the Old South is very much alive and well in this gracious city, even in the center of town, where proud old homes trimmed with iron-grillwork balconies line the streets fanning out from Bienville Square.

Since 1702, the flags of France, England, Spain, the United States, and the Confederacy have fluttered overhead. It wasn't until federal troops occupied the city on April 12, 1865, and firmly planted the Stars and Stripes that Mobile settled down to a life of constancy in its national identity.

Today, in addition to shipping, one of the largest drydock and ship-building centers of the Gulf is located here. Industry also encompasses chemicals, steel, petroleum refining, food processing, and pulp and paper production. All of this makes Mobile a fascinating mixture of the old and the new—and during Mardi Gras, its French heritage takes over, with mystic society parades each evening that rival those in New Orleans.

What to See and Do

Mobile's **Convention and Visitors Bureau,** 1 St. Louis Centre, Suite 2002, Mobile, AL 38602 (tel. 205/433-5100, or toll free 800/666-6282), can furnish full details on all of the city's many attractions. There is also a Welcome Center at Fort Conde, 150 S. Royal Street, at Church—it's a reconstructed French fort from the early 1700s, and staffers wear uniforms from that era.

For a look at a classic "Old South" mansion, visit **Oakleigh,** 350 Oakleigh Place, at Savannah Street (tel. 432-1281). It was built by slaves between 1833 and 1838, and the bricks for the first floor were made on the premises. The Historic Mobile Preservation Society has restored Oakleigh to its pre-1850 period, complete with authentic furnishings. It is open Monday to Saturday from 10am to 3:30pm, Sunday from 2 to 4pm (closed holidays and Mardi Gras and during Christmas week). There is a small admission charge.

The **Richards-DAR House,** 256 N. Joachim Street (tel. 434-7320), is a restored Italianate town house built around 1860. Its furnishings are of that period, and it has a lovely curved, suspended staircase and elaborate ironwork. It is open Tuesday through Sunday (closed Mardi Gras, Easter, Thanksgiving, and Christmas). There's a small admission charge.

There's no admission charge at the **Fine Arts Museum of the South,** Museum Drive (tel. 343-2667), on the south shore of the lake in Langan Park. Featured are southern antique furniture, crafts, paintings, and prints. It is open Tuesday through Sunday (closed holidays).

Battleship USS *Alabama* **Memorial Park,** Battleship Parkway, on the northern shore of Mobile Bay (tel. 433-2703), holds the World War II battleship, the submarine USS *Drum,* and a B-52 bomber—all dedicated to the memory of the Alabama men and women who served in World War II and the Korean war. It's open every day from 8am to sunset except Christmas.

Where to Stay

Stouffer's Riverview Plaza, 54 Water St., Mobile, AL 36602 (tel. 205/438-4000), provides a host of amenities in addition to superior guest rooms. There is also a Luxury Level (The Club), with its own lounge and concierge services. There are a heated pool, a hot tub, tennis and health club privileges, and a shopping arcade. It also has a fine restaurant (see below). The rates range from $90 to $150 for a double room and $80 to $120 for a single room. The Club rates are in the $110 to $150 range for a double room and $100 to $150 for a single room.

Best Western Bradbury Inn, 180 Beltline, Mobile, AL 36608 (tel. 205/343-9345), has a heated pool and cable TV, and some rooms have refrigerators. There's an adjacent restaurant, and hotel rates include a free breakfast. The rooms, single or double, go for $50 to $60; children under 12 stay free with their parents.

The **Malaga Inn,** 359 Church St., Mobile, AL 36602 (tel. 205/438-4701), is a small, utterly charming hotel consisting of restored 1862 twin town houses, with a garden courtyard and fountain. Many of the original furnishings are in evidence in the public rooms. Guest rooms are nicely furnished, many with oversize beds. There's a pool and an excellent restaurant (see "Where to Dine"). You really can't do better if the graciousness for which the South is noted is what you're after. Rates for double rooms start at $70, and children under 12 stay free in a room with their parents. All rates increase slightly during Mardi Gras.

Take U.S. 98 southeast for 23 miles to reach one of the most outstanding resorts of this region, Point Clear. At **Marriott's Grand Hotel,** Point Clear, AL 36564 (tel. 205/928-9201), the key word is *luxury*. From the warm, awe-inspiring lobby that rises two stories and is centered by a huge fireplace and filled with brass, porcelain, and antiques and paneled and beamed in cypress, to the cypress-paneled rooms and cottages, quiet elegance holds sway. The dining room makes each meal an experience, especially if you get there early enough to sit next to the glass-walled end that overlooks the bay. As for facilities, there's a little bit of everything: a 36-hole championship golf course, ten tennis courts, deep-sea fishing, sailing, waterskiing, a pool and a beach area, shuffleboard, dancing and entertainment in the Bird Cage cocktail lounge—and if you have a favorite activity I've left out, it's probably there, too. The hotel will Modified American Plan (breakfast and full-course dinner included in rates) and a European Plan (no meals), and offers rooms in the main building, the Bay House, and cottage units for two to eight people. Rates for double occupancy range from $69 to $200. They offer a wide variety of golf and family package plans.

Where to Dine

As you might suppose, fresh seafood features prominently in Mobile's restaurants. Continental cuisine also appears on many menus.

The Pillars, 1757 Government St. (tel. 478-6341), is a lovely restored plantation home. To reach it, take I-10 to the Michigan Avenue exit. Filet mignon Rossini is a specialty on the continental menu, although fresh local seafood dishes get equal billing. All baking is done on the premises, and the Pillars has an exceptional wine list. It's open for dinner only, from 5 to 10:30pm, every day except Sunday and major holidays, and dinner will run from $12 to $22. Advance booking is a good idea.

At Stouffer's Riverview Plaza, 64 Water Street (tel. 438-4000), **Julia's** is a favorite of residents and visitors alike. Continental-style dishes are featured, with a heavy emphasis on fresh seafood, and all baking is done on the premises. Also very popular is the Sunday jazz brunch (book ahead) at $17. It is open from 6:30am to 2:30pm and 5:30 to 10:30pm. Breakfast is moderately priced, lunch is in the $5 to $12 range, and dinner runs from $8 to $25. It is best to reserve ahead.

For inexpensive family meals, there's a **Morrison's Cafeteria** at 3200 Springdale Plaza W. (tel. 479-0534). It is open from 11am to 8:30pm; both lunch and dinner average $5 or less.

GULF SHORES

Fifty miles southeast of Mobile, Alabama's Gulf Coast consists of just 32 miles. It stretches from Perdido Key at the Florida state line to Mobile Bay at the western tip of Pleasure Island, which lies between the Gulf and the Intracoastal Waterway.

Pleasure Island ("the Island" to residents and most visitors) is one destination that truly earns that overworked phrase "holiday paradise." Its subtropical climate (average temperatures range from 62°F in winter to 87°F in summer) makes it a year-round destination. There are wide, white sand beaches; bays, inlets, and freshwater lakes for fishing; charter boats for deep-sea or backwater fishing; moonlight cruises; golf courses; tennis courts; and horses for riding on the beaches. There also are over 5,000 hotel, motel, and condominium units for lodging and an abundance of good eateries serving up everything from southern-style home cooking to seafood to continental dishes. When you add to all that a historic fort, two nature preserves, and two theme parks, you'd be hard pressed to go looking for anything that isn't there.

What to See and Do

Alabama Gulf Coast Convention & Visitors Bureau, P.O. Box 457, Gulf Shores, AL 36542 (tel. 205/968-7511), furnishes details on all accommodations, dining, water activities, and sightseeing attractions in the area. The bureau is located on Highway 59 just north of the Intracoastal Waterway bridge. You can contact it in advance at the address given above. Ask for the excellent "Gulf Coast Lifestyles" vacation guide.

Entirely surrounded by water and connected to the mainland only by bridges, the Island is a happy hunting ground for those addicted to fishing. Those looking for deep-sea game fish board a party or charter boat and head for the continental shelf, just 31 miles offshore, in search of blue marlin (they've weighed in at up to 700 pounds), sailfish, tuna, barracuda, wahoo, bluefish, amberjack, mackerel, and shark. Closer in, king mackerel, bonita, snapper, and grouper are plentiful. There's freshwater fishing for bream, red drums, speckled trout, and bass in the several bodies of water on the island. As a matter of fact, you'll often find professional fishing enthusiasts elbow to elbow with those of the simple pole-and-worm variety trying their luck from the pier at Gulf State Park or on the banks of the Intracoastal Waterway. And if conditions are just right, it is quite possible to pull both freshwater and saltwater fish from the same spot in the brackish waters of back bays and bayous.

An $8 fishing license, good for one week, is required for freshwater or saltwater fishing. Among the several places to arrange charters or join party boats for half- or full-day fishing are **Orange Beach Marina** (tel. 205/981-9861); **Perdido Pass Marina** (tel. 205/981-6481); and **Sportsman Marine** (tel. 981-6247). Most charter boats carry up to six people, and the rates usually cover bait, tackle, and ice. If you're on your own, almost any of the charter captains will find a space for you with a group already formed. Call the **Perdido Pass Marina** (tel. 981-6481) for information about party boats that carry large groups with no advance booking required.

Because I'm far from a dyed-in-the-wool fishing person but love being on the water, I will opt any time for the ultimate of an on-the-water experience—a 2- or 3-hour voyage aboard that oldest of all vessels, a sailboat. And for those with a taste for fishing, Capt. Fred Saas combines a marvelous sail aboard his 50-foot sailboat, *The Daedalus,* with shrimping in secluded back bay and bayou waters. must admit that it is an interesting experience to see the shrimp net pulled overboard loaded with all sorts of wiggling, flapping sea life that come up with the shrimp, only to be tossed back into the water. *The Daedalus* also gives you a closeup look at birds and other wildlife, as well as playful porpoises who swim alongside to catch those tasty morsels discarded from the shrimp net. Not the least of *The Daedalus's* attractions is Captain Saas, a genuine man of the sea, with long years and thousands of nautical miles behind him. He will entertain you with tales as you sail. Joined at times by his wife, Carol, Captain Fred provides all this at the modest charge of $7.50 per person per hour. He's also been known to perform wedding ceremonies, at no cost at all. Ice is provided—you bring your own beverages. To reserve, contact **Sailboat Charters,** Route 2, Box 615, Pirates Cove, Elberta, AL 36530 (tel. 205/986-7018).

If you've no taste whatsoever for shrimp or any other kind of fishing, Jerry and Monica Davidson, along with their son, Rusty, have just the sail for you aboard the 42-foot *Nonyme* or the 65-foot *Cyrun E. King,* both classic Chesapeake Bay bug-eye ketches of the type that dredged for oysters long before the age of power. Both have been lovingly preserved and restored by the Davidsons, and both are shallow draft, which means that you get to explore not only Gulf waters but also back bays and coves that are inaccessible to deeper draft vessels. Best of all, you can choose just to relax and get that tan or to join them in handling the sails under their expert guidance. There's always ice and an ice chest waiting to receive your favorite beverages, or, if you prefer, the Davidsons will cater drinks and refreshments for you. There are 3-hour afternoon and sunset cruises at $25 per person, as well as dinner cruises (for a minimum of four passengers) at $50 per person for a meal of steak, salad, and wine. The ketches can also be chartered for full-day, morning, overnight, and moonlight sails. For those totally hooked on sailing, the Davidsons provide sailboat rentals, sailing lessons, and even sailboard rentals and lessons. To book, contact the **Island Sailing Center,** Route 1, Box 326, Gulf Shores, AL 32542 (tel. 205/968-6775 or 981-5609).

Wildlife lovers who prefer their feet planted firmly on land are in luck—both **Gulf State Park** and **Bon Secour Wildlife Refuge** promise peaceful hours in which to commune with nature to your heart's content. Together these parks cover some 10,000 acres, with undeveloped beaches that stretch for miles, freshwater lakes for boating and fishing, nature trails, and picnic areas. Both have fully staffed visitor centers that furnish information on the migratory songbirds; white pelicans; blue herons; ospreys; endangered species, such as loggerhead turtles and American alligators, who find a natural habitat within their borders; and monarch butterflies. They also have information about the numerous wildflowers that are especially colorful at that season.

There's golf year round in this wonderful climate, with four excellent courses open to the public: **Cotton Creek Club,** P.O. Box 2288, Gulf Shores, AL 36542 (tel. 205/968-7766), designed by Arnold Palmer; **Gulf Shores Golf Club,** P.O. Box 499, Gulf Shores, AL 36542 (tel. 205/968-7366); **Gulf State Park Resort,** P.O. Box 437, Gulf Shores, AL 36542 (tel. 205/948-4653); and **Lakeview Golf Club,** P.O. Box 9530 Clubhouse Drive, Foley, AL 36535 (tel. 205/943-8000). Green fees range from $15 to $35.

As for tennis, most hotels and condominiums have private courts, and there are six city-owned courts open to the general public. For locations, hours, and fees, call the Convention & Visitors Bureau (tel. 968-7511).

Equestrians can indulge in invigorating rides on those wide beaches by contacting David and Sherry Cook at **Horseback Beach Rides,** 20316 Brinks Willis Road, Foley, AL 36535.

Sightseers will want to visit historic **Fort Morgan,** at the western tip of the Island. The star-shaped fort dates from 1833. As a Confederate stronghold during the Civil War, it was the next-to-the-last fort to fall to Union forces. There's a $2 admission charge to visit the fort and the excellent small museum on its grounds.

On the lighter side, **Waterville, U.S.A.,** offers loads of family fun, with water slides, a wave pool, and a host of other entertainments. Its neighbors are the Zooland Animal Park and Zooland minigolf.

Dedicated shoppers will be in "hog heaven" at the **Riveria Shopping Centre,** a short drive from the beach on Highway 59 South, at Foley, AL (tel. 205/943-8888). There are no less than 36 factory outlets in the complex, with bargains ranging from top brand names in clothing to linens in the West Point Pepperell Mill store.

At some point in your Gulf Shores stay, be sure to drop by the **Sea Oats Studios** (tel. 968-6744) to see the lovely creations of potter Steve Burrow. Steve and his wife, Dee, dig and blend their own clay mixtures before shaping them into outstanding decorative and useful pieces.

Where To Stay

Accommodations at Gulf Shores can be anything you want them to be—from campsites to cabins to budget motels to luxury rooms and suites to condominiums. Almost all offer money-saving package deals, so be sure to inquire when you reserve.

Topping the luxury category is the **Perdido Beach Hilton,** Box 400, Orange Beach, AL 36561 (tel. 205/981-9811, or toll free 800/634-8001). All 345 beautifully appointed rooms and suites have Gulf views (most with balconies), and in addition to a wide beachfront, there are two pools, tennis courts, a gift shop, and a fitness center. Its Voyagers restaurant is one of the most elegant and most popular in this area (see "Where to Dine," below), and casual meals are served in its Café Palm Breeze. There's music nightly in its lobby lounge and live entertainment in its disco, Nightreef. Golfers enjoy guest privileges at the Arnold Palmer–designed Cotton Creek Club (see above). The rates at this highly recommended hotel range from $68 to $88 in the value season (November through February), from $96 to $116 in spring and fall, and from $108 to $136 in summer.

Gulf State Park Resort Hotel, P.O. Box 437, Gulf Shores, Ala., 36542 (tel. 205/948-5998), has a 6,000-acre state park as its setting, and its newly renovated 144-room hotel has a good restaurant, two lounges, and a pool. There are also lighted tennis courts, an 18-hole golf course, shuffleboard, horseshoes, volleyball, nature trails through the park, and a fishing pier on the Gulf. Seasonal hotel rates range from a high of $79 in the summer season to a low of $39 from November through May. In addition to hotel rooms, there are some 21 lakeside cabins available only on a weekly basis at daily rates of $35 to $60 for four people and $50 to $80 for six people. Over 450 campsites run $8 to $20.

Gulf Shores Plantation, P.O. Box 1299, Gulf Shores, AL 36542 (tel. 205/540-2291, or toll free 800/824-2104 in Ala. 800/554-0344 in other states), is really a self-contained resort 13 miles west of the town of Gulf Shores and 8 miles from Fort Morgan. Three hundred tastefully decorated one-, two-, and three-bedroom condominiums face the Gulf in six graceful buildings, with boardwalks leading over the dunes to the 4,000-foot stretch of beach. In addition to that gorgeous beach, there are five outdoor pools, one indoor pool, lighted tennis courts, and sailboats and catamarans for rent. The Cabaña Café is a restaurant for casual meals, and there's a convenience store as well as a gift shop. Seasonal rates range from a high of $76 to $160 to $58 to $110 September through February.

Condominiums at **Summer House** on Romar Beach, P.O. Drawer 2699, Gulf Shores, AL 36547 (tel. 205/981-9711, or toll free 800/222-2512), are all three-bedroom units, some with wraparound balconies and all with Gulf-view balconies. There are indoor and outdoor pools, a Jacuzzi, a health club, tennis courts, a basketball court, and a playground for children. The rates range from $149 to $169.

Three nine-story buildings hold nicely furnished one-, two-, and three-bedroom condominium units at **Seaside Beach & Racquet Club,** P.O. Box 278, Gulf Shores, AL 36542 (tel. 205/981-6971, or toll free 800/662-4438). Other amenities include two outdoor pools and one indoor pool, a sauna, a steam room, a weight room, tennis courts, and shuffleboard. Close to, but not directly on, the beach, are three-story tennis villas. The condominium rates range from $93 to $139; the tennis villa rates range from $73 to $97.

At **Boardwalk,** P.O. Box 1182, Gulf Shores, AL 36542 (tel. 205/948-4400), all the attractively furnished units have one bedroom and a Gulf view. Directly behind Boardwalk is the popular and reasonably priced Sea 'n Suds restaurant. The seasonal rates of $85 to $140 include resort membership with reduced fees at the Cotton Creek Club.

At **Quality Inn Beachside,** P.O. Drawer 1013, Gulf Shores, AL 36547 (tel. 205/948-6874, or toll free 800/888-6913), the tropical atrium has an indoor pool and lots of greenery as its centerpiece. There's also an outdoor pool, a Jacuzzi, a fitness center, a full-service restaurant, and a delicatessen that comes in handy if you opt for one of the reasonably priced suites with a kitchen. Nicely appointed guest rooms go for $94 to $119 from May through Labor Day, $62 to $72 in the fall, and $59 to $69 in March and April. For one-bedroom suites with kitchen, you'll pay $119 to $140, $72 to $94, and $69 to $89, respectively.

Where to Dine

Seafood fresh from Gulf waters clearly dominates the culinary scene along Alabama's Gulf Coast, and you'll find it everywhere you turn—in eateries that range from casual, drop-in establishments to the dressiest of elegant restaurants. Those listed below have my personal recommendation, but they are only a small sampling of places to enjoy good dining in this area.

The most elegant dining along Alabama's Gulf Coast is in **Voyagers,** at the Perdido Hilton Hotel, Hwy. 182, Orange Beach (tel. 981-9811). Wide windows overlook the Gulf, and the décor reflects the flair and sophistication of European design, with luxurious furnishings of light wood, sparkling crystal and fine china, and table linens highlighted by touches of soft pink. The service is as polished and elegant as the surroundings. As for the food, under the direction of award-winning chef Gerhard Brill (executive chef for many years at New Orleans's Commander's Palace), the menu is an exciting mix of Southern and seafood delights, many with a delightful dash of Creole seasoning. Among Chef Brill's specialties are fresh trout with roasted pecans; filet mignon Stanley (cooked with Creole seasonings); a delicate roast duckling; and—not to be missed if they're in season—soft shell crabs topped with a delicious Creole sauce. The desserts are also delectable, with the bread pudding soufflé served with whiskey sauce a real standout. The entrees range from $14 to $22. Dinner is served daily from 5 to 10pm. On weekends, it's best to make reservations.

On Sunday, from 11am to 2:30pm, there's a lavish Champagne Jazz Brunch in the Perdido Hilton's **Café Palm Breeze,** when Chef Brill features a variety of poached-egg dishes, roast round of beef, shrimp au gratin, that fabulous bread pudding, and freshly baked pies. Top jazz groups provide the entertainment. All this is for under $15—and children under 5 eat free. Reservations are required.

There's also more than a touch of New Orleans cuisine at **Hemingways,** on the docks in the Orange Beach marina (tel. 981-9791). This is not surprising because it was the late Eddie Prudhomme (nephew and apprentice of his noted uncle, Paul) who founded the restaurant. Among the creations that have been carried on by owner Cable Outlaw are the pirogue à la Louisianne (an eggplant skiff filled with seafood and cream sauce topped with jumbo shrimp), panéed seafood stuffed catfish, and flounder Bayou Rouge (with a spicy Louisiana tomato sauce). Continental cuisine standouts include steak Oscar Renos and escallops of veal à la Neptune. The desserts fall into the gourmet class, and there's an extensive wine list. The à la carte menu is served from 11:30am to 9:30pm Monday through Saturday. Entrees are in the $9 to $22 range (most hovering around $15). There's also an "all-you-can-eat" plantation-style buffet lunch for a modest $6 that is served from 11:30am to 2:30pm.

Everything is cooked to order at the **Perdido Pass Restaurant,** 27501 Perdido Beach Blvd., in Orange Beach (tel. 981-6312). It's right at the Alabama Point Bridge, and its menu features fresh seafood, and beef and poultry that may be mesquite grilled, broiled, blackened, fried, or sautéed according to your fancy. The prices for complete dinners run under $10 on the extensive menu, which also includes a good selection of sandwiches, burgers, and croissants with a variety of fillings. It is open daily from 11am to 9pm.

The specialty is charcoal-grilled seafood at **Coconut Willie's** Pelican's Landing, 312 East Blvd. (tel. 948-7145), a casual place that decidedly does not take its food casually. The seafood selection is extensive—at $12 to $22 for a complete meal—and there's a good selection of steaks, chicken, and sandwiches. There is also a children's menu for those under 12. The desserts are homemade and feature cheesecake, key lime pie, and fudge pie. It is open daily from 11am to 10pm.

Since 1957 Gulf Shores residents have flocked to **Hazel's Nook,** near the northeast corner of Highways 180 and 59 (tel. 968-7065), and I firmly believe that every visitor to this town should follow their example at least once during every visit. I make it a point to go for breakfast, when I can easily fill up on nothing more than several of the homemade biscuits—they've been dubbed "the official biscuits of Alabama," and they certainly earn that title. Of course, there's much more to the country breakfast, which comes with your choice of sugar-cured bacon, sausage, or ham and costs under $4. For less than $5 there's a country breakfast buffet and fruit bar (children under 4 eat free and those under 9 pay half). Waffles, omelets, and "stuff" (sausage or ham and biscuits and the like) are other breakfast selections; seafood plates ($7 to $10) are the stars at lunch and dinner, along with a good variety of sandwiches that go for under $3. It is open daily: breakfast is served from 6am to 1:30pm, lunch is served from 11am to 2pm, and dinner is served from 2 to 8pm.

INDEX

GENERAL INFORMATION

SIGHTS AND ATTRACTIONS

New Orleans

Excursion Areas

ACCOMMODATIONS

New Orleans

Excursion Areas

KEY TO ABBREVIATIONS: *A* = Apartments; *B* = Budget; *B&B* = Bed-and-Breakfast; *C* = Condominiums; *CG* = Campgrounds; *E* = Expensive; *GH* = Guesthouse; *M* = Moderately priced

RESTAURANTS

New Orleans

Key to Abbreviations: *B* = Budget; *E* = Exceptional, mostly expensive; *FC* = First Class; *M* = Moderately priced

Excursion Areas

NOW, SAVE MONEY ON ALL
YOUR TRAVELS!
Join Frommer's™ Dollarwise® Travel Club

Saving money while traveling is never a simple matter, which is why the **Dollarwise Travel Club** was formed 31 years ago. Developed in response to requests from Frommer's Travel Guide readers, the Club provides cost-cutting travel strategies, up-to-date travel information, and a sense of community for value-conscious travelers from all over the world.

In keeping with the money-saving concept, the annual membership fee is low—$18 for U.S. residents or $20 for residents of Canada, Mexico, and other countries—and is immediately exceeded by the value of your benefits, which include:

1. Any TWO books listed on the following pages.
2. Plus any ONE Frommer's City Guide.
3. A subscription to our quarterly newspaper, *The Dollarwise Traveler*.
4. A membership card that entitles you to purchase through the Club all Frommer's publications for 33% to 50% off their retail price.

The eight-page **Dollarwise Traveler** tells you about the latest developments in good-value travel worldwide and includes the following columns: **Hospitality Exchange** (for those offering and seeking hospitality in cities all over the world); **Share-a-Trip** (for those looking for travel companions to share costs); and **Readers Ask . . . Readers Reply** (for those with travel questions that other members can answer).

Aside from the Frommer's Guides and the Gault Millau Guides, you can also choose from our Special Editions. These include such titles as *California with Kids* (a compendium of the best of California's accommodations, restaurants, and sightseeing attractions appropriate for those traveling with toddlers through teens); *Candy Apple: New York with Kids* (a spirited guide to the Big Apple by a savvy New York grandmother that's perfect for both visitors and residents); *Caribbean Hideaways* (the 100 most romantic places to stay in the Islands, all rated on ambience, food, sports opportunities, and price); *Honeymoon Destinations* (a guide to planning and choosing just the right destination from hundreds of possibilities in the U.S., Mexico, and the Caribbean); *Marilyn Wood's Wonderful Weekends* (a selection of the best mini-vacations within a 200-mile radius of New York City, including descriptions of country inns and other accommodations, restaurants, picnic spots, sights, and activities); and *Paris Rendez-Vous* (a delightful guide to the best places to meet in Paris whether for power breakfasts or dancing till dawn).

To join this Club, simply send the appropriate membership fee with your name and address to: Frommer's Dollarwise Travel Club, 15 Columbus Circle, New York, NY 10023. Remember to specify which single city guide and which two other guides you wish to receive in your initial package of member's benefits. Or tear out the next page, check off your choices, and send the page to us with your membership fee.

FROMMER'S CITY GUIDES

(Pocket-size guides to sightseeing and tourist accommodations and facilities in all price ranges.)

☐ Amsterdam/Holland. $8.95	☐ Montréal/Québec City $8.95
☐ Athens. $8.95	☐ New Orleans $8.95
☐ Atlanta. $8.95	☐ New York. $8.95
☐ Atlantic City/Cape May $8.95	☐ Orlando. $8.95
☐ Barcelona $7.95	☐ Paris. $8.95
☐ Belgium $7.95	☐ Philadelphia. $8.95
☐ Boston $8.95	☐ Rio $8.95
☐ Cancún/Cozumel/Yucatán . . .$8.95	☐ Rome $8.95
☐ Chicago $8.95	☐ Salt Lake City $8.95
☐ Denver/Boulder/Colorado	☐ San Diego $8.95
Springs. $7.95	☐ San Francisco $8.95
☐ Dublin/Ireland. $8.95	☐ Santa Fe/Taos/Albuquerque $8.95
☐ Hawaii $8.95	☐ Seattle/Portland. $7.95
☐ Hong Kong $7.95	☐ Sydney $8.95
☐ Las Vegas $8.95	☐ Tampa/St. Petersburg $8.95
☐ Lisbon/Madrid/Costa del Sol. .$8.95	☐ Tokyo $7.95
☐ London. $8.95	☐ Toronto. $8.95
☐ Los Angeles. $8.95	☐ Vancouver/Victoria. $7.95
☐ Mexico City/Acapulco $8.95	☐ Washington, D.C. $8.95
☐ Minneapolis/St. Paul. $8.95	

SPECIAL EDITIONS

☐ Beat the High Cost of Travel . . .$6.95	☐ Motorist's Phrase Book (Fr/Ger/Sp). . . .$4.95
☐ Bed & Breakfast—N. America $11.95	☐ Paris Rendez-Vous $10.95
☐ California with Kids $14.95	☐ Swap and Go (Home Exchanging) $10.95
☐ Caribbean Hideaways $14.95	☐ The Candy Apple (NY with Kids) $12.95
☐ Manhattan's Outdoor	☐ Travel Diary and Record Book $5.95
Sculpture. $15.95	

☐ Honeymoon Destinations (US, Mex & Carib) $14.95

☐ Where to Stay USA (From $3 to $30 a night) $10.95

☐ Marilyn Wood's Wonderful Weekends (CT, DE, MA, NH, NJ, NY, PA, RI, VT) $11.95

☐ The New World of Travel (Annual sourcebook by Arthur Frommer for savvy travelers) . .$16.95

GAULT MILLAU

(The only guides that distinguish the truly superlative from the merely overrated.)

☐ The Best of Chicago $15.95	☐ The Best of Los Angeles $16.95
☐ The Best of France. $16.95	☐ The Best of New England $15.95
☐ The Best of Hong Kong $16.95	☐ The Best of New York. $16.95
☐ The Best of Italy $16.95	☐ The Best of Paris $16.95
☐ The Best of London. $16.95	☐ The Best of San Francisco $16.95

☐ The Best of Washington, D.C. $16.95

ORDER NOW!

In U.S. include $2 shipping UPS for 1st book; $1 ea. add'l book. Outside U.S. $3 and $1, respectively.
Allow four to six weeks for delivery in U.S., longer outside U.S.

Enclosed is my check or money order for $_____

NAME _____

ADDRESS _____

CITY _____ STATE _____ ZIP ____

0690